Making Sense

A Student's Guide to Research and Writing

Making Sense

Life Sciences

MARGOT NORTHEY
PATRICK VON ADERKAS

OXFORD
UNIVERSITY PRESS

OXFORD
UNIVERSITY PRESS

8 Sampson Mews, Suite 204, Don Mills, Ontario M3C 0H5
www.oupcanada.com

Oxford University Press is a department of the University of Oxford. It furthers the University's
objective of excellence in research, scholarship, and education by publishing worldwide in

Oxford   New York

Auckland   Cape Town   Dar es Salaam   Hong Kong   Karachi   Kuala Lumpur
Madrid   Melbourne   Mexico City   Nairobi   New Delhi   Shanghai   Taipei   Toronto

With offices in

Argentina   Austria   Brazil   Chile   Czech Republic   France   Greece
Guatemala   Hungary   Italy   Japan   Poland   Portugal   Singapore
South Korea   Switzerland   Thailand   Turkey   Ukraine   Vietnam

Oxford is a trade mark of Oxford University Press in the UK and in certain other countries
Published in Canada by Oxford University Press
Copyright © Oxford University Press Canada 2011
The moral rights of the author have been asserted
Database right Oxford University Press (maker)
First Published 2011

Library and Archives Canada Cataloguing in Publication

Northey, Margot, 1940–
Making sense, life sciences : a student's guide to writing and
research / Margot Northey, Patrick Von Aderkas.

Includes bibliographical references and index.
ISBN 978-0-19-543370-8

1. Life sciences—Authorship.   2. Report writing.   I. Von Aderkas, Patrick   II. Title.

QH304.N67 2010   808'.06657   C2010-906154-3

Cover images: Trees: Simonox/iStockphoto.com; Butterfly: BEANS-/iStockphoto.com;
DNA: Mevans/iStockphoto.com; Frog: Kerkla/iStockphoto.com

Screen captures on pages 27-9, 31, 32, 34-6, 38-40: *Web of Knowledge* from Thomson Reuters.

Screen capture on page 30: Reprinted courtesy of JSTOR and The American Association for
the Advancement of Science. JSTOR © 2010. All rights reserved.

Oxford University Press is committed to our environment. This book is printed on Forest
Stewardship Council certified paper, harvested from a responsibly managed forest.

Mixed Sources

Product group from well-managed
forests and other controlled sources
www.fsc.org   Cert no. SW-COC-000952
© 1996 Forest Stewardship Council

FSC

Printed and bound in Canada

1 2 3 4 – 14 13 12 11

CONTENTS

ACKNOWLEDGEMENTS

When you write a book, you wonder who the readers will be. There can be no mystery when it's a student guide. That is not to say that there are not surprises along the way. A big one was how much interest there was from fellow professors. My colleagues at the University of Victoria were full of insight—they offered everything from advice on how to avoid plagiarism to stories of their favourite mistakes. Many professors related to me their own inadequacies when they were budding scientists. It was this wellspring of goodwill and helpful ideas that spirited this book along.

I would like to thank Oxford University Press for inviting me to work on this new edition. Peter Chambers has been a wonderful developmental editor. I am particularly grateful to Janice Evans, whose meticulous copy-editing improved this book in so many ways. I would also like to thank the reviewers whose clever suggestions I incorporated into this incarnation of *Making Sense*. This book was a joint effort with Margot Northey: she provided the strong scaffold with its Canadian touches.

I am indebted to many students in the following UVic courses: General Biology, Cell Biology, Plant Morphogenesis, Higher Plants, Plant Morphology, Plants and People, Forest Biology Graduate Seminar, and most recently Tree Biology. They unwittingly tested many ideas that I had about presentations, examination preparation, essay writing, and research. Student essays even provided some examples found in this text. A number of recent Honours students (Barry Macdonald, Dani Sweetnam-Holmes, and Marie Vance) and graduate students (Andrea Coulter and Natalie Prior) provided text or insights.

I am also indebted to my son Max for reading various bits—he was able to tell me whether, in his undergraduate experience, they rang true. My wife Elizabeth proofed the whole thing, laughed at my jokes, and kept me merrily rolling along. I dedicate this book to my mother, who discovered the joys of university late in her life.

Patrick von Aderkas
University of Victoria

A NOTE TO THE STUDENT

It's a mad, crazy world to be a life sciences student. There are exams, lectures, and labs. As deadlines pile up, topics have to be researched, digested, and then written about in thoughtful reports and essays. A surefire way to make this process easier is to improve your writing and researching skills.

We have designed this edition of *Making Sense* to provide you with a set of writing guidelines. A popular belief is that it takes 10,000 hours to master any skill. But you don't have 10,000 hours! This text presents you with concise information that will substantially reduce the time it takes you to acquire mastery in writing. We present practical advice to help you overcome common pitfalls in grammar, style, punctuation, and usage. We provide a rich variety of examples that will help you improve your writing by example. We even include an annotated problem essay along with its revised version to show you how you can improve your own essays. You will find that once you gain a little bit of control, more follows, and eventually you will be able to write about science with fluidity and ease.

We have also considered the ways in which technologies are changing how you learn. Computers affect the ways you put together posters, presentations, essays, and lab reports; they also influence your research habits. A computer, however, is merely a tool. You still need to develop a good eye for graphic design, a good ear for clarity in presentation, a good sense for the written word, and a full understanding of the research process.

Finally, we have addressed common concerns about working in groups. Life sciences foster cooperative effort in labs and classes; in a scientific career, such cooperation leads to inter-lab collaborations and large-scale projects. We know it is hard for you to focus on getting along with your peers when marks are at stake. To help you learn to work in groups, we have provided advice on lab partnerships, study groups, and other types of cooperative work.

Above all, we have written this text to give you a clear, concise, and readable guide that will help you do well in all your courses and in your future career.

A NOTE TO THE INSTRUCTOR

A strength of the *Making Sense* series is its focus on essays, reports, and resumés. There are chapters to help students improve punctuation, grammar, documentation, word usage, and style. In this edition, we aimed at adapting this content to students in the life sciences. To this end, we added and enhanced material on lab reports, exam preparation, group work, and graphics use.

We also took a fresh approach to research techniques. Students use search engines and browsers in unexpected and surprising ways. I'm not alone in coming to the conclusion that methods of research are changing. Electronic databases not only allow student scholarship to develop along traditional lines—that is, to search ever deeper into a subject—but they also allow non-traditional horizontal searches through citations, cross-references, and similar titles. This type of skimming forces students to alter their search strategies on the fly, which can lead to great success. In short, there is more than one good way to find information these days.

This book is much more than a writing guide. Many courses in the life sciences have little or no assigned written work and may even lack a lab component. Teaching in the life sciences involves getting students to talk about what they have learned. Often, the best way to get students to discuss what they know is to assign them group work. Consequently, this book contains useful advice to help students work collaboratively during classes and labs to complete assignments as well as in study groups to prepare for exams.

CHAPTER 1

Writing and Thinking

OBJECTIVES

- developing strategies for tackling a writing project
- defining your purpose
- avoiding problems in style and tone
- thinking like a scientist—the value of questions

You are not likely to produce clear writing unless you have first done some clear thinking, and thinking can't be hurried. It follows that the most important step you can take is to leave yourself enough time to think. Psychologists have shown that you can't always solve a difficult problem by "putting your mind to it"—by determined reasoning. Sometimes when you are stuck it's best to take a break, sleep on it, and let the subconscious or creative part of your brain take over for a while. Very often a period of relaxation will produce a new approach or solution. Just remember that leaving time for creative reflection isn't the same thing as sitting around listening to music until inspiration strikes out of the blue.

INITIAL STRATEGIES

Writing is about making choices: choices about what ideas you want to present and how you want to present them. Practice makes decision-making easier, but no matter how fluent you become, with each piece of writing you will still have to choose.

You can narrow the field of choice from the start if you realize that you are not writing for just anybody, anywhere, for no particular reason. With any writing you do, it's always a sound strategy to ask yourself two basic questions:

- What is the purpose of this piece of writing?
- What is the reader like?

Your first reaction may be, "Well, I'm writing for my instructor to satisfy a course requirement," but that's not specific enough. To be useful, your answers have to be precise.

Think about the purpose

Depending on the assignment, you may have any one (or more) of the following purposes for writing an essay:

- to show your knowledge of a topic or text;
- to show that you understand certain terms or theories;
- to show that you can do independent research;
- to show that you can apply a specific theory to new material;
- to demonstrate your ability to evaluate secondary sources; and/or
- to show that you can think critically or creatively.

An assignment designed to see if you have read and understood specific material requires a different approach from one that's meant to test your critical thinking. In the first case, your approach will tend to be *expository*, with the emphasis on presenting facts. In the second case, you will probably want to structure your essay around a particular argument or assertion that other people might dispute. Your aim in this kind of *argumentative* or *persuasive* essay is to bring your reader around to your point of view. (Argumentative essays are discussed in greater detail in Chapter 2.)

Think about the reader

Thinking about the reader does *not* mean playing up to the instructor. To convince a particular person that your own views are sound, you have to consider his or her way of thinking. If you are writing a paper on the effects of terrorism for a sociology professor, your analysis will be different than it would be if you were writing for an economics or biology professor. You will have to make specific decisions about the terms you should explain, the background information you should supply, and the details you will need in order to convince that particular reader. In the same way, if you plan to write a paper on long-term effects of genetically modified organisms on the environment and your reader is a big supporter of biotechnology, you will have to anticipate any arguments that he or she may raise so that you can address them. If you don't know who will be reading your paper—your professor, your tutorial leader, or a marker—just imagine someone intelligent, knowledgeable, and interested, skeptical enough to question your ideas but flexible enough to adopt them if your evidence is convincing.

Think about the length

Before you start writing, you will also need to think about the length of your assignment in relation to the time you can spend on it. If both the topic and the length are prescribed, it should be fairly easy for you to assess the level of detail required and the amount of research you will need to do. If only the length is prescribed, that restriction will help you decide how broad or how narrow a topic you should choose (see pages 17–19). You should also keep in mind how much the assignment is worth. A paper that is worth 50 per cent of your final grade will merit more of your time and effort than one that is worth only 10 per cent.

Think about the tone

In everyday writing to friends you probably adopt a casual tone, but academic writing is usually more formal. Just how formal you need to be will depend on the kind of assignment and the instructions you have been given. Life sciences assignments generally require a formal tone, as do most essays and reports. What kind of style is too informal for most academic work? Here are the main signs.

USE OF SLANG

Although the occasional slang word or phrase may be useful for special effect, frequent use of slang is not acceptable in academic writing because slang expressions are usually regional and short-lived. They may mean different things to different people at different times. (Just think of how widely the meanings of *hot* and *cool* can vary, depending on the circumstances.) In a formal essay, where clarity of expression is important, it's better to use words with well-established meanings that will be understood by the greatest number of readers. If you think a word you're using might be slang, look it up in a dictionary or conduct an online search (try typing your word plus *slang* into your search engine to get the most relevant results).

EXCESSIVE USE OF FIRST-PERSON PRONOUNS

Since a formal essay is not a personal outpouring, you want to keep it from becoming *I*-centred. There is no need to begin every sentence with "I think" or "In my view" when the facts or arguments speak for themselves. Over the past thirty years, first-person pronouns have become more common in life sciences writing. First-person narration has even become acceptable in international peer-reviewed journals. This trend can confuse a student who has been told that science is best written about from a detached perspective. If you aren't sure what your instructor expects, it's always best to ask. It's certainly acceptable to use the occasional first-person pronoun if the assignment calls for your point of view—as long as your opinions are backed by evidence. Also, if the choice is between using *I* and creating a tangle of passive constructions (for example, "It is hoped that it can reasonably be concluded, based on the evidence that has been presented, that . . ."), it's almost always better to choose *I*. (A hint: when you do use *I*, it will be less noticeable if you place it in the middle of the sentence rather than at the beginning—this strategy is especially useful when writing resumés.) Here are some examples of ways to avoid both *I*-centred and unnecessarily passive sentences:

✗ Having analyzed the new data, I believe they are flawed.

✗ The new data, having been analyzed, appear to me to be flawed.

✓ When analyzed, the new data seem flawed.

✗ In this essay, Aldo Leopold's portrayal of nature will be investigated, and the repeated conflict between wilderness and civilization will be discussed.

✓ **[better]** In this essay, I will investigate Aldo Leopold's portrayal of nature and discuss the repeated conflict between wilderness and civilization.

✓ **[best]** This essay will investigate Aldo Leopold's portrayal of nature and discuss the repeated conflict between nature and civilization.

FREQUENT USE OF CONTRACTIONS

Generally speaking, contractions such as *can't* and *isn't* are not suitable for academic writing, although they may be fine for letters or other informal kinds of writing—for example, this handbook. This is not to say that you should avoid using contractions altogether; even the most serious academic writing can sound stilted or unnatural without any contractions at all. Just be sure that when you use contractions in a college or university essay you use them sparingly, since excessive use of contractions makes formal writing sound chatty and informal.

Finding a suitable tone for academic writing can be a challenge. The problem with trying to avoid excessive informality is that you may be tempted to go to the other extreme. If your writing sounds stiff or pompous, you may be using too many inflated phrases, long words, or passive constructions (see Chapter 6). When in doubt, remember that a more formal style is the best option.

Think about the structure

Embarking on a career in the life sciences requires you to develop a diverse set of skills—you must master scientific techniques and methods, develop your analytical thinking and learn to design experiments, and ultimately apply these skills in order to discover aspects of nature. Underlying most of this process is an attitude that is based on a questioning spirit. The sooner you learn to approach essays and assignments in this spirit, the faster you will develop a recognizably scientific writing style. The trick is to think like a scientist. Simply put, you must question everything.

In your early studies, you are given *descriptive* assignments, but very soon you will be given more *analytical* assignments. You may be asked to test a hypothesis, to question the truth of a statement. A solid strategy for approaching analytical assignments involves asking questions of increasing sophistication. The first questions that you should ask are always the simplest, least sophisticated questions: Did the test prove or disprove the statement? Did it work? Once you have answered these questions in your assignment, you can elaborate on your conclusions by providing evidence from the experiments and, if required, from the scientific literature.

More advanced scientific thinking happens when you move your questioning up a level and query the nature and components of the hypothesis. By asking questions, you will find it easier not only to think through a problem but to get downright creative. You will also find it easier to write a longer analysis, as each question requires an answer. Bit by bit, you will create a substantial critical appraisal of the subject.

I'll provide a simple example. In biology, a typical laboratory assignment involves students pollinating two types of flowers: some that have just opened and some that have been open for two days. The students are testing the hypothesis that newly opened flowers are more likely to be pollinated and to set seed than are older flowers. The students—behaving as bee surrogates—

dust on the pollen. After a number of weeks, the students count the seeds per flower and analyze the data.

The first question to be answered is the easiest, as it comes directly out of the hypothesis: Did the newly opened flowers pollinate more readily and produce more seeds? Then the student can ask other questions by picking away at the hypothesis: Were the newly opened flowers already pollinated while in the bud? Were the older flowers diseased? Are bees more selective than their human surrogates, choosing to pollinate only newer flowers in nature? These questions cast doubt on some of the assumptions of the experiment. At this point a good student might suggest how to design a better experiment. Another way to identify similar shortcomings is to ask the question, "What is the matter with this experiment?" Following up this line of thinking stirs up good questions. Oddly enough, negative thinking—that is, asking what's *wrong*—is much more effective than asking what's right. It's probably not the best strategy in life, but in science it's a winner.

GUIDELINES FOR WRITING

Whenever you embark on a writing project, try to keep the following guidelines in mind:

- Think about your audience, the reader or readers of your writing.
- Be clear about your subject and your purpose, what it is you hope to achieve.
- Define your terms.
- Include only relevant material; don't pad your writing to achieve a certain number of words.
- Strive for consistency of expression throughout the work.
- Make sure you are accurate in all of your statements, in your analysis and presentation of data, and in your documentation of sources.
- Order your information logically.
- Be simple and clear in expressing your ideas.
- Make sure that your argument is coherent.
- Draw conclusions that are clearly based on your evidence.
- Allow yourself lots of time to work on drafts before completing the final copy.
- Make sure to edit and proofread your work carefully.

In the chapters that follow we will consider these guidelines in greater detail.

USING BIAS-FREE LANGUAGE

As concern with political correctness has grown, it has become more important than ever to avoid bias in the language we use—both spoken and written. Just as you give thought to your reader and to the kind of tone you wish to create, you will also want to take pains to use language that steers clear of any suggestion of bias, no matter how unintentional it may be.

The potential for bias is far-reaching, involving factors that include gender, race, culture, age, disability, occupation, religion, and socio-economic status. Although our society hasn't come up with ideal solutions in every case, developing an awareness of sensitive issues will help you to avoid using biased language. To avoid bias in your writing, hew to the following guidelines.

Gender

At one time, it would have been acceptable to refer to a person of either sex as "he," a practice still preferred by some traditionalists:

> For an ecologist to study bears in the wild, he will need tracking devices.

But as sensitivity to sexist language has increased, we have become more careful about this use of a generic pronoun. Here are some options for avoiding the problem:

- Use the passive voice:

  Tracking devices will be needed by an ecologist studying bears in the wild.

- Restructure the sentence:

  An ecologist who studies bears in the wild will need tracking devices.

- Use "he or she", although this is cumbersome and should be used sparingly:

  For an ecologist to study bears in the wild, he or she will need tracking devices.

- Use the plural form:

  For ecologists to study bears in the wild, they will need tracking devices.

Another option is to alternate, using the masculine form in one instance and the feminine form in the next.

Recently, some writers have used the neutral "they" to refer to a singular antecedent:

> When a writer aims for simplicity, they will occasionally break with grammatical convention.

Be careful, however. This may still raise the hackles of a traditional reader.

Another trouble spot involves gender-specific nouns, such as *stewardess*, *waitress*, and *fireman*. The solution in these cases is to look for gender-free words—for example, *flight attendant*, *server*, and *firefighter*.

Race and culture

The names used to describe someone's racial or cultural identity often carry negative connotations for some readers although they are acceptable to others. For example, consider the term *Negro*. The search for neutral language has produced alternatives such as *black* and *African Canadian*, but no single term has gained universal approval. We have similar problems with the term *Indian*, with alternatives such as *Aboriginal*, *Native*, and *First Nations*. The best approach is to find out what term the racial or cultural group in question prefers. You should also remember that concepts of race differ according to context even within a university or a college, with social scientists, philosophers, and students themselves each using quite different points of reference.

The impact of genomics on life sciences has raised the issue of race, with the result that great sensitivity is required, especially when discussing current hot topics such as personalized medicine, race-targeted pharmaceuticals, and human evolution. Today, racial terms are often used in a slightly bewildering fashion, serving as substitutes for descriptions of undefined genetic characteristics. When discussing genetics, avoid generalizations about race by using concrete, scientifically valid descriptions.

There are many other areas where the effort to develop and use neutral language has made an impact. To be politically correct, writers usually refer not to *old people* but to *seniors* and to someone as *having special needs* rather than *being handicapped*. Occasionally the search for neutral language leads to ever-changing terms or vague euphemisms, such as when *garbage collector* became *waste collector* and then *sanitation engineer*. Whatever the situation, be sensitive to the power of the words you use and take the time to search for language that is bias-free but not cumbersome.

SUMMARY

Writing for the life sciences is generally formal in style. Outside of the usual requirements of restraining use of the first person and avoiding slang and contractions, science-related writing demands a slightly different tone—life sciences writers generally affect a neutral, impersonal tone. When proving or disproving hypotheses, you can enrich your analytical writing by developing a framework around questions that naturally arise from the work. This is where careful thought to the purpose of the writing pays dividends. The time you spend considering the assignment's value, length, and readership will also help you to achieve clarity in your writing.

CHAPTER 2

Planning an Essay

OBJECTIVES

- planning an essay
- establishing the type of writer you are
- structuring your essay
- differentiating between descriptive essays and argumentative essays
- working from the core idea—the thesis
- knowing the difference between a thesis and a hypothesis
- using the three-C approach
- creating an outline

If you are one of the many students who dread writing academic essays, you will find that following a few simple steps in planning and organizing will make the task easier—and the result better.

This is not a one-size-fits-all process, and the amount of time you spend on each stage will depend on the nature of the assignment. For a short, straightforward essay requiring little research, you will likely spend most of the time drafting and editing. For a more complex essay, when you must take into account what others before you have said, it's likely that over half of your time will be spent on research and planning. Understanding the total process of completing a written assignment will serve you well, whether you are a first-year undergraduate or a post-graduate student.

THE PLANNING STAGE

Know the pros and cons of preplanning

Some students claim they can write essays without any planning at all, driven entirely by enthusiasm. On the rare occasions when they succeed in creating a well-written essay, their process is usually not as spontaneous as they think. In most cases they have thought or talked a good deal about the subject in advance and have come to the task with fully formed ideas. More often, students who try to write a lengthy essay without planning just end up frustrated. They get stuck in the middle and don't know how to finish, or they suddenly realize that they're rambling.

Many writers believe that the planning stage is the most important part of the whole writing process. Certainly the evidence shows that poor planning usually leads to disorganized writing. In the majority of students' essays the single greatest improvement would be not better research or better grammar but better organization.

Organizing your thoughts before you start to write has its immediate advantages. As with any complex task, the more you plan your strategy, the better your results. Once you have planned a few essays and developed a system for organizing your ideas before you write, you will find that you can write any essay—even one on a subject that you simply don't like—without difficulty. This is a powerful position to be in.

Yet planning can get in the way. Some students prefer to write essays that evolve slowly, maturing and changing along the way. They need to warm to the task with a bit of exploratory writing (see pages 45–6).This style can be summed up in one phrase—*getting something down on paper so that the rest will follow*. The hard decisions about organization come later.

Whether you organize before or after you begin to write, however, at some point you need to plan.

Read primary material

Primary material is the direct evidence—usually journal articles, sometimes books—on which you will base your essay. Surprising as it may seem, the best way to begin working with this material is to give it a fast initial skim. If you are consulting a book, don't just start reading from cover to cover; first look at the table of contents, scan the index, and read the preface or introduction to get a sense of the author's purpose and plan. In the case of a journal article, skim the abstract, the introduction, the results, and the opening paragraph of the discussion; skip the sections on materials and methods. Getting an overview will allow you to focus your questions for a more purposeful and analytic second reading. Make no mistake: a superficial reading is not all you need. You still have to work through the material carefully a second time. But an initial skim followed by a focussed second reading will give you a much more thorough understanding than one slow plod ever will.

Secondary sources

In the life sciences, secondary sources are analyses of the primary material. While primary literature is the literature of invention and discovery, secondary literature is the literature of summation, discussion, and commentary. The first is peer-reviewed, meaning the articles have been vetted by experts, whereas the second is not. Secondary sources include textbooks, reviews, encyclopedias, government reports, and other similar sources. Instructors and professors give *much* more weight to primary sources. In some disciplines, instructors discourage secondary reading in introductory courses. They know that students who turn to commentaries may be so overwhelmed by the weight of authority that they will rely too heavily on them.

In some instances—and especially in the sciences—your instructor will encourage you to review recent secondary literature on your chosen topic to see where your views stand in relation to those of the experts in the field. However, if you turn to commentaries as a way around the difficulty of understanding the primary source, or if you base your argument solely on the interpretations of others, you may end up producing a trite, second-hand essay. Your interpretation could even be downright wrong, because at this stage you might not know enough about a subject to be able to accurately evaluate the commentary.

Always be sure you have a firm grasp of the primary material before you turn to secondary sources. Secondary sources are an important part of learning and are essential to many research papers, but they can never substitute for your own active reading of the primary material. Once you get a feel for the subject, you should never be afraid of holding and developing your own views.

Analyze your subject

Whether the subject you start with is one that has been assigned or suggested by your instructor or is one that you have chosen yourself, it is bound to be too broad for an essay topic. You will have to analyze your subject in order to find a way of limiting it.

Ask questions

How do you form useful questions? Journalists approach their stories through a six-question formula: *who? what? where? when? why?* and *how?* For example, starting with the question *what?* and applying it to a biological problem, you might ask, "What kind of organism is it?"; "What makes study of this organism interesting?"; "What are the biological problems associated with this group of organisms?" In the life sciences, which rely heavily on experimental and descriptive investigation, *how* questions form the most common line of enquiry. *How?* leads to interpretation and analysis, whereas *why?* can mislead students into ascribing purpose and design where there may be none. But you should also embrace *why* questions, as they often serve a broader purpose. *Why* questions range from simple questions such as "Why were these organisms chosen?" to deeper speculative questions such as "Why did this behaviour evolve among these organisms?" Questions such as "Who are the experts on this organism?" are very useful and can lead you quickly to discover the more important facts, theories, and controversies. The life sciences are built on expert evidence enshrined in journals, so asking *who?* is always very useful.

To take another subject, consider some of the same kinds of questions you could ask about the effect of global climate change on polar bears in the Canadian Arctic:

- *What* are the likely effects of ice loss due to global warming on the polar bear's ability to hunt and to reproduce? *What* are the mathematical models that predict polar bear populations in various climate change scenarios?
- *Where* are the polar bears found? *Why* is the distribution not random throughout the North?
- *Who* are the experts on polar bear population biology? *Why* are there so few?
- *Why* is there no intergovernmental organization on arctic mammals?
- *How* will polar bears be affected by a 10 per cent loss of spring sea ice? *How* will polar bears be affected by a 50 per cent loss of sea ice?

Most often, the questions you ask initially—and the answers to them—will be general, but they will stimulate more specific questions that will help you refine your topic and develop a thesis statement.

TRY THE THREE-C APPROACH
A more systematic scheme for analyzing a subject is the three-C approach. It forces you to look at a subject from three different perspectives, asking basic questions about *components*, *change*, and *context*.

Components:
- What parts or categories can the subject be broken down into?
- Can the main divisions be subdivided?

Change:
- What features have changed?
- Is there a trend?
- What caused the change?
- What are the results of the change?

Context:
- What is the larger issue surrounding the subject?
- In what tradition or school of thought does the subject belong?
- How is the subject similar to, and different from, related subjects?

What are the *components* of the subject?

This question forces you to break down the subject into smaller elements. It helps you avoid oversimplification and easy generalization.

Suppose that your assignment is an interdisciplinary essay, one in which you are expected to discuss two divergently different disciplines in one essay. Science and society essays are often of this nature. Let's take an essay on the role of religion in genotype conservation of trees. If you consider the components, you might decide that you can split the subject into (1) religious beliefs concerning the biological world and (2) religion's role in conservation efforts. Alternatively, you might divide it into (1) the relationship between trees and religion, (2) the genotype diversity of trees that have religious significance, and (3) the relationship between conservation practices and religions. Since these are still broad topics, you might break them down further, for example splitting the relationship between conservation practices and religions into (1) Christian, (2) Muslim, (3) Buddhist, (4) Hindu, and so on. You could use similar religion-based subdivisions to highlight tree species that have religious associations, which in turn could be broken down into the types of associations, such as (1) trees associated with temple gardens and sacred sites, (2) trees directly associated with religious practices, and (3) trees that have cultural links to a religion's development.

Similarly, if you were analyzing the signal transduction pathway in a stress response in yeast, you could ask, "What are the extracellular components?" (e.g., ligands, membrane-bound proteins, composition of the extracellular matrix) and "What are the intracellular components?" (e.g., enzymes, signalling molecules, transcription factors, metabolic responses, genes). Or you could ask, "What are the content groupings?" (e.g., low-molecular-weight signalling molecules, proteins, genes). If you were writing an essay on predator–prey relations in the tundra, you could ask, "What are the major predators and their prey?" and "Is there a mathematical relationship between predator populations and prey populations?"

Approaching your subject this way will help you appreciate its complexity and avoid making wide-sweeping generalizations that don't apply to all areas of the subject. In addition, asking questions about the components of your subject may help you find one aspect of it that is not too large for you to explore in detail.

What features of the subject suggest change?

This question helps you to think about trends. It can also point to antecedents or causes of an occurrence as well as to the likely results or implications of a change.

For the essay on tree conservation and religion, you could ask, "Has a religion developed more associations with trees through the ages or did it merely absorb pre-existing tree associations at an early stage of its development?" You might also ask, "What is the future of these associations?"; "Has a particular religion's outlook on tree conservation evolved over time?"; or "How have recent changes in religious practices affected widespread views on tree conservation?"

Suppose you have decided to focus on stress-induced signal transduction pathways in yeast. You might ask, "What are the effects of changes in gene expression on stress tolerance?" or "Do proteins in this pathway change their physical conformation, resulting in an altered function?" If the experiment does not reveal or explain the complete pathway, you might also question how future research might change the general understanding of how pathways are controlled.

On the subject of predator–prey relations in the tundra, you might ask, "Have there been changes or trends in the population growth of predators that are not influenced by prey availability, such as disease, habitat alteration, or some human influence?" or "Have there been changes in the type or abundance of prey available?" Then ask, "What are the causes and reasons for such changes?"

What is the *context* of this subject?

This question forces you to see the bigger picture. What are the similarities and differences between your chosen subject and related ones? To what particular school of thought or tradition does the subject belong? Questions about context are *rarely* posed by first- and second-year students, largely because rote learning in the first two years of study tends to ignore that many fields in the life sciences presently are—or have always been—in intellectual ferment, with theories hotly debated. The following are typical context questions:

- How do tree-conservation efforts inspired by religion compare to similar efforts inspired by extra-religious influences? How do conservation efforts in countries where religion has a strong impact on government decisions compare to similar efforts in countries where religion does not play a role in government decisions?
- How does stress-induced signal transduction compare with other types of signal transduction? Does the pathway in yeast differ from pathways found in other organisms?
- What theories exist to explain predator–prey relations? How do these theories apply to the organisms in your paper?

General as most of these questions are, you will find that they stimulate more specific questions—and thoughts—about the material from which you can choose your topic and decide on your controlling idea. Remember that the ability to ask intelligent questions is one of the most important, though often underrated, skills that you can develop for any work, in school and elsewhere.[1]

Analyze a prescribed topic

Even if the topic of your essay is supplied by your instructor, you still need to analyze it carefully. Try underlining key words to make sure that you don't neglect anything. Distinguish the main focus from subordinate concerns. A common error in dealing with prescribed topics is to emphasize one portion while giving short shrift to another. Give each part its proper due, and make sure that you actually do what the instructions tell you to do. For example, consider the instructions implicit in these verbs:

Outline	State simply, without much development of each point (unless asked).
Trace	Review by looking back—on stages or steps in a process, or on causes of an occurrence.
Explain	Show how or why something happens.

Discuss	Examine or analyze in an orderly way. This instruction allows you considerable freedom, as long as you take into account contrary evidence or ideas.
Compare	Examine differences as well as similarities. (For a more detailed discussion, see pages 48–9.)
Evaluate	Analyze strengths and weaknesses, providing an overall assessment of worth.

These and other verbs tell you how to approach the topic; don't confuse them.

Develop a thesis

Every essay needs a controlling idea around which all the material can be organized. This central idea is usually known as a thesis, though in the case of an expository essay you may prefer to think of it as a theme. Consider these statements:

THEME: Agriculture plays a role in plant extinction in Canada.

THESIS: Canada would have greater plant biodiversity if Canadian agriculture was better regulated.

The first is a straightforward statement of fact; an essay centred on such a theme would probably focus on simply describing agriculture's habitat-altering influence on plant biodiversity. By contrast, the second statement is one with which other people might well disagree; an essay based on this thesis would have to present a convincing argument. The expository form can produce an informative and interesting essay, but many students prefer the argumentative approach because it's easier to organize and is more likely to produce strong writing.

If you have decided to present an argument, you will probably want to create a working thesis as the focal point around which you can start organizing your material. This working thesis doesn't have to be final: you are free to change it at any stage in your planning. It simply serves as a linchpin, holding together your information and ideas as you organize. It will help you define your intentions, make your research more selective, and focus your essay.

At some point in the writing process you will probably want to make your working thesis into an explicit thesis statement that can appear in your introduction. This is not always necessary: as you gain experience, you may choose to present your thesis later or to imply it rather than state it. Even if you don't intend to include it in your final draft, though, you need to know what your thesis statement is and to keep it in mind throughout the writing process. It's worth taking the time to work this statement out carefully. Use a complete sentence to express it, and above all make sure that it is restricted, unified, and precise.[2]

THESIS VERSUS HYPOTHESIS—WHAT'S THE DIFFERENCE?

Science students should not confuse a *thesis* with a *hypothesis*. A thesis is a statement that needs to be proved and generally serves as an organizing principle for an essay or book. It relates directly to the central theme of a writing assignment. A hypothesis is the core idea of an experiment. In short, proving a thesis depends on rallying written fact and opinion, whereas testing a hypothesis depends on repeatable acquisition of data. A thesis is central to an essay; a hypothesis is central to a lab report. For information on how to formulate a hypothesis, see Chapter 5.

A RESTRICTED THESIS

A restricted thesis is one that is narrow enough for you to examine thoroughly in the space you have available. Suppose, for example, that your general subject is evolution. Such a subject is much too broad to be handled properly in an essay of one or two thousand words; you must restrict it in some way and create a line of argument for which you can supply adequate supporting evidence. Following the analytic questioning process, you might find that you want to restrict it by time: "After 150 years, evolution still has its controversies." Or you might prefer to limit it to a discussion of neo-Darwinism: "Evolution as described by Darwin has had a rough ride over the last twenty years, but neo-Darwinists will prevail."

As another example, suppose that your general subject for a two-thousand-word essay is the work of the famous nineteenth-century explorer and scientist Alexander von Humboldt. You might want to limit your essay by discussing a prominent theme in his journals: "Humboldt's personal comments reveal that he yearned to create a unified system that could explain the interrelatedness of the thousands of organisms he had seen." Or you could focus on some aspect of Humboldt's thought: "During his trip to South America, Humboldt developed an idealized perception of nature because he ignored the influence of humans on the biogeographic regions that he visited." Whatever the discipline or subject, make sure that your thesis is restricted enough that you can explore it in depth.

A UNIFIED THESIS

A unified thesis must have one controlling idea, for example, "The aquaculture industry in the coastal waters of British Columbia is a growing enterprise." Beware of the double-headed thesis: "The aquaculture industry in the coastal waters of British Columbia is a growing enterprise, but its failure to address sea lice is an increasing concern." What is the controlling idea here? Is it the history of aquaculture or the concern about fish pathology? It's possible to have two or more related ideas in a thesis, but only if one of them is clearly in control, with all the other ideas subordinated to it: "Recent trends in capital investment have led to the growth of aquaculture in the coastal waters of British Columbia, but too little is being invested in studying biological diseases." In this example, the controlling element is investment of capital in aquaculture.

A PRECISE THESIS

A precise thesis should not contain vague terms such as *interesting* and *significant*, as in "The Government of Ontario's development of policy concerning water quality is one of the most interesting cases of environmental regulation." Does *interesting* mean "effective," "daring," "controversial," or "intriguing"? Don't say simply, "The role of honeybees in pollination is important" when you can be more precise about the role of bees in plant reproduction and the advantages that plants get out of their relationship with bees: "The numerous types of pollination that bees are able to perform improve the fitness of plants."

Remember to be as specific as possible when creating a thesis in order to focus your essay. Don't just make an assertion—give the main reason for it. Instead of saying, "Canadians are more accepting than Americans of evolution" and leaving it at that, add an explanation: "Canadians are more accepting than Americans of evolution because Canadian public schools and government agencies are less influenced by religious principles than are their American counterparts." If these details make your thesis sound awkward, don't worry; a working thesis is only a planning device, something to guide the organization of your ideas. You can change the wording in your final essay.

Create an outline

Individual writers differ in their need for a formal plan. Some say they never have an outline, while others maintain they can't write without one; most fall somewhere in between. Since organization is such a common problem, though, it's a good idea to know how to draw up an effective plan. Of course, the exact form your plan takes will depend on the pattern you use to develop your ideas—whether you are defining, classifying, or comparing, for example (see pages 46–9).

If you tend to have problems organizing your writing, your outline should be formal and written in complete sentences. On the other hand, if your mind is naturally logical, you may find it's enough just to jot down a few words on a scrap of paper. For most students, an informal but well-organized outline in point form is the most useful model. If you have used index cards to organize your research materials (see Chapter 3), these cards can provide a simple way to begin your outline. Rearranging the cards in different orders will give you an idea of how topics fit together before you put the outline down on paper. Try arranging the cards into potential paragraph groupings, with the most important subjects first. You can then easily work these groupings into an outline. You can also use coloured pencils to code the index cards; this will help you to sort the cards quickly and keep track of topics if you decide to change their order. If you prefer to work on a computer, you can use any of the various outline styles offered by your word processor. Choose the system that allows you to see, at a glance, the overall outline of your work.

You may even find that you prefer laying paper out on a desk or a floor to scrolling through pages on a computer.

The following is an example of an outline for an argumentative essay:

THESIS: Trophy hunting in British Columbia is an unsustainable elitist sport whose origins and regulation are not in wildlife management, as claimed by the government of British Columbia, but in the long-discredited practice of placing a bounty on wildlife.

I.   Trophy hunting in British Columbia
    A.   Trophy species
        1.   Current species
        2.   Former species
    B.   Effect of hunting on population structure of trophy species
        1.   Historical populations, quotas, and policies
        2.   Current populations, quotas, and policies
    C. Types of trophy hunters
        1.   Hunter's citizenship
        2.   Hunter's income
    D. Types of trophy hunting
        1.   In natural settings
        2.   In restricted settings

    E. Trophy hunting policies
       1. BC versus the rest of Canada
         a) With similar species
         b) With different species
       2. BC versus the rest of the world
         a) With similar species
         b) With different species

II. Bounty hunting
    A. Bounty species—wolves and bears
       1. History of wolf and bear bounties in Canada
       2. Comparison to history of wolf and bear bounties in the U.S.
    B. Effect of bounty on species populations
       1. In Canada: ineffectual
       2. In the U.S.: devastating
    C. Elimination of the bounty in Canada
       1. Opposition to bounty
       2. Legislative response for wildlife management
    D. Trophy hunting in BC
       1. Government justification
       2. Sporting association justification
       3. Opposition
    E. Today's trophy hunters are tomorrow's bounty hunters
       1. Interest in new forms of bounty hunting
       2. Goals of hunters' lobby groups

Conclusion

The following example shows an outline for an expository essay with a more descriptive theme:

THEME: Because of their importance for survival, refined navigational skills are found throughout the animal kingdom. These skills are based on a wide variety of different cues.

I. Orienting and navigating seen in many different kinds of animals
    A. Birds
       1. Arctic tern
       2. Homing pigeon

B. Insects
   1. Army ant
   2. Monarch butterfly
C. Fish
   1. Salmon
   2. Eels
   3. Tuna

II. Navigating serves different purposes
   A. Migration
      1. Favourable climate
         a) Going south
         b) Going north
      2. Food availability
      3. Breeding grounds
   B. Locating local food sources
      1. Honeybee
      2. Ant

III. Navigating animals use different cues
   A. Celestial cues
      1. Sun compass
      2. Star navigation
   B. Terrestrial cues
      1. Geomagnetism
      2. Barometric pressure
      3. Odour trails
      4. Landmarks
   C. Neurobiology of cue interpretation
      1. Eye and brain
      2. Antennae

Conclusion

The guidelines for both types of outline are simple:

- **Code your categories**. Use different sets of markings to establish the relative importance of your entries. The examples here move from Roman numerals to uppercase letters to Arabic numerals to lowercase letters, but you could use a different system. Computer programs have a default format but also offer alternatives.

- **Categorize according to importance**. Make sure that only items of equal value are put in equivalent categories. Give major points more weight than minor ones.
- **Check lines of connection**. Make sure that each of the main categories is directly linked to the central thesis, then see that each subcategory is directly linked to the larger category that contains it. Checking these lines of connection is the best way of preventing essay muddle.
- **Be consistent**. In arranging your points, use the same order every time. You may choose to move from the most important point to the least important, or vice versa, as long as you are consistent.
- **Be logical**. In addition to checking for lines of connection and organizational consistency, make sure that the overall development of your work is logical. Does each heading/idea/discussion flow into the next, leading your reader through the material in the most logical manner?
- **Use parallel wording**. Phrasing each entry in a similar way makes it easier for your reader to follow your line of thinking. For a discussion of parallel structure, see pages 122 and 123.

Be prepared to change your outline at any time in the writing process. Your initial outline is not meant to put an iron clamp on your thinking but to relieve anxiety about where you're heading. A careful outline prevents frustration and dead ends—that "I'm stuck. Where do I go from here?" feeling. But since the very act of writing will usually generate new ideas, you should be ready to modify your original plan. Just remember that any new outline must have the consistency and clear connections required for a unified essay.

SUMMARY

Writing essays in the life sciences can be a creative and imaginative experience. This process is easier if you have a well-organized set of hooks on to which you can hang information. As you develop your writing abilities and organizational style, particularly in the first years of university or college, take time to explore the different methods for structuring an essay provided in this chapter. Whatever style you choose, organizing your ideas and posing the questions that will drive your essay—whether it's descriptive or argumentative—are important first steps.

CHAPTER 3

Researching an Essay

If your topic requires more facts or evidence than the primary material provides, or if you want to know other people's opinions on the subject, you will need to do some research. Some students like to read around in the subject area before they decide on an essay topic; for them, the thesis comes after the exploration. You may find this approach useful for some essays, but generally it's better to narrow your scope and plan a tentative thesis before you turn to secondary sources—you'll save time and produce a more original essay.

EXPLORE LIBRARY RESOURCES

Before you begin your first research assignment, get to know your way around your school's library. This step is essential. You don't want to be so overwhelmed by the library's size and complexity that you either scrimp on required research or waste time and energy trying to find information. Most academic libraries have orientation seminars specifically designed to show you where and how to find what you want. Take advantage of these services. Librarians will be glad to show you the bibliographies, indices, online databases, and other reference tools for your field of study. Once you are familiar with these basic resources, you will be able to check systematically for available material.

 In addition to on-site resources, libraries offer a wealth of online services that you can access from remote locations. These services allow you to conduct your initial search for materials from your own home computer.

Online catalogues provide remote access to a list of all the holdings at your library, including books, videos, microforms, and print journals. A search by keyword will give you a list of relevant sources in your library and possibly in other libraries as well. Interlibrary loan services enable you to access these off-campus resources quickly at little or no cost. Give yourself lots of time to conduct your preliminary online search. Even if you have a good idea of what's available from the online catalogue, you will still need to go to the library to verify that the content of the shelf holdings matches the content described in the online catalogue. If you find that your library's resources are not extensive enough for what you need, you should consider interlibrary loans, which are fast, but only fast *enough* if you plan in advance.

Electronic databases simplify your search for information because they make millions of journal articles available from a single source. Libraries subscribe to online database services such as Web of Science, JSTOR, PubMed, and EBSCOhost that index a subset of smaller databases, thereby acting as gateways to a huge network of online journals. A single search gives you access to articles in thousands of different journals.

To conduct a database search from a remote computer, simply go to your library's website and follow the link to the database service of your choice. You can then search by subject, author, or title. In addition, there are usually options for narrowing the search, for example by restricting it to a specific journal, date of publication, or discipline.

Your search results will provide you with a list of articles on your subject, some of which are available in full text; this format allows you to read the material online as well as save, print, or email it.

BROWSE ONLINE DATABASES

How to use Web of Science, PubMed, and other online database services

Most libraries subscribe to online database services that allow you to access articles published in international peer-reviewed journals. PubMed, Web of Science, EBSCOhost, JSTOR, and BIOSIS Previews (ISI) are large database services that allow you to search multiple databases at once, but there are also a host of useful discipline-specific databases—for example, CABI, which provides material related to applied life sciences. Web of Science is suitable for any life sciences or health sciences essay, and it is fairly easy to navigate. PubMed is narrower in focus, restricting itself mainly to medicine and peripherally related subjects. JSTOR is an interdisciplinary resource, focussing generally on the humanities, social sciences, and sciences; it doesn't always provide the most recently published articles, but its archive contains many complete collections, some dating back to the nineteenth century. These older articles can be very valuable if you are looking at the history of an idea or field. BIOSIS has the largest catchment of all the database services, but it can be difficult to use.

Do NOT confuse database services with Internet search engines. Google, Yahoo, Bing, and similar search engines find links to content published on the Internet; PubMed and Web of Science find links to primary literature published in peer-reviewed journals. You are after peer-reviewed primary literature, so you must master these database services.

You can effectively navigate databases if you realize one thing: the value of database services resides not in the amount of information they can retrieve—which is truly overwhelming—but in the ease with which they allow you to link papers through time. You can search backwards or forwards; you can often find the first paper published in a field; and, in a click or two, you can find the most recent publication in that same field. Database services also allow you to link papers based on other factors, such as citation rate (e.g., to find the most important papers) or place of origin (e.g., to find papers written by scientists in a particular laboratory).

Let's look at three different case studies that illustrate how to search databases for useful material.

CASE 1: RESEARCHING A SCIENTIST'S BODY OF WORK

Imagine that you are writing an essay entitled "David Schindler's Contribution to Aquatic Ecology." Professor Schindler, of the University of Alberta, is one of the world's foremost experts on freshwater biology. How do you know he's a world expert? How would you write a retrospective on this Canadian's contributions to the field of aquatic biology? As you plan your approach, remember that scientists produce science, and you can use their international peer-reviewed papers as currency to assess the value of their work.

To begin your search for papers written by David Schindler, open the "Search" page, type "Schindler" into the "Author" search field, and press return. This search will find approximately 8,700 papers. Next, try searching for "Schindler D"—your results will drop to roughly 240. As you look down the list of results, you will see a number of papers that have nothing to do with aquatic ecology. After a bit of research, you discover that the David Schindler you are searching for is known as D.W. Schindler. Start the search over, typing "Schindler DW" into the "Author" field.

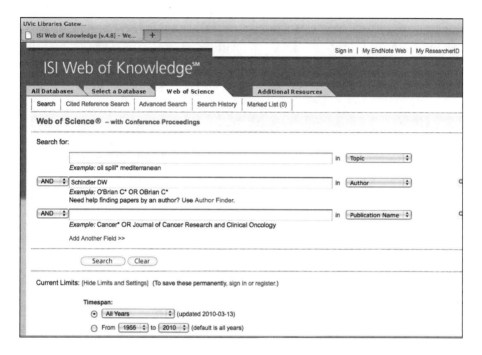

The result will be just over 200 papers on aquatic ecology, all written by David W. Schindler. (This format, last name followed by initials, works for author searches in most databases.)

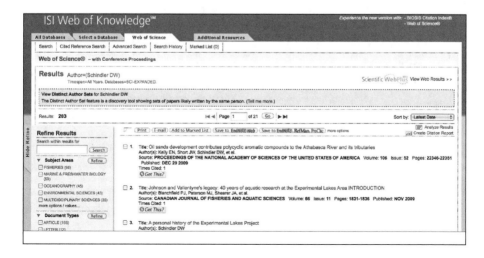

Is it possible for a scientist to produce so many papers? Yes. Some scientists produce over 300 papers during their careers. But the value of the papers lies not in their number but in their quality. Good papers present useful information that other scientists will want to read and then cite. If you look down this first page of results, you will instantly realize that the papers displayed have recently been published, as the citation numbers are low. (To find the number of times a paper has been cited, look at the "Times Cited" entry that appears below the publication date in each entry. A zero indicates that a paper has never been cited.)

Before you read Schindler's most recent work, take a look at his early career. If you look above the list of returns, you will that this is page 1 of 21 pages. Click on the double arrow to the right of this "Page" field; it will take you to the last page of results, which displays the oldest papers. Here you will see that his first paper was published in the journal *Science* in 1963.

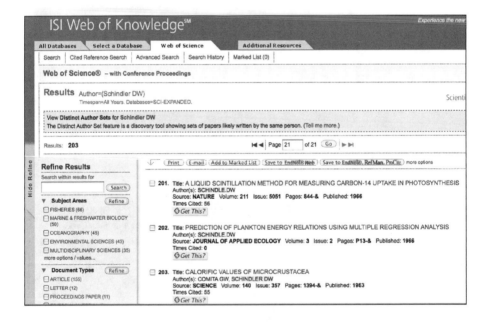

If you search through the results, you will notice that many of Schindler's papers have extraordinarily high citation rates. For example, on page 16 of the results you will find a paper (no. 165) from 1977 that is cited over one thousand times. The average citation rate for a peer-reviewed paper is about one (1), so you can see that David Schindler's output is highly cited. In fact, his papers are among the most cited in Canadian scientific publishing history.

Next, click on the title of paper 165, "Evolution of Phosphorus Limitation in Lakes." A new window that is dedicated to this article will appear.

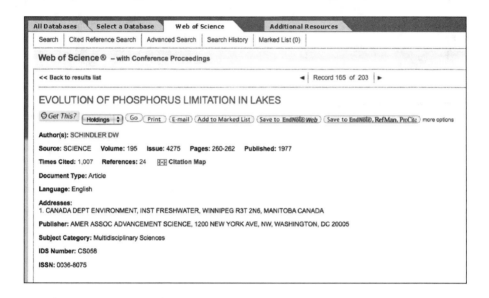

You can, at any point, send this information to your personal email account by hitting the "Email" button (located above and to the right of the author's name) and then filling in the address fields when prompted. This is one way to keep track of papers that you might want to revisit; the other is to create a marked list by clicking on the "Add to Marked List" button, which is located beside the "Email" button. When writing essays for first- or second-year classes, you will rarely need to reference a large number of papers (in this example, you would limit your research to David Schindler's most important papers), so you can stick to the first option.

So how do you access a paper? There are two ways. The first is to click on the "Get This?" button, located on the left-hand side of the page (some library pages label this button as "Find it/SFX"). In some cases, a new page that tells you where you can get the paper will appear (in this case, the paper is available from JSTOR). This page will provide a link that you can click on to go directly to the article.

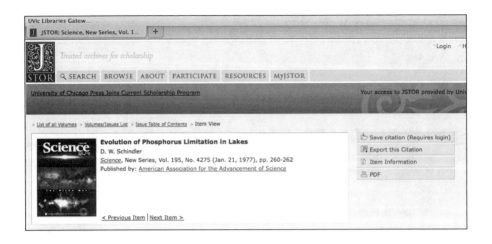

From here, you can download the entire article by clicking the "PDF" button, located in the menu on the right.

In this example, JSTOR was probably not your only choice. Often, you can access journal archives with a single click. If not, it is relatively easy to go your library's online catalogue and find a link to the *Science* archives, from which you can directly access the article you want.

The second way to access a paper is to retrieve a printed copy from your library. You will need to use this method if your library does not have access to electronic back issues of *Science*. To begin, find the journal in the online library catalogue and check that your library has a bound copy of the volume that you want. Write down the call number, volume, issue, and page information, then go to the stacks, get the volume, and photocopy the pages.

Once you've found your primary literature, how do you begin to evaluate the impact of David Schindler's work on the field of aquatic ecology? One way is to read recent analyses of his work. To do this, return to your Web of Science search results, then click on the field that displays the number of citations for one of the articles that you have chosen to use. A new window will pop up.

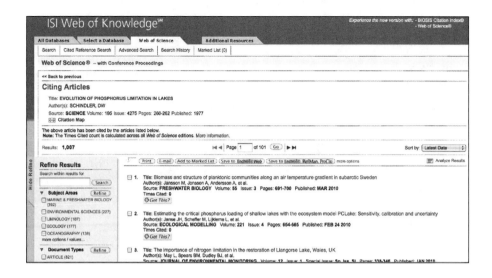

This window displays a list of peer-reviewed papers—displayed in reverse chronological order—that have cited this particular paper. It might take some scrolling and careful reading of titles before you find the most relevant articles.

How do you decide which of Schindler's articles have had the greatest impact on other researchers? Return to your original list of search results and note the menu bar on the right-hand side of the page that currently displays "Latest Date." If you pull down the menu, you can choose "Times Cited"; this option will reorder all of David Schindler's publications from most to least cited.

It turns out that there is a faster way to find Schindler's most cited articles. To begin, type "Schindler DW" into Google Scholar—you will get over 40,000 hits.

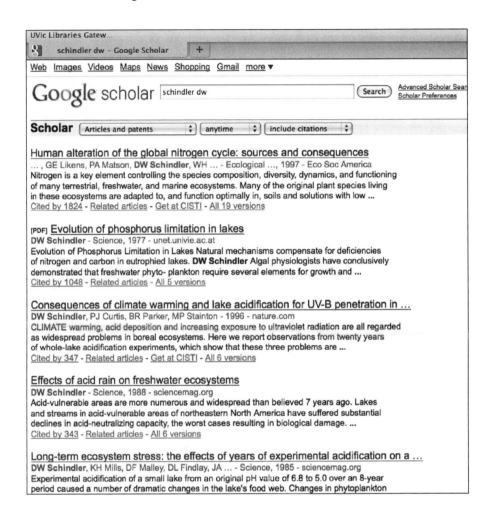

Before you cry out "argh!" in frustration, look at the first entry—"Human Alteration of the Global Nitrogen Cycle: Sources and Consequences"—and look to the bottom left-hand corner of this entry, where you will see "Cited by 1824." The next entry, "Evolution of Phosphorus Limitation in Lakes," is cited in more than one thousand other papers. Surely this is too easy! It's a list of Schindler's papers beginning with the most cited!

On that last search, both Web of Science and Google Scholar were useful. This comparison illustrates a far deeper truth: we are all flicking and bouncing through information in ways that are not actually systematic but nevertheless work. Instead of digging deeper and deeper into a single source of information, we often skip horizontally through databases. How many databases will you have open on your computer when you're researching? Probably more than one.

How we research topics today is not how we conducted our searches thirty years ago. Indeed, your professors are doing just what you are doing— skimming more and reading less. Is this because we don't like reading as much as we did in the past? I don't think so. Skimming is a superficial but very efficient way of filtering information. We're busy and we want answers quickly, and Internet-based searches spare us a great deal of laborious hunting around libraries. Online searches can also surprise us with unexpected information, forcing us to quickly revise our search strategies. The modern method is actually more fun, turning research into an exciting, fast-paced hunt. When we compare electronic research methods with traditional scholarship over the centuries, we find that we're in the midst of a revolution in research behaviour.

CASE 2: RESEARCHING INTERSECTING SUBJECTS

Now imagine that you are writing an essay on proteomics and its contribution to our understanding of sleeping sickness. How do you find material on a recently emerged, rapidly expanding field such as proteomics? How do you find relevant information on a topic such as sleeping sickness that researchers have been studying for over a hundred years?

It is best to remember that science advances along fronts, sometimes very rapidly. Usually, instructors and TAs are only interested in what's modern and topical. This means that you must restrict your search to very recent articles. In this case, let's limit our search results to articles published in the past 10 years. To restrict the search in Web of Science, go to the "Search" page and scroll down to the "Current Limits" section.

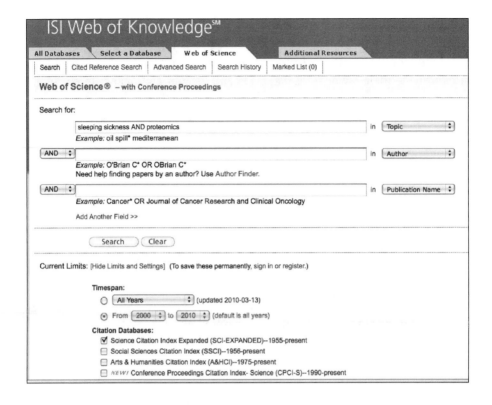

In the "Timespan" section, select the second option and change the range to read "From 2000 to 2010." In the "Citation Databases" section, make sure that "Science Citation Index Expanded" is the only option selected. To begin your search, type "sleeping sickness AND proteomics" into the "Topic" field and click on the "Search" button.

The screen that pops up indicates that there are only two papers that meet your requirements: one by Nett et al. from 2009 and one by Holzmüller et al. from 2010.

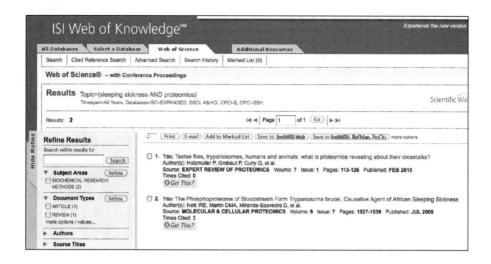

But now you have a problem—you have so little choice and such a big essay to write. Surely there are more papers?

One good way to find papers related to your topic is to look at the citations within one of these papers. Let's select the paper by Nett et al.

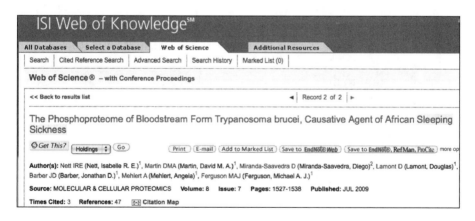

To find out what papers the authors referenced, click on the "References" button (located below the journal information, to the left of the "Citation Map" button), which indicates that the authors have cited 47 other papers. A list of those papers, arranged in alphabetical order, will pop up.

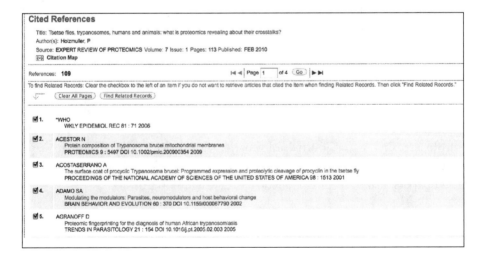

☑ 44. TU XM
Pairwise knockdowns of cdc2-related kinases (CRKs) in Trypanosoma brucei identified the CRKs for G(1)/S and G(2)/M transitions and demonstrated distinctive cytokinetic regulations between two developmental stages of the organism
EUKARYOTIC CELL 4 : 765 DOI 10.1128/EC.4.4.755-764.2005 2005

☑ 45. TU XM
The involvement of two cdc2-related kinases (CRKs) in Trypanosoma brucei cell cycle regulation and the distinctive stage-specific phenotypes caused by CRK3 depletion
JOURNAL OF BIOLOGICAL CHEMISTRY 279 : 20519 DOI 10.1074/jbc.M312862200 2004

☑ 46. USACHEVA A
The WD motif-containing protein receptor for activated protein kinase C (RACK1) is required for recruitment and activation of signal transducer and activator of transcription 1 through the type I interferon receptor
JOURNAL OF BIOLOGICAL CHEMISTRY 276 : 22948 2001

☑ 47. WARD P
Protein kinases of the human malaria parasite Plasmodium falciparum: the kinome of a divergent eukaryote
BMC GENOMICS 5 : ARTN 79 2004

References: 47   ⊨◄ Page 2 of 2 (Go) ► ►⊨

This list reveals that similar studies, with slightly different titles, are available.

As you scroll through the list of cited references, you will notice that many are not relevant, but a few look promising. There is a paper by Ward P. entitled "Protein Kinases of the Human Malaria Parasite *Plasmodium falciparum*: The Kinome of a Divergent Eukaryote." *Kinome* is a more specific term to describe a proteomic survey of kinases. Unfortunately, this article is not about sleeping sickness, but malaria.

So perhaps *sleeping sickness* is not the best term to include in your search. Try using the causative organism's name. Go back to the "Search" page and type "*Trypanosoma brucei* AND proteomics" into the "Topic" field. This search yields a total of 34 papers, a number of which are very close to your topic. Now you have choice concerning what to write about in your essay. Using the techniques for retrieving papers (outlined in Case 1), you should be able to find copies of most of the papers.

Finally, return to the paper written by Holzmüller et al. in 2010. Click on the "References" button, and a list of 109 papers will appear.

Cited References

Title: Tsetse flies, trypanosomes, humans and animals: what is proteomics revealing about their crosstalks?
Author(s): Holzmuller, P
Source: EXPERT REVIEW OF PROTEOMICS Volume: 7 Issue: 1 Pages: 113 Published: FEB 2010
Citation Map

References: 109   ⊨◄ Page 1 of 4 (Go) ► ►⊨

To find Related Records: Clear the checkbox to the left of an item if you do not want to retrieve articles that cited the item when finding Related Records. Then click "Find Related Records."
(Clear All Pages) (Find Related Records)

☑ 1. *WHO
WKLY EPIDEMIOL REC 81 : 71 2006

☑ 2. ACESTOR N
Protein composition of Trypanosoma brucei mitochondrial membranes
PROTEOMICS 9 : 5497 DOI 10.1002/pmic.200900354 2009

☑ 3. ACOSTASERRANO A
The surface coat of procyclic Trypanosoma brucei: Programmed expression and proteolytic cleavage of procyclin in the tsetse fly
PROCEEDINGS OF THE NATIONAL ACADEMY OF SCIENCES OF THE UNITED STATES OF AMERICA 98 : 1513 2001

☑ 4. ADAMO SA
Modulating the modulators: Parasites, neuromodulators and host behavioral change
BRAIN BEHAVIOR AND EVOLUTION 60 : 370 DOI 10.1159/000067790 2002

☑ 5. AGRANOFF D
Proteomic fingerprinting for the diagnosis of human African trypanosomiasis
TRENDS IN PARASITOLOGY 21 : 154 DOI 10.1016/j.pt.2005.02.003 2005

Even a quick glance down the first of the four pages provides a number of on-topic papers. To find even more potential resources, click on the "Clear All Pages" button, select a paper that sounds useful, and hit "Find Related Records"; you can further sort these records by relevance. These tools can be very useful, and gaining familiarity with them now will substantially shorten the time you need to spend preparing for your next paper.

CASE 3: RESEARCHING A BROAD TOPIC

In the third case, imagine that you're researching a very broad essay topic—stem cell research. This subject involves significant political, philosophical, and ethical issues. How can you tackle such a vast subject? How do you, as an undergraduate student, find your way into this complex field and come out alive?

You may want to consult general-reference sources before you turn to the primary literature. While these types of sources are generally not acceptable as references in your essay, they can give you a basic overview. The reference section of your school's library is a good place to start—reference books provide brilliantly succinct introductions to complex subjects. You might also find useful books dedicated to a summary of your topic. Wikipedia often contains useful articles on big subjects, and these articles are usually accurate because the self-editing community is vigilant, especially on controversial topics. The Wikipedia entry on stem cell research even has a list of related specialist research journals.

In addition, socially important scientific subjects usually create a wave of books, magazine articles, and newspaper editorials that you can consult. News publications such as *The Globe and Mail*, *The New York Times*, *The New Yorker*, *The Guardian*, *The Independent*, and *The Times* often print editorials and articles that present pithy appraisals of controversial topics. You can also use Web of Science to find relevant articles published in generalist journals such as *Scientific American* and *New Scientist*, both of which excel in scientific journalism. Their articles tend to be very undergraduate-friendly, as they're written for non-specialists.

Once you have a general understanding of your topic, you will be ready to consult the primary literature. Begin a new search in Web of Science. Restricting your search for the phrase "stem cell research" to papers published in the last ten years returns 5,261 articles. Even if you restrict your search to the past two years, you will end up with 223 results.

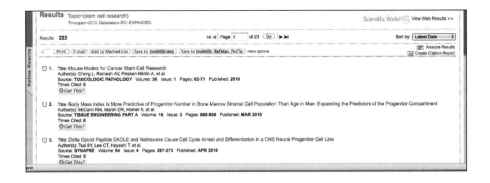

This mountain of papers is smaller but still unmanageable, so you need to redefine the search. Remember: you don't need to find all of the most technically advanced articles, just enough to form a reasonable review. Begin by restricting your search to papers published in the current year, then click on the "Refine Results" tab (located on the left-hand side of the "Results" page), which will bring up a new menu.

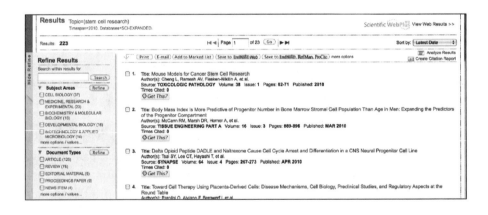

Click on the "more options/values" link that appears at the bottom of the "Document Types" section. This link will reveal more options, one of which ("Review") reveals that there are 76 peer-reviewed reviews.

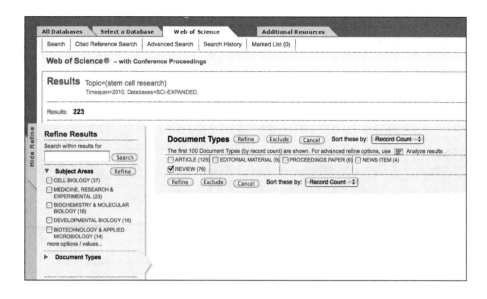

Seventy-six is a manageable number of reviews. To see a list of these reviews, check off the box beside "Review" and click the "Refine" button. A new list will tumble out. You can further refine this list by clicking first on the triangle beside "Source Titles" (located in the "Refine Results" box on the left-hand side of the screen) and then on the new "more options/values" button that appears.

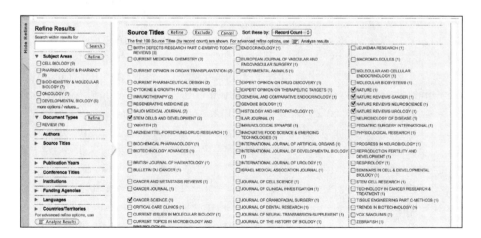

Now you can choose which journals you'd like to consult (the number of reviews available in a journal appears in square brackets after the journal's name). You could focus on journals that specialize in stem cell research or you could restrict your search to journals that you know your library carries. A surefire way to find relevant articles is to make your choice based on publication date. To find the most recent papers, expand the "Publication Years" option on the left-hand menu. You can then click the "more options/values" button, but in this case that isn't necessary, as the only two options—2009 and 2010—are already displayed.

This menu reveals that there are 54 reviews from 2010. Check the box beside "2010," then hit the "Refine" button. Now you should be able to sort through these 54 results in a matter of minutes; once you have decided on the articles that you would like to read, check whether they are available in your library.

Before you begin your first research project, play around with the many features offered by Web of Science. You will find that you can refine searches in very complex ways. You are not restricted to searching by topics, authors, and publication names, as the category buttons provide drop-down menus that allow you to select half-a-dozen other categories. For example, you could combine two topics—say, stem cell research and fraud—and find ten articles published over the last decade. In comparison, you could enter the same words, select "Title" as the search category, and find just two articles published in the same period. You can also find useful articles by searching for unusual terms within the text of the articles. Alternatively, you can use a cited reference as a starting point for a search, create citation maps that go forwards and backwards, and search through these maps—this method is very effective when you want to conduct a narrow search. With a bit of imagination coupled to experience, you can learn to quickly find what you need. Once you know how to use Web of Science, branch out and try other database services, such as PubMed or BIOSIS. All are relatively easy to learn if you start with the help page.

SEARCH THE WEB

In addition to the online services provided by your library, you may wish
to access the huge volume of information available on the Internet. No
doubt you already have favourite search engines and are accustomed to
finding information on just about anything. Your search engine can access bil-
lions of sites—a wealth of information—almost instantly. Be careful, though.
You will want to invest a little time and energy in making sure that the information you get is reliable and accurate. When writing essays for first- and
second-year courses, you can use the Web to help orient some of your questions, but you should rely only on peer-reviewed journal articles to support
your points in an essay.

Evaluating online sources

Unlike academic journals, which are peer reviewed and tend to be reliable
sources of information, many websites do not have editorial boards and publish material that has not undergone any review process. Remember that anyone can publish online, as the current proliferation of blogs will attest. You
want to be sure that the author or publisher of any material you use has the
necessary authority to lend credibility to the site.

Here are some tips for evaluating websites:

- **Pay attention to domain names**. In June 2008, the Internet
  Corporation for Assigned Names and Numbers (ICANN) made
  sweeping changes to the way top-level domains (TLDs) are
  assigned. The new system is less structured, with virtually any TLD
  allowed. However, until this system is widely adopted, the following URL guidelines will provide you with some means of assessing
  the nature and reliability of a site.

  .ca (Canada): This is an example of a country code top-level
  domain, other examples being *.uk* (United Kingdom), *.de*
  (Germany), and *.eu* (European Union). A *.ca* domain can be
  bought by any corporation or resident satisfying the Canadian
  Presence Requirement. These sites may be useful but can be
  authored by a wide range of companies or individuals, so be
  alert for a particular slant or perspective.

  .com (commercial): These domains are the most popular and can be
  bought by any individual or company, usually for the purpose

of doing business online. However, publishers such as Oxford University Press host academic journals—with the stated goal of bringing high-quality research to a wide audience—under *.com* domains. Other examples are online encyclopedias and dictionaries, newsletters, newspapers, and magazines. These organizations, as well as having a commercial purpose, have the intention of disseminating sound information. Don't discard any *.com* site out of hand, but do investigate it thoroughly.

.edu (education): This domain is used almost exclusively by educational institutions in the U.S. Educational domains used in other countries include *.ac.uk* (United Kingdom) and *.edu.mx* (Mexico). Canadian universities typically use the *.ca* domain.

.gc.ca (Government of Canada): This domain is privately held by the Canadian government, with control over subdomains held by organizations and departments, for example, Health Canada or Environment Canada. Information on these sites is usually factual, but you need to be alert for political bias.

.gov (government): These sites are used by government entities of the United States. As with *.gc.ca* sites, they usually contain factual information, but they can also be selective in which facts they include, so be on the lookout for a specialized agenda.

.net (network): This domain is traditionally used by organizations involved in Internet infrastructure, but there are no formal restrictions on who may register a *.net* domain name.

.org (organization): Originally designated for not-for-profit firms and non-governmental organizations, *.org* domains can now be registered by any individual or business. Check these sites carefully to determine who publishes them and assess their potential accuracy.

There may be additional clues in the URLs of some sites. For example, a tilde (~) indicates a personal page where you are likely to find expressions of opinion.

- **Look for information about the site host**. You should be able to find a statement, usually on the home page, that identifies the host, lists contact information, and gives details about the credentials of any contributors to the site.

- **Determine the currency of the site**. Individual sites (and pages) should include a clear indication of when the material was written, published, and last revised.
- **Evaluate the accuracy of the information**. Be sure to cross-reference facts and figures against other sources. Data published on the site should be documented in citations or a bibliography, and research methods should be explained.
- **Avoid wikis**. These are collaborative websites that allow anyone to contribute or modify content. A free encyclopedia that anyone can edit may allow you to find information quickly and easily, but it doesn't contain the kind of sound research you want to base your essay on. Although editors may continually check the veracity of contributions to the site, there is no guarantee that what you are reading is accurate.
- **Be wary of blogs**. Although some companies have official blogs that can offer good advice about subjects such as cell biology, many are simply online diaries published by a rapidly increasing number of people who are expressing personal opinion and nothing more. Using such unverified material can seriously undermine your essay, as many a student has discovered.
- **Assess the overall quality of the site**. A major clue to the reliability of the site is its level of correctness and writing standard. Typos and grammatical errors are clear indications of unprofessional work that has not been monitored for correctness and accuracy. A Web author who doesn't pay attention to these details probably doesn't have fastidious research methods either.

MAKE CLEAR NOTES

Finding your research material is one thing; taking notes that are dependable and easy to use is another. With time you will develop your own best method, but for a start you might try the index-card system. Record each new idea or piece of evidence on a separate card. The number of cards you need will depend on the range and type of research you're doing. When you've finished with your note-taking, you can easily arrange the cards in the order in which you will use them.

You might prefer to interpret the information as you're reading it and to record your notes on a computer. Then you can easily cut and paste your notes to arrange them in a logical order.

Whatever method you follow, remember that exact records are essential for proper references. For every entry, check that the bibliographic details are complete, including the name of the author, the title of the source, the place and date of publication, and the page number. For online sources, record the URL, date of publication, and date of access. Nothing is more frustrating than using a piece of information in an essay only to find that you aren't sure where it came from. Record the bibliographic details in the citation format you plan to use for your paper; that way, when you're preparing your list of references later on, you can copy the source directly. (For a detailed discussion of when to use references and how to avoid plagiarism, see pages 56–8; for detailed information about citation formats, see Chapter 11.)

SUMMARY

Research in the life sciences involves conducting new experiments in the context of previous research. Consequently, learning to find peer-reviewed papers that are relevant to your essay topic is probably the most important step you will take in your development as a scholar of science. You must learn how to use library resources and retrieve relevant information from electronic databases. Practise searching for articles in Web of Science—if you can master such a powerful database, you will have the confidence to learn others. Once you develop these literature-searching techniques, you will be better prepared to enter the wider world of experimentation.

CHAPTER 4

Writing an Essay

OBJECTIVES

- developing your ideas
- writing an effective introduction and conclusion
- knowing the difference between a summary and a conclusion
- using quotations
- avoiding plagiarism
- editing what you've created
- learning by example—an annotated essay
- backing up your work

WRITING THE FIRST DRAFT

Rather than striving for perfection from the moment they begin to write, most writers find it easier to compose the first draft as quickly as possible and do extensive revisions later. However you begin, you can't expect the first draft to be the final copy. Skilled writers know that revising is a necessary part of the writing process and that care taken with revisions makes the difference between a mediocre essay and a good one.

Many writers find it difficult to start writing. Facing down writer's block is not easy. If you are a student who suffers from this problem, remember that you don't need to write all parts of the essay in the same order as they will appear in the final copy. In fact, the introduction is often the hardest part to write. If you face the first blank page with a growing sense of paralysis, try leaving the introduction until later and start with the first idea in your outline. If you feel so intimidated that you haven't even been able to draw up an outline, you might try the approach suggested by John Trimble[1] and begin anywhere: just write, "Well, it seems to me that . . ." and begin talking on paper.

Instead of sharpening pencils or running out for a snack, just try to get going. Don't worry about grammar or wording; at this stage, the object is to get your writing juices flowing. Begin small: start linking your bits of evidence together to support your ideas, then assemble these ideas into an argument.

Of course, you can't expect this kind of exploratory writing to resemble the first draft that follows an outline. You will probably need to do a great deal more changing and reorganizing, but at least you will have the relief of seeing words on a page. Experienced writers—and not only those with writer's block—consider this the most productive way to proceed.

DEVELOPING YOUR IDEAS: SOME COMMON PATTERNS

The way you develop your ideas will depend on your essay topic, and topics can vary enormously. Even so, most essays follow one or another of a handful of basic organizational patterns. Here are some of the patterns, along with suggestions for using them effectively.

Defining

Sometimes a whole essay is an extended definition, explaining the meaning of a term that is complicated, controversial, or simply important to your field of study—for example, *evolutionary biology* in medicine, *ethics* in animal biology, or *biotechnology* in agriculture. Rather than making your whole paper an extended definition, you may decide to begin your paper by defining a key term before shifting to a different organizational pattern. In either case, make your definition exact; it should be broad enough to include all the things that belong in the category but narrow enough to exclude things that don't belong. A good definition builds a kind of verbal fence around a term, herding together all the members of the class and cutting off all outsiders.

For any discussion of a term that goes beyond a bare definition, you should give concrete illustrations or examples. Depending on the nature of your essay, these could vary in length from one or two sentences to several paragraphs or even pages. If you are defining *biotechnology*, for instance, you will probably want to discuss at some length the theories of leading biotechnologists.

In an extended definition, it's also useful to point out the differences between the term you're defining and any others that may be related to or confused with it. For instance, if you're defining *parthenogenesis*, you might want to distinguish it from *cloning*; if you're defining *restoration ecology*, you might want to distinguish it from *conservation*; if you're defining *backcrossing*, you might want to distinguish it from *hybridization*.

Classifying

Classifying means dividing something into its separate parts according to a given principle of selection. The principle or criterion may vary. You could classify crops, for example, according to how they grow (above the ground or below the ground), how long they take to mature, or what climatic conditions they require. As another example, you could classify members of a given population according to age, occupation, income, race, religion, or gender. If you are organizing your essay by a system of classification, remember the following guidelines:

- You must account for all members of a class. If any are left over, you need to alter some categories or add more.
- You can divide categories into subcategories. You should consider using subcategories if there are significant differences within a category. If, for instance, you are classifying the workforce according to occupation, you might want to create subcategories according to income level.
- You should include at least two items in each subcategory.

Explaining a process

Explanations of processes show how something works or has worked—whether it is the weather cycle, the Linnaean system of classification, or the stages in an insect's development. You need to be systematic, to break down the process into a series of steps or stages. Although the order of the steps will vary, most often it will be chronological, in which case you should see that the sequence is accurate and easy to follow. Whatever the arrangement, you can generally make the process easier to follow if you start a new paragraph for each new stage.

Tracing causes or effects

A cause-or-effect analysis is really a particular kind of process discussion in which you explain how certain events have led to or resulted from other events. Usually you are explaining why something happened. When exploring causes and effects, always avoid oversimplifying relationships. If you are tracing causes, distinguish between a direct cause and a contributing cause, between what is a condition of something happening and what is merely a correlation or coincidence. For example, if you discover that both the age of the average driver in Canada and the number of accidents caused by drunk drivers are increasing, you cannot jump to the conclusion that older drivers are the cause of the increase in drunk-driving accidents. Similarly, you must be sure that the result you identify is a genuine product of the event or action.

Comparing

Students sometimes forget that comparing things means showing differences as well as similarities—even if the instructions do not say "compare and contrast." Suppose, for instance, that you were comparing negative and positive opinions on the effects of conservation on the population biology of some rare animals. The easiest method for comparison—though not always the best—is to discuss the first subject in the comparison thoroughly and then move on to the second:

Positive views: population figures
conservation efforts
public opinion

Negative views: population figures
conservation efforts
public opinion

The problem with this kind of comparison is that it often sounds like two separate essays slapped together.

To make a successful comparison, you must integrate the two subjects, first in your introduction (by putting them both in a single context) and again in your conclusion (by bringing together the important points you have made about each subject). When discussing the second subject, try to refer repeatedly to your findings about the first ("In contrast to the rosy view of free trade offered by its supporters in the manufacturing sector, critics maintain that . . ."). This method may be the wisest choice if the subjects you are comparing seem so different that it is hard to create similar categories by which to discuss them.

If you can find similar criteria or categories for discussing both subjects, however, the comparison will be more effective if you organize it by category:

Population figures: negative views
positive views
Conservation efforts: negative views
positive views
Public opinion: negative views
positive views

Because this kind of comparison is more tightly integrated, the reader will find it easier to see the similarities and differences between the subjects. As a result, the essay is likely to be more forceful.

WRITING INTRODUCTIONS

The beginning of an essay has a dual purpose: to indicate your approach to the topic and to whet your reader's interest in what you have to say. There are many ways to catch your reader's attention; the following sections discuss four of the most common methods. However you choose to begin your essay, your lead must relate to your topic: never sacrifice relevance for originality. Also, whether your introduction is one paragraph or several, make sure that by the end of it your reader clearly knows the purpose of your essay and how you intend to accomplish it.

The funnel approach

One effective way of introducing a topic is to place it in a context—to supply a kind of backdrop that will put it in perspective. The idea is to step back and discuss the area into which your topic fits and then gradually narrow in on your specific topic. Sheridan Baker[2] calls this the *funnel approach* (see page 50). For example, suppose that your topic is the growing demand for personalized medicine. You might begin with a more general discussion of the growing influence of DNA in crime-analysis procedures or in disease-screening techniques.

You can use a funnel opening in almost any kind of essay. The following example comes from an essay on phenotypic plasticity:

> Scientists once believed that one gene was responsible for one trait. Even today, popular language suggests that a single gene—for example, the "intelligence" gene or the "fat" gene—can control complex behaviour or morphology. However, more recently-discovered complex interactions such as pleiotropy and epistasis prove that phenotypic traits are not simply a matter of genetics. Over the past decades, genetic researchers have increasingly focussed on the occurrence and causes of phenotypic plasticity, an aspect of organismal life that merges genetics, anatomy, and physiology. Plasticity, in the developmental sense, is a property of the reaction norm for a specific expressed trait. Norms of reaction model the variability of phenotypes across different environments. Genes must interact with the environment, and that environment has a number of variable elements—temperature, climate, water availability, day length, soil

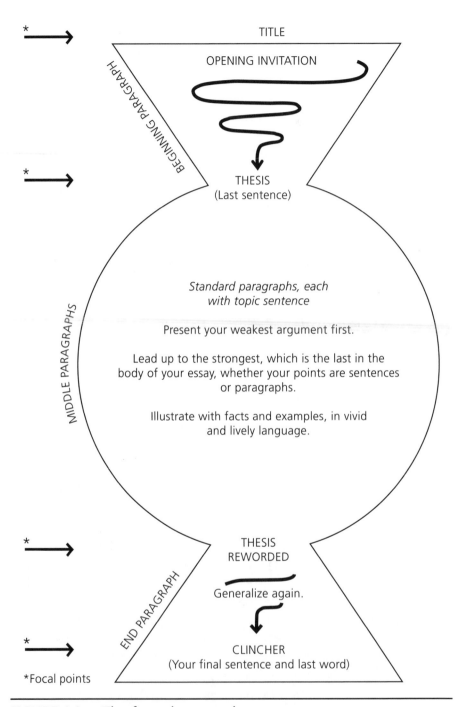

FIGURE 4.1. The funnel approach

The Canadian Practical Stylist, by Sheridan Baker and Laurence B. Gamache, 1998, pg. 65, Addision Wesley. Reprinted with permission by Peasrson Education Canada, Inc.

nutrition, insects, and disease. Genes also interact with one another. When it comes to the biology of organisms, gene–environment interactions have far-reaching and often elusive consequences.

You should try to catch your reader's interest right from the start. You know from your own reading how a dull beginning can put you off a book or an article. The fact that your instructor must read on anyway makes no difference. If a reader has to get through thirty or forty similar essays, it's all the more important for yours to stand out.

The quotation

This approach works especially well when you use a quotation from the person or work that you will discuss in your essay. Here is an example from an essay on the effects of overfertilization on Canadian lakes:

> Lakes around dense human habitation are in danger of dying. This is an international problem, according to David Schindler in *The Algal Bowl: Overfertilization of the World's Freshwaters and Estuaries*. In a recent interview, Schindler said, "We really need to treat a feedlot with 50,000 cattle like we treat a small city." Pigs, cattle, and humans produce abundant waste that seeps into water systems, accumulating in lakes where it causes eutrophication: nutrient levels spike, causing algal blooms, which in turn deplete the water of oxygen, killing fish and other organisms. In Canada, this problem affects lakes located south of 51 degrees latitude in a band stretching from coast to coast.

You can also use a quotation from an unrelated source or author, as long as it is relevant to your topic and not so well known that it will appear trite. A dictionary of quotations can be helpful, allowing you to search for quotes by author, key words, or even topic.

The question

A rhetorical question will only annoy the reader if it's commonplace or if the answer is obvious, but a thought-provoking question can make a strong opening. For example, you might begin an essay on the issue of court fines for environmental damages with the question, "How do you put a price on the cultural and biological damage of chopping down the Golden Spruce on Haida Gwaii?" Just be sure that you do actually answer the question somewhere in your essay.

The anecdote or telling fact

This is the kind of concrete lead that journalists often use to grab their readers' attention. For example, a biology paper on collagen in scurvy patients might begin: "By the time Magellan's ship, the *Trinidad*, had crossed the Pacific, only a dozen men were left functioning in his crew. Scurvy had taken twenty souls already. Another twenty were too sick from the disease to be of any use. Magellan was just one of many long-distance sailors whose crews would pay a high price for a diet too low in fresh fruits and vegetables." Save this approach for your least formal essays—and remember that the incident must really highlight the ideas you will discuss in your essay.

WRITING CONCLUSIONS

Endings can be painful—sometimes for the reader as much as for the writer. Too often, writers feel that they ought to say something profound and memorable, so they end up writing a pretentious or affected ending. You know the sort of thing:

> In summary, gene therapy is going through a period of technical revolution. The advances being made in this field will undoubtedly save thousands of lives in the future.

Experienced editors say that many articles and essays would be better without their final paragraphs; in other words, when you have finished saying what you have to say, the best thing to do is to stop. This advice may work for short essays, where you can keep the central point firmly in the foreground. However, for longer pieces, where you have developed a number of ideas or a complex line of argument, you should provide a sense of closure. Readers welcome an ending that helps to tie the ideas together; they don't like to feel as though they've been left dangling. And since the final impression is often the most lasting, it's in your interest to finish strongly. Simply restating your thesis or summarizing what you have already said isn't forceful enough. The following sections discuss several alternatives.

The inverse funnel

The simplest conclusions restate the thesis in different words and then discuss its implications. Sheridan Baker calls this the *inverse funnel approach*, as opposed to the *funnel approach* of the opening paragraph.[3]

The sample essay on phenotypic plasticity, which opened with a "funnel" approach, concludes with an "inverse funnel":

> The evidence supplied in this essay shows that temperature, climate, water availability, day length, soil nutrition, insects, and diseases can all affect phenotypic plasticity. The complex gene interactions generated by these factors result in a wealth of developmental and adaptive responses. Far from a simple one gene–one phenotype model, organisms show a variety of reaction norms. This evidence suggests that phenotypic plasticity is a key component of an organism's ability to adapt to its environment.

One danger in moving to a wider perspective is that you may try to embrace too much. When a conclusion expands too far, it tends to lose focus. It's always better to discuss specific implications than to trail off into vague generalities in an attempt to sound profound.

The new angle

A variation on the basic inverse funnel approach is to reintroduce your argument with a new twist. Suggesting a fresh angle can make your ending more compelling or provocative. Beware of introducing an entirely new idea, though, or one that's only loosely connected to your original argument; the result, if it's too far off-topic, could detract from your argument. The following example is a short and very effective conclusion to a highly focussed essay on the function of tapetal cells:

> Ultimately, understanding the factors that control a tapetal cell's molecular and physical triggers will lead to deeper insights into conifer sterility. The tapetal layer is essential to conifer reproduction, as it creates the megaspore wall. As the guardian of the seed, the megaspore wall protects the developing seed from both the elements and the surrounding tissues of the tree. Although this structure has been considered vestigial and useless by some investigators, its role is possibly more dynamic than previously thought. Without a megaspore wall, the ovule would abort and the seed would die.

The full circle

If you begin your essay by relating an anecdote, posing a rhetorical question, or citing a startling fact, you can complete the circle by referring to it again in your conclusion, relating it to some of the insights revealed in the main body of your essay. This technique provides a nice sense of closure for the reader.

The stylistic flourish

Some of the most successful conclusions end on a strong stylistic note. Try varying the sentence structure: if most of your sentences are long and complex, make the last one short and punchy, or vice versa. Sometimes you can dramatize your idea with a striking phrase or a colourful image. When you are writing your essay, keep your eyes open and your ears tuned for fresh ways of putting things, and save the best for the end. If you want good examples of short and long essays that finish with a flourish, have a look at articles published in the generalist journal *New Scientist*.

SUMMARY OR CONCLUSION—WHAT'S THE DIFFERENCE?

A summary restates the aim and then outlines the major premises of an essay. A conclusion may contain elements of summary, but it often introduces opinion or perspective into the writing. Conclusions can discuss future research directions, or they can evaluate the merit of research in a particular field. Remember: you draw a conclusion, but you don't draw a summary. The former involves opinion, the latter is a mere shopping list of highlights. Life science students find it much more difficult to write a conclusion than do students in the humanities; science students often feel that they cannot diverge from the objectivity and neutrality of scientific method.

So when should you end your essay with a conclusion rather than a summary? This decision will depend on your topic. When science methodology meets its limitations, when science meets or even creates controversy, or even when science meets society—and they tend to meet very often—then opinion and conjecture have their place. You might say that to not have an opinion in a conclusion leads the reader to conclude that the writer is either naive or uncritical.

INTEGRATING QUOTATIONS

A quotation can benefit an essay in two ways. First, it can add depth and credibility by showing that your position or idea has the support of an authority. Second, it can provide stylistic variety and interest, especially if the quotation is colourful or eloquent. The trick to using quotations effectively is to make sure that you properly integrate them into your own discussion—they should neither dominate your ideas nor seem tacked on. To ensure that a quotation has the desired effect, always refer to the point you want the reader to take from it; don't let a quotation dangle on its own. Usually, the best way to do this is to make the point before the quotation:

> Shortly after receiving the Nobel Peace Prize in 1962, Linus Pauling expressed his dismay at the effects of radioactive fallout from nuclear bombs: "I like people. I like animals, too—whales and quail, dinosaurs and dodos. But I like human beings especially, and I am unhappy that the pool of human germplasm, which determines the nature of the human race, is deteriorating."

Sometimes, however, a quotation can precede the explanation. This format is common in introductory paragraphs, as illustrated earlier in this chapter. You must make sure, however, that you explain the significance of the quotation so that your reader is not left wondering why you have added it.

If a complete sentence precedes the quotation, use a colon at the end of the introductory phrase; if you work the quotation into the syntax of your own sentence, you do not need to add any punctuation before the quoted material; to otherwise introduce a quotation, use a comma:

> John Polyani put it best: "Nothing is more irredeemably irrelevant than bad science."

(or)

> Was John Polyani being merely rhetorical when he said that "[n]othing is more irredeemably irrelevant than bad science"?

(or)

> John Polyani felt strongly, insisting, "Nothing is more irredeemably irrelevant than bad science."

If the quoted passage comes at the end of a sentence, finish with a period before the closing quotation mark—unless the sentence is a question, in which case finish with a question mark after the quotation marks. If you need to adjust any element of the quoted material (e.g., changing a capital letter to a lowercase letter), place your modification in square brackets.

The length of a quotation can vary from a short phrase woven into the middle of a sentence to a paragraph or more. Just remember that the longer the quotation, the greater the danger that it will overshadow rather than reinforce your own viewpoint. Don't quote any more than you really need. You should also know that writers in certain disciplines, especially those in the life sciences, tend not to include direct quotations; when they do use them, the quotations are usually very short. If you're unsure about the conventions for your own discipline, you can always ask your instructor.

AVOIDING PLAGIARISM

Plagiarism is intellectual theft; as with other crimes, ignorance is no excuse. Most students caught plagiarizing are not criminals, but just lazy, and are often unaware of how incredibly sensitive the academic community is on this issue. Be warned: plagiarism is a form of cheating, and your instructors will view it as no less than an abomination. Why? Research is a collaborative exercise. Scientific information is built up paper by peer-reviewed paper, and these papers cannot include plagiarized material. As a student new to the essay-writing process, you must learn to write within this tradition. Plagiarism is a form of disinformation, masking the truth. It flies in the face of the originality of discovery, invention, and individual expression, as it is merely parroting.

Plagiarism flourishes in ambiguous situations, often because students do not default to the norm of science, which is to never use a piece of knowledge without attribution. If you use someone else's idea, acknowledge it, even if you have changed the wording or just summarized the main points. Don't be afraid that your work will seem weaker if you acknowledge the ideas of others. On the contrary, it will be all the more convincing; serious academic treatises are almost always built on the work of preceding scholars, with credit duly given to the earlier work.

Let's say you are writing an essay on new directions in the field of ecology. The following passage comes from Charles Hall's article on ecology[4] in the *Encyclopedia of Earth*, a Creative Commons (cultural free-share) site:

> More recently ecology has included increasingly the human-dominated world of agriculture, grazing lands for domestic animals, cities, and even industrial parks. Industrial ecology is a discipline that has recently been developed, especially in Europe, where the objective is to follow the energy and material use throughout the process of, e.g., making an automobile with the objective of attempting to improve the material and energy efficiency of manufacturing.

One student's essay includes the following passage. It is plagiarized because the student repeated exact phrases from the original article without acknowledging the source:

✗   Ecology has begun to include **the human-dominated world of agriculture, grazing lands for domestic animals, cities, and even industrial parks.** Additionally, **industrial ecology** as **a discipline, especially in Europe,** follows **energy use throughout the process of** production, such as **making an automobile. The objective** is **to attempt to improve the material and energy efficiency of manufacturing.**

To avoid a charge of plagiarism and its unpleasant and sometimes disastrous consequences, all you need to do is acknowledge your source. In the correctly documented passage below, the writer has used quotation marks to identify words and phrases taken directly from the original article; the writer has also included a parenthetical text citation. (See Chapter 11 for alternative citation styles.) In this case, the writer would provide a bibliography, at the end of the essay, that gives complete publication information for the source.

✓   According to Hall (2009), ecology has begun to include the **"human-dominated world of agriculture, grazing lands for domestic animals, cities, and even industrial parks. Industrial ecology is a discipline that has recently been developed, especially in Europe, where the objective is to follow the energy and material use throughout the process of, e.g., making an automobile with the objective of attempting to improve the material and energy efficiency of manufacturing."**

The following passage shows a variant on plagiarism. This form of plagiarism is more common in students' essays for life sciences courses, as science essays usually do not include direct quotations. This student has made the mistake of assuming that putting the information in his own words is good enough. It's not. The concept of industrial ecology is still "borrowed":

✗   Ecology has shifted some of its focus to agriculture and industry. Industrial ecology is a recent development that uses ecological models to study the energy efficiency of manufacture.

Remember that plagiarism involves not only using someone else's words but also expressing their ideas without referencing the original source.

In the correctly documented passage below, proper acknowledgment takes the form of an in-text reference to the original author:

✓ Recently, ecology has begun to include studies of human activities, particularly agriculture and industry. An example is the new field of industrial ecology that creates models of the energy efficiency of manufacturing processes (Hall 2009).

Where should you draw the line on acknowledgements? As a rule, you don't need to give credit for anything that's common knowledge. You wouldn't provide a reference for the fact that DNA is present in a cell's nucleus or that Darwin and Wallace developed theories of evolution, but you should acknowledge any clever turn of phrase that is neither well known nor your own. And always document any fact or claim—statistical or otherwise—that is unfamiliar or open to question.

For all students, online material presents a particular hazard and can cause a lot of grief. Even though websites are instantly accessible, the material is not common property. In fact, it is the property of the individual or organization that publishes it and is protected by copyright in the same way that printed material is. (Information about the proper procedure for documenting online material is included in Chapter 11.) It is crucial that you properly acknowledge the information you find on a website.

In the life sciences, unlike in the arts and humanities, writers usually avoid using direct quotations. As a student, you must learn to interpret what you read and rewrite it in your own words, a process that often involves reorganizing and synthesizing information from a number of different sources. Subsequently, avoiding plagiarism in your life sciences undergraduate essays can be difficult, but it can be done. (For examples of proper paraphrasing and a name–year style of in-text citation in a life sciences essay, see the sample annotated student essay on pages 62–77.)

A last note on plagiarism: in the event you are falsely accused, remember that the best offense is defense. Hand in a file folder containing your research notes or old drafts. This should clear things up immediately.

THE EDITING STAGE

Often the best writer in a class is not the one who can dash off a fluent first draft but the one who is the best editor. To edit your work well you need to see it as the reader will, and in order to do that you have to distinguish between what you meant to say and what you have actually put on the page. For this reason it's a good idea to leave some time between drafts so that when you begin to edit you will be looking at the writing afresh rather than reviewing it from memory. This is the time to do something that will take your mind off your work, to go to a movie or the gym. Without this distancing period, you can become so involved in your paper that it's hard to see your writing objectively.

Editing doesn't mean simply checking your work for errors in grammar or spelling. It means looking at the piece as a whole to see if the ideas are well organized, well documented, and well expressed. It may mean making changes to the structure of your essay by adding some paragraphs or sentences, deleting others, and moving others around. Experienced writers may be able to check several aspects of their work at the same time, but if you are inexperienced or in doubt about your writing, it's best to look at the organization of the ideas before you tackle sentence structure, diction, style, and documentation.

What follows is a checklist of questions to ask yourself as you begin editing. Far from all-inclusive, it focusses on the first step: examining the organization of your work. Since you probably won't want to check through your work separately for each question, you can group some together and overlook others, depending on your own strengths and weaknesses as a writer.

Checking for organization

- Is the title concise and informative?
- Are the purpose and approach of this essay evident from the beginning?
- Are all sections of the paper relevant to the topic?
- Is the organization logical?
- Are the ideas sufficiently developed? Is there enough evidence, explanation, and illustration?
- Would an educated person who hasn't read the primary material understand everything? Do any points need additional clarifications or explanations?
- Does the discussion take into account opposing arguments or evidence?
- Do the paragraph divisions make the ideas more coherent? Do these divisions signal where one idea transitions to the next? Are similar ideas grouped together in each paragraph?

- Do any parts of the essay seem disjointed? Would more transitional words or logical indicators make the sequence of ideas easier to follow?
- Do the conclusions accurately reflect the argument in the body of the work?

If you have difficulty visualizing the overall organization of your paper onscreen, try printing the pages and placing them beside one another on the floor, bed, or desk. This process should help you to see what is not always apparent on a computer—namely, the number of lines or pages that you have devoted to various parts of your argument or description. You can then decide whether any of your discussions seem too long or too short.

You can also devise your own checklist based on comments you have received on previous assignments. These questions will be particularly useful when you move from the overview of your paper to the close focus on sentence structure, diction, punctuation, spelling, and style. If you have a particular weak area—for example, irrelevant evidence or run-on sentences—you should give it special attention. Keeping a personal checklist will save you from repeating the same old mistakes.

Your word-processing program will catch typing as well as spelling errors, but remember that it may not point out actual words that are used incorrectly (such as *there* when you need *their*). Think of a computer-based spell check as a useful first pass rather than a final one. Similarly, grammar checkers are not reliable. They will pick up common grammar errors and stylistic problems, but they do make mistakes and will likely never equal the judgment of a good human editor.

Always read over your work with a critical eye and take the time to change anything that is unsatisfactory. If you have doubts about your essay, read it aloud to yourself—boring bits, illogical lines of argument, poor style, awkward phrasing, and bad grammar will become immediately obvious. If you're still unsure, try recording your reading and replaying it to yourself, or read your essay to a friend, loyal roommate, or willing family member.

Keep in mind, too, that for final editing most good writers suggest working from the printed page rather than from the computer screen. Print a draft and use the hard copy for your editing and proofreading. You will read more slowly and with greater acuity, and the final product will be more polished as a result.

FORMATTING YOUR ESSAY

We've all been told not to judge a book by its cover, but the very warning suggests that we have a natural tendency to do so. Readers of essays have this same tendency. A well-typed, attractive essay creates a receptive reader and, fairly or unfairly, often gets a higher mark than a sloppy paper that is more difficult to read. Good looks won't substitute for good thinking, but they will certainly enhance it.

Number each page. Always double-space your work and use margins of at least one inch to frame the text in white space and allow room for your reader to write comments. Provide a neat, well-spaced cover page that includes the title, your name, and the name of your instructor and course. Make good use of formatting features such as bold and italics for emphasis, and choose appropriate font faces. One rule of thumb is to use a serif font such as Times New Roman, usually 12-point, for the body of the essay and a sans-serif font such as Arial for the title and headings. However, most instructors will provide you with guidelines specifying their particular preferences for presentation and formatting.

Keep in mind that while a computer can make your work look good, fancy graphics and a slick presentation won't replace intelligent thinking.

SAMPLE ANNOTATED STUDENT ESSAY

The following essay on aspects of chromatin (pages 62–77) illustrates various style problems that are common in student-written essays. As you read through the essay, examine the annotated comments and think about how they might help you to improve your own work. Compare the original "bad" version with the revised "good" version—you will notice what an improvement a few simple edits can make. The student received a B– for the original essay—the content was good, but the writing contained many problems with style, grammar, and overall effect. After receiving her instructor's suggestions, the student re-edited and then resubmitted the paper. The "good" version received an A. In almost every case, improving your style and grammar will earn you a higher grade. Remember that you won't often have the opportunity to resubmit your essay for a higher grade, as this student did, so edit your work as carefully as you can before handing it in.

BAD

There are mistakes
in the use of commas
throughout the essay.

This last clause is
unnecessary, as the
sentence already
lists what the
reader can expect.

Chromatin function

The organelles within eukaryotic cells, contain thousands of structures that allow for intricate and complex functions, that are responsible for life of an organism. The nucleus is one of the most prominent membrane bound organelles, which contains DNA organized into chromosomes that are composed of compact chromatin fibers (Horn &Peterson, 2002). There are many functions associated with the structure of chromatin, which include gene transcription and replication, positioning of the chromosomes, and gene silencing, which will be the basis of this essay.

The primary structure of chromatin consists of 147 base pairs of DNA coiled in a left-handed helix 1.7 times around a histone, forming a "beads-on-a-string" appearance. Each histone contains separate functional domains, which include a motif, an amino terminus and a carboxy "tail" terminus, that contain sites for post-modification such as methylation, or phosphorylation (Horn et al. 2002). Histones then interact with each other through tail mediated nucleosome interactions, forming the 30 nm fiber, secondary structure. Formation of the tertiary structure is driven by magnesium ions through tail-mediated interactions forming chromonema fibers (Hornet al., 2002).

References are
incorrect.

The opening paragraph is a classic funnel type, but it suffers from having three long sentences in a row. The reader needs to be drawn in, not bored.

This paragraph builds logically from the chromatin molecule to the tertiary structure, but it has many little errors and too many long sentences.

GOOD

The opening paragraph is more direct and slightly shorter.

Chromatin function

Organelles within eukaryotic cells carry out complex functions that are responsible for maintaining the life of the organism. Most prominent among the organelles is the nucleus, which contains DNA and chromatin fibers organized into chromosomes (Horn and Peterson 2002). The structure of chromatin is associated with many functions, including gene transcription and replication, chromosome positioning, and gene silencing.

The primary structure of chromatin consists of 147 base pairs of DNA coiled in a left-handed helix 1.7 times around a histone complex, forming a "beads-on-a-string" appearance. Histone proteins have separate functional domains. These domains include a characteristic motif, an amino terminus, and a carboxy "tail" terminus. Post-translational modification occurs by either methylation or phosphorylation (Horn and Peterson 2002). Histones interact with each other through tail-mediated nucleosome interactions, forming 30 nm fibers, which are secondary structures. Magnesium ions drive the formation of the tertiary structure through tail-mediated interactions to create chromonema fibers (Horn and Peterson 2002).

1

Generally, run-on sentences have been broken up. In the second paragraph, the underlined material denotes instances where the author has corrected inaccuracies.

BAD

The first sentence of a paragraph needs to be more dynamic.

→ Chromatin can exist in two distinct forms within the nucleus, which are euchromatin and heterochromatin. Euchromatin is considered to be in a transcriptional "on" state, becoming uncoiled during interphase, while heterochromatin is condensed and remains in an "off" state (Jenuwein and Allis, 2001).

Repetition obscures meaning.

One of the key functions of chromatin is its critical involvement in gene expression. There are many suggested mechanisms that imply chromatin is associated with the process of transcription, via many associated proteins, mechanisms, and complexes as described below.

The first proposed mechanism involved in the enhancement of transcription involves nucleosomes that are continuously destabilized by nucleosome remodeling complexes. These complexes respond to stimuli within the cell and disturb the interactions between the histone octamers and the DNA, which cause lateral movements of nucelosomes along the DNA strand (Catez, Lim, Hock, Postnikov, & Bustin 2003). This results in modifications such as acetylation of lysine residues and phosphorylation of serine residues in the aminotermini of the histones (Catez et al. 2003). The extent of modification is dependent on the enzymes including histone acetyle transferases (HAT), histone deacetylases (HDACs), kinases and phosphatases. Researchers have found that enzymatic activity of these modifying

In both paragraphs, the numerous run-on sentences cause problems in clarity.

The reference style is inconsistent. This mistake recurs throughout the essay.

GOOD

Chromatin can exist either as euchromatin or heterochromatin. Euchromatin is in a transcriptional "on" state, uncoiling during interphase. Heterochromatin is condensed and remains in an "off" state (Jenuwein and Allis 2001). One of chromatin's key functions is in gene expression. Many suggested mechanisms imply that chromatin is associated with transcription via many complexes and their associated proteins.

The first mechanism researchers proposed involves nucleosome remodeling complexes. Transcription is enhanced because of continuous destabilization of nucleosomes by nucleosome remodelling complexes. Responding to stimuli within the cell, complexes disturb the interactions between histone and DNA. This reaction causes lateral movements of nucleosomes along the DNA strand (Catez et al. 2003). A consequence is modification of the amino terminal of the histone by acetylation of lysine residues and phosphorylation of serine residues(Catez et al. 2003). The extent of modification is dependent on particular enzymes. These include histone acetyletransferases (HAT), histone deacetylases (HDACs), kinases, and phosphatases. Researchers have found that enzymatic activity of these

2

The author has combined the third and fourth paragraphs to form a single, more unified paragraph.

BAD

enzymes leads to the recruitment of regulatory machinery of the cell, and thus promotes structural alterations that ultimately lead to transcription, replication or DNA repair (Catez and colleagues 2003).

Other proteins that are thought to be associated with transcription are included in the HMGN family of proteins, which are found in all mammalian and vertebrate cells.HMGN1 and HMGN2 bind without specificity to the nucleosome core particle and form complexes containing two molecules of either HMGN1 or HMGN2 (Catez et al., 2003). The function of the HMGN proteins is to unfold the higher order compaction of the chromatin structure, and thus enable chromatin to undergo transcription and replication more readily. Evidence for this unfolding mechanism is observed in HMGN mutants in that they do not unfold chromatin and therefore, there is no increase in transcription (Catez et al. 2003).

Further research has also suggested that the HMGN proteins do not remain stationary on the chromatin, but rather exhibit movement along the chromatin in response to the metabolic state of the cell. Researchers have hypothesized that the mobility of the HMGN proteins resembles transcription regulatory factors that are known to redistribute through out the cell cycle and more importantly during transcription (Catez et al. 2003). As well the

This paragraph is in need of a rewrite; the information is structured logically, but it could be structured more effectively.

The objective of this paragraph is not clear, and the first line needs to be rewritten.

Many paragraphs start with run-on sentences, which gives a breathless aspect to the essay. There is almost no rhythm to the words.

GOOD

modifying enzymes leads to the recruitment of regulatory machinery of the cell. Subsequent structural alterations ultimately lead to transcription, replication, or DNA repair (Catez et al. 2003).

The HMGN family of proteins are generally associated with transcription in all vertebrates. HMGN1 and HMGN2 bind without specificity to the nucleosome core particle, forming complexes. Characteristically, a complex is made up of two molecules of either HMGN1 or HMGN2 (Catez et al. 2003). The function of the HMGN proteins is to unfold the higher-order compaction of the chromatin structure. Doing so enables chromatin to undergo transcription and replication. Nonfunctional mutants that have altered HMGM structure are unable to unfold chromatin. The lack of transcription provides evidence that this essential process requires functional HMGM (Catez et al. 2003).

HMGN proteins are influenced by events in the cell metabolism and cell cycle. These proteins do not remain stationary on the chromatin, but exhibit movement along the chromatin in response to the metabolic state of the cell. Researchers have hypothesized that the mobility of the HMGN proteins resembles

3

The new opening sentence emphasizes the focus of the paragraph—why HMGMs are important.

BAD

The last line in the paragraph is completely unnecessary. It should be omitted.

HMGN proteins are also subject to post-translational modification, which affects their interaction with chromatin considerably. Therefore, it has been concluded that chromatin organization associated with the HMGN proteins is reflected in transcriptional activity (Calez et al., 2003).

Paragraph beginnings are weak.

Another recent breakthrough in the investigation of chromatin transcriptional function occurred by examining large scale chromatin fibers in vivo by immunoelectron microscopy. The heterochromatic regions were found to condense immediately prior to DNA replication and as chromatin condensed, a transcription activator, VP16, was activated to the two heterochromatin chromosome regions (Tsukamoto, Hashiguchi, Janicki, Tumbar, Belmont and Spector 2000). It was also observed by Tsukamoto and colleagues that after activating genes with doxycyline (a transcriptional stimulant) for eight hours, chromatin condensed without movement as expected (Tsukamoto et al., 2000). From these parallel findings researchers suggest that changes in chromatin sturcutre, such as condensing, are associated with the recruitment of transcriptional machinery (Tsukamoto 2000).

Another significant function of chromatin is the regulation of chromosome position and movements within the nucleus, which was investigated by Bickmore and co-workers in 2002. In their study, a Lac operator was integrated into the human genome and

The most important information in this paragraph—the nature of the breakthrough—is buried in the last line. This information should appear in the first sentence

Here, the discussion focuses on Bickmore's work and interpretations, but the citations refer to other sources. Perhaps the writer didn't really read all of these papers but rather copied the citations directly from Bickmore's paper. This kind of carelessness suggests inaccuracy.

GOOD

that of transcription factors that redistribute throughout the cell cycle, especially during transcription (Catez et al. 2003). HMGN proteins are also subject to post-translational modification, which affects their interaction with chromatin considerably (Catez et al. 2003).

Parallel studies in microscopy and molecular biology revealed that changes in chromatin structure affected recruitment of transcriptional machinery. Large-scale chromatin fibers examined by immunoelectron microscopy showed heterochromatic regions that condensed immediately prior to DNA replication. As chromatin condensed, a transcription activator, VP16, was activated to the two heterochromatin chromosome regions (Tsukamoto et al. 2000). Furthermore, after activating genes with a transcriptional stimulant, doxycycline, chromatin also condensed (Tsukamoto et al. 2000).

An additional function of chromatin is regulating chromosome position within the nucleus (Spector 2003). Researchers integrated a Lac operator into the human genome. They then observed specific chromosomes, each with a single locus of the Lac operator

4

The writer has removed the ambiguous reference to Bickmore, revealing that the discussion stems from the paper written by Chubb et al.

The themes that link the paragraphs are better highlighted (in a major redraft, the author could also choose to combine and condense some of the paragraphs).

BAD

then specific chromosomes containing a single locus of the Lac operator were selected for observation (Spector 2003; Chubb, Boyle, Perry and Bickmore 2002). Bickmore observed that the chromatin within the nucleolus or the nuclear periphery had more restricted movements than chromatin in other nuclear regions. Using FRAP, it wa confirmed that chromatin was restricted to a radius of 0.25 μm(Spector, 2003; Chubb et al., 2002). Bickmore suggested that the restricted movement maybe due to steric interactions between large tangled DNA polymers or that perhaps the chromatin attaches to structures within the nucleus such as the nucleolus, nuclear periphery or nuclear matrix (Spector 2003; Chubb et al. 2002). These observations allowed her to conclude that chromatin within the nucleolus may act as an anchoring structure for chromosomes (Spector, 2003; Chub et al. 2002).

As well studies investigating Drosophila spermatocytes have indicated limited chromatin movements within the nucleus. Researchers found that over short periods of time, chromatin movement was restricted to less than 0.3 μm/s in nuclear regions indicating a "random walk" as no deliberate movements were observed, while the average diffusion coefficient was estimated to be 0.001 μm²/s (Spector 2003). Although minimal confined movements were apparent in nuclear chromatin, the position in of the chromosomes remained unchanged bound to specific nuclear

Again, a wealth of long sentences is not doing the student any favours.

GOOD

(Chubb et al. 2002). Chromatin within the nucleolus or the nuclear periphery had more restricted movement than in other nuclear regions. Using FRAP, it appears that chromatin movement was restricted to a radius of 0.25 μm. The researchers suggested that this restriction may be caused by steric interactions between large tangled DNA polymers. Alternatively, chromatin may have attached itself to structures within the nucleus such as the nucleolus, nuclear periphery, or nuclear matrix. This led the researchers to conclude that chromatin within the nucleolus may be acting as an anchor for chromosomes (Chubb et al. 2002).

Limited chromatin movement within the nucleus is supported by studies of *Drosophila* spermatocytes. Researchers found that over short periods of time, chromatin movement was restricted to less than 0.3 μm/s in nuclear regions. This was a sign of restricted random movement (Spector 2003). Although minimal confined movements were apparent in nuclear chromatin, the position of the chromosomes was unchanged. The chromosomes remained bound to specific nuclear territories. These studies suggest that chromatin

5

The first few words in each paragraph now create an outline of the entire essay—a quality that will help readers who want to skim the text to get a good idea of what the essay is about.

BAD

territories. These studies suggest that chromatin has distinct role in the positioning of chromosomes within the nucleus and restricts their movements, anchoring them to specific territories (Spector 2003).

Another function of chromatin is the regulation of gene silencing, which is the process of inactivating a gene or a set of genes (Spector 2003). In recent studies, heterochromatin was integrated into the brown gene of Drosophila, which caused the gene to undergo a mutation resulting in a brown Dominant (bw^D) allele. The mutated gene then misdirected itself to interact with centrometric heterochromatin, causing the gene to become silenced (Spector 2003; Fisher and Merkenschlager, 2002). Subsequent observations also suggest that developing B cells inactive transcriptional states are situated away from heterochromatin, while many inactive genes are positioned in close proximity to heterochromatin. These recent observations clearly provide evidence that heterochromatin is greatly involved in gene silencing (Spector, 2003; Fisher et al., 2002).

The function of chromatin has been clearly implicated in an array of nuclear activities. Research indicates that chromatin plays a distinct functional role in many aspects of gene transcription and replication, silencing, and chromosomal positioning. The dynamic nature of chromatin structure and function allows for

The first and last sentences of the last paragraph say the same thing. The final sentence should be omitted.

GOOD

has distinct role in the positioning of chromosomes within the nucleus and restricts their movements, anchoring them to specific territories (Spector 2003).

Chromatin also plays a role in gene silencing, the process of inactivating one or many genes (Spector 2003). Researchers integrated heterochromatin into the brown gene of *Drosophila*, which caused the gene to undergo a mutation resulting in a dominant brown (bw^D) allele. The mutated gene then misdirected itself to interact with centromeric heterochromatin, causing the gene to become silenced (Fisher and Merkenschlager 2002; Spector 2003). Subsequent observations also suggested that in developing B cells active transcriptional states are situated away from heterochromatin, while many inactive genes are positioned in close proximity to heterochromatin.

Researchers have clearly implicated the function of chromatin in an array of nuclear activities. Research indicates that chromatin plays a distinct functional role in many aspects of gene transcription and replication, silencing, and chromosomal positioning. The dynamic nature of chromatin structure and function allows it to continually adapt to changing nuclear

6

BAD

continual adaptation to changing nuclear environments, due to a diversity of stimuli within the nucleus (Catez, 2003). Chromatin's involvement in chromosome organization and gene regulation imply its functional responsibility in the complexity and intricacy of the nucleus.

Currently, researchers have the ability to visualize specific gene characteristics within the nucleus of living cells. However, future advances in cellular technology will allow for simultaneous observation of the interactions within the genome in 'real' time, to better interpret gene regulation (Spector, 2003). Improvements in technology will promote the understanding of the organization and dynamics of the genome in attempt to define mechanisms that ensure proper gene expression and nuclear activity, that are facilitated by the diversity of chromatin functions (Spector 2003).

References

Catez F, Lim J, Hock R, Postnikov YV, Bustin M. 2003. HMGN dynamics and chromatin function. Biochem Cell Biol. 81(3):113–122.

Chubb JR, Boyle S, Perry P, Bickmore WA. 2002. Chromatin motion is constrained by association with nuclear compartments in human cells. Curr Biol. 12(6):439–445.

The last paragraph provides a new perspective, but it ends weakly with run-on sentences. It is also overwritten. The writer is struggling to square future technological advances with the goals of the essay. It would have been better if the writer had revised the opening paragraph to connect with this discussion. Sadly, the ending limps to a conclusion.

GOOD

environments in response to a diversity of stimuli within the nucleus (Catez 2003).

Currently, researchers can visualize specific gene characteristics within the nucleus of living cells. In the future, advances in cellular technology will allow researchers to observe simultaneous interactions within the genome in "real" time. These observations will aid in our interpretation of chromatin's role in gene regulation, chromosome behaviour, and nuclear activity (Spector 2003). Chromatin modifications result in complex responses. It only takes one element to malfunction for a chromatin-related disease to occur. There are nearly a dozen such diseases found in humans (Hendrich and Bickmore 2001). To provide better treatments and comfort to sufferers, we must continue to unravel the diverse functions of chromatin.

References

Catez F, Lim J, Hock R, Postnikov YV, Bustin M. 2003. HMGN dynamics and chromatin function. Biochem Cell Biol. 81(3):113–122.

Chubb JR, Boyle S, Perry P, Bickmore WA. 2002. Chromatin motion is constrained by association with nuclear compartments in human cells. Curr Biol. 12(6):439–445.

7

The new closing paragraph is shorter and more concise, and the writer has added a new perspective, tying the conclusion to the introduction.

BAD

Fisher AG, Merkenschlager M. 2002. Gene silencing, cell fate and nuclear organization. Curr Opin Genet Dev. 12(2):193–197.

Horn PJ, Peterson CL. 2002. Chromatin higher order folding: wrapping up transcription. Sci. 297(5588):1824–1827.

Jenuwein T, Allis CD. 2001. Translating the histone code. Sci. 293(5532):1074–1079.

Spector DL. 2003. The dynamics of chromosome organization and gene regulation. Annu Rev Biochem. 72:573–608.

Tsukamoto T, Hashiguchi N, Janicki SM, Tumbar T, Belmont AS, Spector DL. 2000. Visualization of gene activity in living cells. Nat Cell Biol. 2(12):871–878.

Considering that this essay was written in 2003, the references were very up-to-date. They were all from top-notch journals, and even the reviews were from quality periodicals. But the missing reference to Bickmore raises suspicions about how the information was gathered and suggests plagiarism.

GOOD

Fisher AG, Merkenschlager M. 2002. Gene silencing, cell fate and nuclear organization. Curr Opin Genet Dev. 12(2):193–197.

Hendrich B, Bickmore W. 2001. Human diseases with underlying defects in chromatin structure and function. Hum Mol Gen. 10(20):2233–2242.

Horn PJ, Peterson CL. 2002. Chromatin higher order folding: wrapping up transcription. Sci. 297(5588):1824–1827.

Jenuwein T, Allis CD. 2001. Translating the histone code. Sci. 293(5532):1074–1079.

Spector DL. 2003. The dynamics of chromosome organization and gene regulation. Annu Rev Biochem. 72:573–608.

Tsukamoto T, Hashiguchi N, Janicki SM, Tumbar T, Belmont AS, Spector DL. 2000. Visualization of gene activity in living cells. Nat Cell Biol. 2(12):871–878.

8

As you can see, this essay is shorter. That's what a good edit will do—cut out the dross. Some students feel that they need to meet the word requirement in their first draft, but it's always better to be clear. If you find that your essay is too short after you've edited it, look for places where you could add useful content—for example, by adding the suggested paragraph about disease.

PROTECTING YOUR WORK

Because lost files are a common problem of high school students and the computer innocent, loss is no longer a credible excuse for a university or college student. Keeping adequate copies of your work will protect you from losing it as a result of a computer or disk problem. The following practices will ensure that your work is adequately protected:

- Save regularly to protect against a computer failure—once every 15 minutes is a good policy.
- Create a backup once a day, so that you have copies on both your hard drive and a USB flash drive or a server.
- Keep a copy of your file at least until you receive your grade for the course.
- Print an extra hard copy just to be on the safe side.

Getting into the habit of following these steps is a good investment of your time and will give you valuable peace of mind.

SUMMARY

Any piece of writing inevitably begins with an introduction and ends with a conclusion—pay attention to these sections because they create first and last impressions. Whenever possible, try to tie your introduction to your conclusion to create a unified essay. If you incorporate someone else's material, use quotations correctly and cite literature when appropriate to avoid the crime of plagiarism. When editing your work, pay particular attention to improperly cited material, which can lead to accusations of plagiarism, as demonstrated in the sample annotated student essay. Make sure to review your organization to ensure that you present your ideas logically. Always leave enough time to polish your work so that you will receive the best mark possible—this is where style comes into play, as you have already taken care of the content. Remember to make backup copies of your assignments, both during the writing process and at the time of submission. It's always a good idea to keep your notes, as well as an extra hardcopy and a digital copy of every assignment, until you get your final mark for the course.

CHAPTER 5

Writing a Lab Report

OBJECTIVES

- assessing the purpose and the reader
- understanding the format
- learning the style, section by section
- formulating a hypothesis
- avoiding common pitfalls and writing errors

Students in the life sciences often write formal reports on the results of scientific experiments. Although lab reports generally conform to a basic format, every scientific discipline (chemistry, physics, biology, psychology, etc.) has slightly different requirements.

Any kind of academic writing should be clear, concise, and forceful, but for scientific writing there is one more imperative: be objective. Scientists are interested in exact information and the orderly presentation of factual evidence to support theories or hypotheses. When making a case for a particular hypothesis, you need to separate the facts you are reporting from your own speculations about them. You must never allow your preconceived opinions or expectations to interfere with the way you collect or present your data. If you do, you run the risk of distorting your results.

Always ask yourself the following questions: "Would anyone with an adequate background be able to repeat my results if they followed my instructions?" and "Would their interpretation be similar?" If you can answer "yes" to both questions, you have likely succeeded in remaining unbiased in your interpretations. You must conduct your experiment as objectively as possible and present the results in such a way that anyone who reads your report or attempts to duplicate your procedure will be likely to reach the same conclusions that you did.

PURPOSE AND READER

You will most often write lab reports to demonstrate that you understand a theory or a phenomenon or that you know how to test a certain hypothesis. Since your reader is either an instructor or a teaching assistant, you can assume that he or she will be familiar with scientific terms; therefore you do not need to define or explain them. You should take care to use precise scientific terms—for example, rather than describing a lizard basking in the sun as a warm cold-blooded animal, describe it as an endothermic poikilothermic animal. While scientific terminology may not be beautiful, it is precise. You can also assume that your reader will be on the lookout for weaknesses in methodology or analysis and omissions of important data. Usually your reader will expect you to give details of your calculations, but even when you only need to provide the results of your calculations, you should be sure to note any irregularities in the experiment that might affect the accuracy of your results.

FORMAT

Since the information in scientific reports must be easy for the reader to find, it should be organized into separate sections, each with a heading. One of the differences between writing lab reports and writing essays is that in a report you must use headings and subheadings as well as graphs, tables, or diagrams (see Chapter 10). By convention, most lab reports follow a standard order:

1. *Title Page*
2. *Abstract*
3. *Introduction*
4. *Materials and Methods*
5. *Results*
6. *Discussion*
7. *Conclusions*
8. *References*
9. *Attachments or Appendices*

The order of these sections is always the same, and it matches that found in journal articles. You may decide to combine sections (e.g., *Results and Discussion*), or you may want to separate sections (e.g., *Materials* presented separately from *Methods*); you might even choose to give the sections slightly different names, depending on what type of information you cover in each one. Different disciplines also have slightly different rules, but the following discussion will give you an overview of what you should include in each section of your report.

Title page

The title page is always the first page of the report. It should include your name, the title of the experiment, the date on which the experiment was performed, and the date of submission; for practical purposes, it should also include the name of your course and the name of your instructor. Your title should be brief—no more than ten or twelve words—but informative, and it should clearly describe the topic and scope of your experiment. Avoid meaningless phrases, such as "A Study of . . ." or "Observations on . . ."; simply state what it is you are studying, for example "Enzyme Kinetics of 6-Phosphofructo-1-Kinase." Sometimes you may want to emphasize the result you obtained, for example, "Specialized Techniques for Mark–Recapture of Mammals, Especially Rabbits, in Winter."

Abstract

Your instructor might not ask you to write an *Abstract* section for most lab reports, but when you finally do have to create one, remember to write this section last. The abstract appears on a separate page following the title page. It is a brief but comprehensive summary of your report that should be able to stand alone; that is, someone should be able to read it and know exactly what the experiment was about as well as what the most important results were. The abstract should never mention any literature and usually does not contain any interpretation or discussion. Your summary should describe the purpose of the experiment, the experimental materials, the procedure, the results, and your conclusions. For a simple experiment, your abstract may be only a few lines, but even for a complex one you should keep it to less than two hundred words. For this reason, you should avoid vague or wordy phrases—for example, don't say, "The reason for conducting the experiments in this study of X was to examine the effect of . . ." when you can be more concise: "X was studied to examine the effect of. . . ."

You must always write abstracts in the third person and in the past tense, and you can often include passive constructions that emphasize the subject of the experiment rather than the researcher. Remember: brevity is the goal of this section. To achieve this goal, you will need to draft and redraft your writing. Consult journal abstracts to get a feel for the impersonal, tight writing style required. Imitation is an excellent way to learn this somewhat awkward compositional style.

To avoid common pitfalls,

- make sure that your *Abstract* doesn't sound like an introduction,
- do not include implications for future work, and
- only mention material that appears in the report.

Introduction

The *Introduction* section gives a more detailed statement of purpose or objective. It should describe the problem you are studying, the reasons for studying it, and the research strategy you used to obtain the relevant data. If, as is often the case, your purpose is to test a hypothesis about a specific problem, you should state both the nature of the problem and what you expected to find. Your introduction should include the theory underlying the experiment and any pertinent background data or equations. Although you may refer to papers relevant to the experiment, it's best to avoid quoting extensively.

Many students find the introduction to be the easiest section to write. While the structure of a lab report is generally constrained, the structure of the introduction is fairly flexible. Here, you can use imagination and creativity to discuss sources and opinion. You can introduce controversies, or you can use a unique quotation to highlight key issues. You also have more freedom in terms of tense, as you can vary the tense of the introduction based on the content. For example, you could discuss a controversy or a quotation in the past tense, then switch to the future tense to present some aspect of the experiment that will be important in the future, then switch to the present tense to build up an argument based on current sources of information.

If you decide to use a quotation, you can reference almost anyone, provided that the quote is appropriate to the experiment. A scientist, such as Darwin, is good for something venerable, but even a children's author, such as Lewis Carroll, is game: after all, where would we be in evolutionary theory without the Red Queen's statement, "It takes all the running you can do, to keep in the same place"? (Evolutionary biologist Leigh Van Valen used these words to formulate his Red Queen Hypothesis, a statement on the eternal arms race between organisms.)

In most scientific papers, the purpose appears at the end of the introduction, ideally in a one-sentence hypothesis or statement of purpose. A common approach to writing an introduction is to think of it as a one-page essay that builds up to the statement of purpose. This mini-essay must include the ideas, concepts, and context necessary for the reader to understand the purpose of the experiment. Putting the purpose of the experiment in the final sentence also provides an excellent bridge to the following sections. Above all, your statement of hypothesis, objective, or purpose must be clear. Spend extra time clarifying this statement, because without clarity of purpose, the whole reason for doing the experiment could seem shaky.

To avoid common pitfalls,

- make sure your *Introduction* is less than two pages in length,
- make your hypothesis and purpose as unambiguous as possible, and
- avoid anticipating your results.

FORMULATING A HYPOTHESIS

Before you write your introduction, you should understand the scientific method. In the life sciences, the scientific method has four basic steps. The first step is to consider experimental experience—both your own observations and the published observations of others. The second step is to formulate a conjecture or a hypothesis based on this experience. The third element is to combine the hypothesis with a prediction. The fourth step is to test the truth of this prediction. You must follow these steps when you are designing an experiment, as scientific advancement depends on a logical, repeatable sequence of actions. Once you have completed your experiment, others must be able to repeat your actions and, in turn, create their own hypotheses and predictions based on the most recent experience. These new hypotheses and predictions can then be tested by other researchers, and so on.

How do you formulate a hypothesis? One way is to follow these eight steps:

1. Start with a simple statement (e.g., "lead can cause poisoning").
2. Make the statement conditional by phrasing it as an *if/then* statement (e.g., "*if* lead causes poisoning, *then* people exposed to lead paint in their homes could suffer from lead poisoning").
3. Determine the variables (e.g., house lead content and number of cases of poisoned inhabitants). Note: an experiment to test a hypothesis requires at least two variables.
4. Determine the subject group (e.g., people who live in houses that have lead-painted surfaces).

5. Identify a treatment that will make the statement testable (e.g., exposure to lead paint in houses).
6. Consider the outcome (e.g., frequency of poisoning among occupants in houses with lead-painted surfaces).
7. Consider whether a control group (a non-treated subject group) is possible (e.g., people who live in houses that have never had any lead paint).
8. Put the elements together to form your hypothesis (e.g., "if lead causes poisoning, then people exposed to lead paint in their homes face a greater chance of poisoning than people who live in houses free of lead paint").

If you consider the example given in this list, you can see how it might be possible to have an introduction that has three paragraphs—the first discussing lead in paints, the second discussing widespread use of lead in house paint, and the third discussing toxicology of lead—followed by the final paragraph containing the hypothesis.

Materials and Methods

The *Materials and Methods* (M&M) section contains a description of the materials and the equipment you used, some explanation of how you physically set up the experiment, an overview of the experimental design (treatments, controls, statistical tests and analyses, etc.), and a step-by-step description of your actions. This final element is essential, as readers must be able to repeat your experiment.

Make sure to list every material and piece of equipment you used. For biological material, include the source and the full Latin name of any organism(s): for example, "California sea cucumbers, *Parastichopus californicus*, were purchased from a biological supply house (WestWind SeaLab Supplies, Victoria, BC)." If any of your equipment or materials are standard, commercially available items, some departments require that you specify the name of the manufacturer, the model number (if applicable), and the name of the source or supplier: for example, "Ethanol (analytical grade purity) was obtained from Sigma-Aldrich, Oakville, ON."

You should also include a simple diagram—produced on a computer or by hand—to help your reader visualize the arrangement of the equipment. If the diagram is too large to fit on a regular page, you can label it and attach it at the end of the report. Just remember to refer to the attachment within the body of the report.

The *methods* portion is a step-by-step description of how you carried out the experiment. Remember to describe the procedures in the order in which you actually performed them. If your experiment consisted of a number of tests, you should begin your discussion of methods with a short summary statement listing the tests so that the reader will be prepared for the series. When you describe the tests in full, discuss them in the same order as they appear in this summary statement to avoid confusion.

As you describe your methods, use enough detail so that others would have no difficulty repeating the experiment in all its essential details. If you are following instructions in a lab manual, you should not copy them out word for word, since this might be considered plagiarism. In some cases, your lab instructor may permit you to simply refer to the instructions and add details of any deviation. When a certain procedure is long, complicated, or not necessary to a full understanding of the experiment, you may describe it in a labelled attachment at the end of the report.

Although you should be concise in your description of the experimental method, make sure that you don't omit essential details. If you heated a test tube in a water bath, for example, you must report the temperature and the duration. If you performed a chromatography test or other process at a faster or slower rate than usual, you must indicate the rate. Readers must know exactly what controls to apply if they try to perform the experiment themselves.

The past tense is standard in all M&M sections. In terms of voice, there has been some debate among scientists who write for scientific journals about whether to use the active or passive voice (e.g., "I *heated* the beaker" versus "The beaker *was heated*"). Thirty years ago, only the passive voice was used for this kind of writing because it emphasized the procedure rather than the person. However, the last two decades have seen a sharp rise in the tendency to use the active voice because it is clearer and less likely to produce awkward, convoluted sentences. Some researchers have also argued that third-person reporting is merely a pretense of objectivity. Using the first person is more honest, as it addresses the more modern sentiment that the scientist is not separable from his or her science. Ask your instructor or teaching assistant about his or her preferences, but also use your own judgment about what sounds best. Your goal, whichever voice you use, is to achieve clarity and objectivity.

To avoid common pitfalls,

1. use lots of details and
2. remember to discuss controls.

Results

This is the section of most interest to scientists, and they depend on its accuracy. It usually contains a mix of data, graphics, and verbal description. It will also likely contain some statistical calculations.

Ask your instructor whether he or she expects you to give the details of your calculations or only the results of those calculations. In either case, you should pay special attention to the units of any quantities; to omit or misuse them is a serious scientific mistake. Taking care to include all units will also reveal mistakes in your calculations that you might not have detected otherwise. Also, remember to use scientific notation when your calculations deal with very large or very small numbers.

You should also make sure, where possible, that the calculated values you report include the "uncertainty" in each of them. For example, you might report that the calculated average diameter of the alga *Volvox* is 80.05 ± 0.35 ml. When reporting any calculations or measurements, check to see if you need to include either the standard deviation, the standard error of the mean, or the coefficient of variation. You should also keep in mind the difference between accuracy and precision: accuracy is a description of how close the values are to the true value(s), whereas precision is an indication of how repeatable the values are. If you get the same value over and over, it may be precise, but if it is far off the true or expected value, it may not be accurate.

The format of the *Results* section depends on the type of experiment you performed. Generally it begins with the main finding and then deals with secondary ones—you will spark your reader's interest if you put the best results first. Whenever possible, summarize your results in a graph or a table. A graph is usually preferable to a table since it has greater visual impact. However, if you have made several measurements, you might not be able to include your results in a single figure and are probably best to report them in tabular form.

 Today's computer programs have sophisticated charting features that will help you to create eye-catching figures quickly and easily (see Chapter 10 for a discussion of graphs and tables).

Whatever type of figure or table you use, label it clearly and be sure to refer to it and explain it in the text. Give each illustration a caption that includes a number and a title, and refer to it by number in your report. You should always number and present the figures in the order in which they are mentioned in the text. Avoid the common error of positioning figures based on where they look best—Figure 5 must appear before Figure 6 even if it means reformatting some of your material. Never allow layout to dictate the order of the figures. The caption should allow the figure and stand on its own. Do not simply write "Figure 1"; instead, describe it in full: "Figure 1:

Graph of average lengths (cm ± SE) of maturing turtles versus time (wk). n = 5. Asterisks indicate significant differences determined by one-way ANOVA, at $p < 0.01$." If the illustration is a photo of two turtles and a dime (for scale), write, "Figure 1: Photograph of immature (left) and mature (right) turtles with a dime for comparison." Full descriptions help readers keep track of information as they flip back and forth through your report.

Graphs can be highly effective for displaying information, but they also require a lot of planning. Remember the following guidelines when you are creating graphs for your lab report:

- Use a scale that will allow you to distribute your data points as widely as possible on the page.
- Put the independent variable (the one you manipulated) on the horizontal axis and the dependent variable (the one you measured) on the vertical axis.
- Make the vertical axis approximately three-quarters the length of the horizontal axis.
- Use large and distinctive symbols, with different symbols for each line on the graph.
- Put error bars (±) on data points where known.
- Label the axes clearly and always include the units of measurement so that the reader knows exactly what you have plotted on the graph.
- Include a legend, when necessary, to indicate the different units and to explain what the different symbols represent.
- Remember to give the graph a title and a caption.

In most cases, you will use the past tense to discuss your results, as you are reporting the outcome of a completed experiment. As in the M&M section, you may choose to use either the active or the passive voice. Do not include any references in the *Results* section. You should use references in the *Introduction*, *Material and Methods*, and *Discussion*, but never in the *Abstract* or *Results* sections.

To avoid common pitfalls,

- do not repeat data in the text when it is illustrated in the tables and figures (or vice versa),
- write this section so that it can be read aloud—it should not sound like a lab book, and
- do not use point form.

Discussion

The *Discussion* section of the lab report allows you the greatest intellectual freedom, since it is here that you analyze and interpret the test results and comment on their significance. In this section, you should show how the test produced its outcome—whether expected or unexpected—and discuss those elements that influenced the results. For a good discussion, remember to think critically not only about your own work but also about how it relates to previous work. In determining what details to include in your analysis, you might try to answer the following questions:

- Do the results reflect the hypothesis or purpose of the experiment?
- Do the results agree with previous findings as reported in the literature on the subject? If not, how can you account for the discrepancy between your own data and the values accepted or obtained by other students and scientists?
- Could the results have another explanation?
- Did the procedures you used help you accomplish the purpose of the experiment? Does your experience in this experiment suggest a better approach for next time?
- What (if anything) may have gone wrong during your experiment and why? What are the sources of error and are they included in the statistical method of analysis?

Since the discussion explores the experiment and its relevance to the literature (i.e., previous published experiments), you need to highlight the logic behind these experimental approaches. You will achieve clarity more easily if you take the time to reread your writing and correct any mistakes. This extra effort is worth it, because this section leaves the biggest and most lasting impression on the reader.

If you do find errors in your experiment, try to break them down into instrument errors (e.g., due to an improperly calibrated measuring device), method errors (e.g., due to uncontrolled elements, such as room temperature, that varied from batch to batch), and finally—every student's familiar foe— human errors. On this final point, always be diplomatic and avoid accusing your lab partners of incompetence.

You should always discuss the most important result and whether the hypothesis is true or false in the first paragraph of the *Discussion* section. No matter how frustrating the lab experience has been, do not begin with a discussion of the problems you faced—they have little to do with the purpose of the experiment. Poor results are usually the fault of poor experimental design, not a poor hypothesis. You should examine difficulties in experimental execution in the body of the *Discussion* rather than at the beginning or end, where they leave a distinctly bitter impression. Similarly, you should bury your suggestions for improvements to the experiment in the middle. You can end your *Discussions* in one of two ways. If your instructor has requested a formal *Conclusions* section, then you should end your *Discussion* with a brief summary. Otherwise, you can end this section with a final paragraph that presents future perspectives and conclusions.

You do not need to write the *Discussion* section in the past tense, unlike the *M&M* and *Results* sections. You should avoid referring to a figure or table in this section. Why? The *Discussion* section is about the *implications* of the data, not the data itself—the *Results* section is the place to describe and note values. You may be tempted to say, "The data in Figure 1 compares favorably with that of Davidson and coworkers (2009)," but it is better to write, "Our sample of maturing snapping turtles show length increases similar to a recent study of the same species (Davidson et al. 2009)."

To avoid common pitfalls,

- spend enough time editing this section to make your ideas as clear as possible,
- write dynamically and avoid using one long sentence after another, and
- use a punch finish—do not let your discussion drift to its death.

Conclusions

The *Conclusions* section is a brief statement of the conclusions that you have drawn from the experiment. You don't necessarily need a separate section for your conclusions; they can also appear as a short summary paragraph at the very end of the *Discussion* section. You may include a chart (or table or graph) if you think it will better model and clarify the conclusion.

References

The only way to avoid suspicion of plagiarism is to support every non-original statement with a reference citation. Each time you refer to a book or an article in the text of your report, cite the reference; then, at the end of the paper, make a list of all the sources you have cited. The precise format of the citations and reference list varies among disciplines, so you should check with your instructor or TA to see which style you should use. For details on the correct form for scientific documentation, see Chapter 11.

Some sections in a lab report require references, while others are always free of references. You will include lots of references that support your line of reasoning in the *Introduction* and *Discussion* sections. In the *M&M* section, you may need to reference methods that you found in the literature if they are necessary for the reader to understand how to repeat the experiment. Though common, such references are usually few in number. However, *never* include even a single reference in the *Abstract* or *Results* sections. Some students are surprised by this last convention, but, after all, your results are your own and you must describe them, not refer to someone else's results. Including outside work constitutes a comparison, which would, logically enough, turn a *Results* section into a *Discussion* section.

To avoid common pitfalls,

- follow the citation style for your discipline,
- make sure you haven't used references in the wrong sections, and
- check your references line-by-line to make sure you haven't missed anything.

Attachments or appendices

In some cases you may wish to include various raw data, supplementary photos, and detailed calculations as attachments or appendices. These additions should be placed on separate pages at the end of the report.

PUTTING THE SECTIONS TOGETHER

Should you write the sections of your report in order? No!

It is far, far easier to write these sections out of order. Even professional scientists do not write straight through from the *Abstract* to the *Conclusions*. In your own lab reports, begin by writing the *Material and Methods* section, which is often the easiest to compose because it requires the least analysis. Then, turn to the *Results* section, which also tends to be straightforward because it involves graphic interpretation and description of analyses. Next, write your *Introduction* to remind yourself of the purpose and the context of your experiment. This will prepare you to write an effective *Discussion*, where you can elaborate on the importance of your results within the context of the primary literature, some of which you will have referenced in the *Introduction*. After the *Discussion*, write your brief *Conclusions*. Once you have prepared these sections, you will be ready to write a succinct summary for the most difficult of all the sections—the *Abstract*.

WRITING STYLE

Scientific reports, like essays, must be written with the reader in mind. Since your reader is your instructor, you don't need to define basic scientific terms or explain a method that would be familiar to anyone with scientific training. At the same time, you should avoid filling your report with technical jargon when non-technical language will do the job. The watchwords are clarity and precision: your goal is to make it as easy as possible for the reader to understand exactly what you mean.

Although the basic rules for writing a lab report are the same as for any other kind of writing, scientific reports do pose special problems for students. The following sections present some words of advice (for more information on common stylistic problems, see Chapter 6).

Avoid using too many nouns as adjectives
Clusters of nouns used as adjectives can create cumbersome phrases:

orig.   adult male kidney disease

rev.   kidney disease in adult males

orig.   apparatus construction

rev.   construction of the apparatus

Of course, some nouns are frequently and quite acceptably used as adjectives: for example, _kidney_ disease, _hydrogen_ bomb, _reaction_ time, _S.I._ units. Your ear is probably the best judge of what is clear and what is not.

Avoid using too many abstract nouns
Whenever possible, choose a verb rather than an abstract noun:

orig.   The addition of acid and subsequent agitation of the solution resulted in the formation of crystals.

rev.   When acid was added and the solution shaken, crystals formed (passive).

rev.   When I added acid to the solution and shook it, crystals formed (active).

Avoid vague qualifiers

As a scientist you must be exact. In particular, you should avoid words such as *quite*, *very*, *fairly*, *some*, or *many* when you can use a more exact term. The word *relatively* is especially dangerous unless you are actually comparing two or more things. If you say that something is significant, you must mean that it is statistically significant—you cannot use the word *significant* in any other context. Avoid adverbs of a general nature, such as *importantly* and *generally*. If you have presented your point clearly, the importance or generality of your topic will be self-evident.

Avoid unnecessary passive constructions

As noted on page 85, there is some debate among scientists about whether it is more appropriate to use the active voice or the passive voice to describe an experiment. Even if you prefer to use passive verbs for describing methods and results, you should try to use active verbs in your *Introduction*, *Discussion*, and *Conclusions* sections. Your sentences will be clearer and more direct:

orig. A pH of 4 is needed for the enzyme to react.

rev. The enzyme needs a pH of 4 to react.

orig. It was reported by E.A. Robinson that . . .

rev. E.A. Robinson reported that . . .

Avoid ambiguous pronouns

A pronoun will cause confusion if the reader can't tell which noun it refers to:

orig. The seed required water to germinate. It must be warm.

Is it the seed or the water that must be warm? If there is any chance of ambiguity, you should repeat the noun:

rev. The water must be warm.

(or)

rev. The seed must be warm.

Be especially careful that the demonstrative pronoun *this* clearly refers to a specific noun:

orig.   When water was withheld, the stalk lost its leaves. <u>This</u> occurred over eight hours.

rev.   When water was withheld, the stalk lost its leaves. <u>This loss</u> occurred over eight hours.

SUMMARY

Lab reports are the most common writing assignments you will face as an undergraduate in the life sciences. These reports follow formal conventions found in scientific papers, so you must learn to write within these conventions in order to publish as a scientist. Lab reports are traditionally divided into seven sections: *Abstract, Introduction, Materials and Methods, Results, Discussion, Conclusions,* and *References.* Each of these sections has its own content requirements and stylistic constraints. The *Abstract* is the most specific, and you can learn this style by reading and imitating published journal abstracts. The *Introduction* and *Discussion* sections must tie together—one ends where the other begins. The *Introduction* is where you can make arguments that build to support the logic of the hypothesis or purpose. The *Discussion* is where you can explore whether you have proven or achieved this same hypothesis or purpose. The *Materials and Methods* section is fairly straightforward, but you have to be careful to include every detail relevant to the experiment. The *Results* section requires a clear, illustrated version of what you recorded during the experiment. Your conclusions, whether they appear in their own section or at the end of the *Discussion* section, should be brief and highlight the most important implications of your experiment. Finally, the references must be listed correctly—edit them slowly and carefully to achieve a professional finish.

CHAPTER 6

Writing with Style

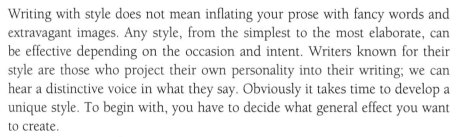

OBJECTIVES

- finding your voice
- achieving clarity
- choosing your words carefully
- controlling clauses, sentences, and paragraphs
- writing with force and purpose

Writing with style does not mean inflating your prose with fancy words and extravagant images. Any style, from the simplest to the most elaborate, can be effective depending on the occasion and intent. Writers known for their style are those who project their own personality into their writing; we can hear a distinctive voice in what they say. Obviously it takes time to develop a unique style. To begin with, you have to decide what general effect you want to create.

Taste in style reflects the times. In earlier centuries, many respected writers wrote in an elaborate style that we would consider much too wordy. Today, journalists have led the trend towards short, easy-to-grasp sentences and paragraphs. Writing in an academic context, you may expect your audience to be more reflective than the average newspaper reader, but the most effective style is still one that is clear, concise, and forceful.

Learning to find your voice in writing is important, and achieving clarity does not mean eliminating your personality. Occasionally, a student expresses the mistaken belief that there must be a universal, neutral style common to the sciences. The more you read scientific literature, the more styles and voices you will encounter. In the last three decades, sciences in general have become more accepting of first-person narration. Getting a handle on when to use *I* and *we* takes time, but it is worth mastering. But be warned: there are still many instructors, TAs, and professors who think writers should avoid using the first person. Before you begin a written assignment, ask your instructor whether he or she will penalize you for using the first person.

BE CLEAR

Use clear diction

A dictionary is a wise investment. A good dictionary will help you understand unfamiliar words and archaic and technical senses of common words. Some dictionaries will help you use words properly by offering example sentences that show how certain words are typically used. A dictionary will also help you with questions of spelling and usage. If you aren't sure whether a particular word is too informal for your writing or if you have concerns that a certain word might be offensive, consult a good dictionary.

You should be aware that Canadian usage and spelling may follow either British or American practice but usually combines aspects of both. There are a number of Canadian dictionaries available today that will help you to be consistent in your approach. It's also a good idea to make sure that the *Language* feature of your word-processing program is set to *English (Canada)*.

A thesaurus lists words that are closely related in meaning. It can help when you want to avoid repeating yourself or when you are fumbling for a word that's on the tip of your tongue. Your word-processing program also has a thesaurus feature that allows you to look up synonyms and antonyms easily. Be careful, though: make sure you distinguish between denotative and connotative meanings. A word's *denotations* are its primary (or "dictionary") meanings. Its *connotations* are any associations that it may suggest; they may not be as exact as the denotations, but they are part of the impression the word conveys. If you examine a list of synonyms in a thesaurus, you will see that even words with similar meanings can have dramatically different connotations. For example, alongside the word *indifferent*, your thesaurus may give the following entries: *neutral, aloof, callous, moderate, unenthusiastic, apathetic, unprejudiced,* and *fair*. Imagine the different impressions you would create if you chose one or the other of those words to complete this sentence: "Questioned about the experiment's chance of success, he was _____ in his response." In order to write clearly, you must remember that a reader may react to the suggestive meaning of a word as much as to its "dictionary" meaning.

USE PLAIN ENGLISH

A side-effect of having to master heaps of life sciences terminology and field-specific jargon is that it inspires insipid prose. You should use jargon only when it is required for plain illustration. A high concentration of technical jargon may give you an increased sense of sophistication, but you risk confusing your readers by forcing them to decipher and remember complex terminology when they should be focussing on your arguments. Another unfortunate effect of using jargon is that it tempts young life sciences writers into using fancy words and phrases. It can also tempt writers to use unnecessary or unclear abbreviations:

orig. EtOH was used to sterilize the hood.

rev. Ethanol was used to sterilize the laminar flow hood.

Plain words are almost always more forceful than fancy ones. If you aren't sure what plain English is, think of the way you talk to your friends (apart from swearing and slang). Many of our most common words—the ones that sound most natural and direct—are short. A good number of them are Anglo-Saxon in origin and are among the oldest words in the English language. In contrast, most of the words that English has derived from other languages are longer and more complicated; even those that have been used for centuries can sound artificial. For this reason you should beware of words loaded with prefixes (*pre-*, *post-*, *anti-*, *pro-*, *sub-*, *maxi-*, etc.) and suffixes (*-ate*, *-ize*, *-tion*, etc.). These Latinate attachments can make individual words more precise and efficient, but putting a lot of them together will make your writing seem dense and hard to understand. In many cases you can substitute a plain word for a fancy one.

Fancy	*Plain*
accomplish	do
cognizant	aware
commence	begin, start
conclusion	end
determinant	cause
fabricate	build
finalize	finish, complete
firstly	first
infuriate	anger
maximization	increase

modification	change
numerous	many
obviate	prevent
oration	speech
prioritize	rank
remuneration	pay
requisite	needed
sanitize	clean
subsequently	later
systematize	order
terminate	end
transpire	happen
utilize	use

Suggesting that you write in plain English does not mean that you should never pick an unfamiliar word or a foreign derivative; sometimes those words are the only ones that will convey precisely what you mean. Inserting an unusual expression into a passage of plain writing can also be an effective means of catching the reader's attention—as long as you don't do it too often.

BE PRECISE

Always be as specific as you can. Avoid all-purpose adjectives such as *major*, *significant*, and *important* and vague verbs such as *involve*, *entail*, and *exist* when you can be more specific:

> **orig.**   Running traplines <u>entailed significant effort</u> by the summer students.

> **rev.**   Running traplines <u>exhausted</u> the summer students.

Here's another example:

> **orig.**   Exploration of the fossil cliffs at Joggins, on the Bay of Fundy, lead to <u>major</u> discoveries in paleoecology.

> **rev.**   Exploration of the fossil cliffs at Joggins, on the Bay of Fundy, lead to <u>revolutionary</u> discoveries in paleoecology.

AVOID UNNECESSARY QUALIFIERS

Qualifiers such as *very*, *rather*, and *extremely* are overused. Saying that something is *very beautiful* may have less impact than saying simply that it is *beautiful*. An easy way to eliminate this problem in your writing is to type a word (e.g., *very*) into your word processor's *Find* function and then eliminate or replace each one. For example, compare these sentences:

> The flower's fame rests on its <u>very</u> unusual form.

> The flower's fame rests on its <u>strikingly</u> unusual form.

Which has more impact? When you think that an adjective needs qualifying—and sometimes it will—first see if it's possible to change either the adjective or the phrasing. Instead of writing

> Multinational Drugs made a <u>very big</u> profit last year,

write a precise statement:

> Multinational Drugs made an <u>unprecedented</u> profit last year,

or (if you aren't sure whether or not the profit actually set a record):

> Multinational Drugs had a profit increase of 40 per cent last year.

In some cases, qualifiers not only weaken your writing but are redundant because the adjectives themselves are absolutes. To say that something is very unique makes as little sense as saying that someone is slightly pregnant or extremely dead.

Create clear paragraphs

Paragraphs come in so many sizes and patterns that no single formula could possibly cover them all. The two basic principles to remember are these:

1. a paragraph is a means of developing and framing an idea or impression;
2. divisions between paragraphs aren't random but indicate a shift in focus.

DEVELOP YOUR IDEAS

You are not likely to sit down and consciously ask yourself, "What pattern shall I use to develop this paragraph?" What comes first is the idea you intend to develop; the structure of the paragraph should flow from the idea itself and the way you want to discuss or expand it.

You may take one or several paragraphs to develop an idea fully. For a definition alone you could write one paragraph or ten, depending on the complexity of the subject and the nature of the assignment. Just remember that ideas need development, and that each new paragraph signals a change in idea.

CONSIDER THE TOPIC SENTENCE

Skilled skim readers know that they can get the general drift of a book or an article simply by reading the first sentence of each paragraph. The reason is that most paragraphs begin by stating the central idea to be developed. In a formal essay, each topic sentence should relate to the section in which the paragraph appears.

Like the thesis statement for the essay as a whole, the topic sentence is not obligatory; in some paragraphs you might not state the controlling idea until the middle or even the end, and in others you might not state it at all but merely imply it. Nevertheless, it's a good idea to think out a topic sentence for every paragraph. That way you'll be sure that each one has a readily graspable point and is clearly connected to what comes before and after. When revising your initial draft, check to see that each paragraph is held together by a topic sentence, either stated or implied. If you find that you can't formulate one, you should probably rework the whole paragraph.

MAINTAIN FOCUS

A clear paragraph should contain only those details that are in some way related to the central idea. It should also be structured so that the details link naturally to one another. One way of showing these relationships is to keep the same grammatical subject in most of the sentences that make up the paragraph. When the grammatical subject keeps shifting, a paragraph loses focus, as in the following example:

orig.   Cell membranes have been the subject of much research for many decades. In 1972, Singer and Nicolson found that these membranes are composed of a lipid bilayer in which proteins are randomly distributed. Within a few years, scientists discovered that biomembranes have heterogeneous regions called microdomains or rafts. Clusters of sphingolipids and cholesterol typify these zones. Biochemists have been able to create artificial membranes that replicate these regions. Microdomains remained a peripheral idea, until glycosphingolipid clustering in Golgi membranes was found to occur just before vesicles are released. This new information was used to frame the lipid raft hypothesis of Simons and Ikonen in 1997.

Here the grammatical subject (underlined) changes from sentence to sentence. Notice how much stronger the focus becomes when all the sentences have the same grammatical subject—either a variation on the same noun, a synonym, or a related pronoun:

> **rev.** Researchers have studied cell membranes for many decades. Early on, scientists discovered that these membranes are composed of a lipid bilayer in which proteins are randomly distributed (Singer and Nicolson 1972). Later, biochemists discovered that these biomembranes have heterogeneous regions, called microdomains or rafts, characterized by high concentrations of sphingolipids and cholesterol. Biochemists have been able to create artificial membranes that replicate these regions. Subsequently, they have discovered Golgi membranes with regions of high glycosphingolipid concentration just prior to vesicle formation. More recently, others have used this information to form the lipid raft hypothesis of membrane structure (Simons and Ikonen 1997).

Naturally it's not always possible to retain the same grammatical subject throughout a paragraph. If you were comparing topics from different fields of study, for example, you might have to switch back and forth. In the same way, you have to shift when you are discussing examples of an idea or exceptions to it.

AVOID MONOTONY

If most or all of the sentences in your paragraph have the same grammatical subject, how do you avoid boring your reader? There are two easy ways:

1. **Use substitute words**. Pronouns—including personal (*I, we, you, he, she, it, they*), demonstrative (*this, that, these, those*), and indefinite (*someone, everyone, many, others,* etc.) pronouns—can replace the subject, as can synonyms (words or phrases that mean the same thing). The revised paragraph on cell membranes, for example, includes the pronouns *they* and *others*, which substitute for *researchers*. Most well-written paragraphs have a liberal sprinkling of these substitute words.

2. **"Bury" the subject by putting something in front of it**. When the subject is placed in the middle of the sentence rather than at the beginning, it's less obvious to the reader. If you take another look at the revised paragraph, you'll see that in a few sentences there is a word or phrase in front of the subject—*early on, later, subsequently, more recently*. As you can see, even a single word will do the trick.

LINK YOUR IDEAS

To create coherent paragraphs, you need to link your ideas clearly. Linking words are those connectors—conjunctions and conjunctive adverbs—that show the relationship between one sentence, or part of a sentence, and another. They're also known as transition words, because they form a bridge from one thought to another. Make a habit of using linking words when you shift from one grammatical subject or idea to the next, whether the shift occurs within a single paragraph or as you move from one paragraph to another. Here are some of the most common connectors and the logical relations they indicate:

Linking word	Logical relation
and also again furthermore in addition likewise moreover similarly	addition to previous idea
alternatively although but despite, in spite of even so however in contrast nevertheless on the other hand rather yet	change from previous idea
accordingly as a result consequently hence for this reason so therefore thus	summary or conclusion

Numerical terms such as *first*, *second*, and *third* also work well as links.

A few words on the above list pose problems for students. One example is *however*. This word is often used incorrectly as a conjunction (it is actually a conjunctive adverb; see the discussion of commas in Chapter 8 for more on conjunctions and conjunctive adverbs). To add to the woes, *however* can mean different things depending on its place in a sentence. When used at the beginning of a sentence but not followed by a comma, it means "in whatever way":

However you conduct this experiment, the electrodes will fail.

But *however* can also mean "nevertheless." When used in this second sense, its placement can vary depending on what the writer wants to emphasize, but it must be restricted by commas:

However, we succeeded in getting the electrodes to function.

We, however, succeeded in getting the electrodes to function.

We succeeded, however, in getting the electrodes to function.

Languages evolve, and to be a good writer you need an ear for what rings true and an eye for what reads well.

VARY PARAGRAPH LENGTH, BUT AVOID EXTREMES

Ideally, academic writing will have a balance of long and short paragraphs. However, it's best to avoid the extremes—especially the one-sentence paragraph, which can only state an idea without explaining or developing it. A series of very short paragraphs is usually a sign that you have not developed your ideas in enough detail or that you have started new paragraphs unnecessarily. On the other hand, a succession of long paragraphs can be difficult to read. In deciding when to start a new paragraph, consider what is clearest and most helpful for the reader.

BE CONCISE

At one time or another, you will probably be tempted to pad your writing. Whatever the reason—because you need to write two or three thousand words and have only enough to say for one thousand, or because you think length is strength and hope to get a better mark for the extra words—padding is always a mistake.

Strong writing is always concise. It leaves out anything that does not serve some communicative or stylistic purpose, and it says as much as possible in as few words as possible. Concise writing will help you do better on both your essays and your exams.

Use adverbs and adjectives sparingly

Don't sprinkle adverbs and adjectives everywhere and don't use combinations of modifiers unless you are sure they clarify your meaning. One well-chosen word is always better than a series of synonyms:

> **orig.** As well as being <u>costly</u> and <u>financially extravagant</u>, the experiment is <u>reckless</u> and <u>risky</u>.

> **rev.** The experiment is <u>risky</u> as well as <u>costly</u>.

Another problem with adverbs in life sciences essays and reports is that they generally serve as woolly filler. *Interestingly, importantly, approximately, definitely, absolutely, roughly,* and *fairly* are only a few examples of the kinds of adverbs that you should always eliminate in favour of more concise descriptions or arguments.

Avoid noun clusters

A recent trend in some writing is to use nouns as adjectives (as in the phrase *noun cluster*). This device can be effective occasionally, but frequent use can produce a mess. Noun clusters have a predictable "right-handedness," with the important noun always being the one furthest to the right. Piling up nouns in front of this one is like building with Lego. Unfortunately, the brevity achieved does not result in greater clarity. Breaking up noun clusters may not always result in fewer words, but it will make your writing easier to read:

> **orig.** experiment plan revision summary

> **rev.** summary of the revised experiment plan

Many noun clusters have become commonly accepted in the life sciences. While you won't be able to entirely avoid these clusters, you should avoid cluttering your writing with new noun combinations.

Avoid chains of relative clauses

Sentences full of clauses beginning with *which*, *that*, or *who* are usually wordier than necessary. Try reducing some of those clauses to phrases or single words:

orig.   The solutions that were discussed last night have a practical benefit, which is easily grasped by people who have no technical training.

rev.   The solutions discussed last night have a practical benefit, easily grasped by non-technical people.

Try reducing clauses to phrases or words

Independent clauses can often be reduced by subordination. Here are a few examples:

orig.   The report was written in a clear and concise manner, and it was widely read.

rev.   Written in a clear and concise manner, the report was widely read.

rev.   Clear and concise, the report was widely read.

orig.   His plan was of a radical nature and was a source of embarrassment to his employer.

rev.   His radical plan embarrassed his employer.

Eliminate clichés and circumlocutions

Trite or roundabout phrases may flow from your pen automatically, but they make for stale prose. Unnecessary words are deadwood; be prepared to slash ruthlessly to keep your writing vital:

Wordy	*Revised*
due to the fact that	because
at this point in time	now
consensus of opinion	consensus
in the near future	soon
when all is said and done	[omit]
in the eventuality that	if
in all likelihood	likely
it could be said that	possibly, maybe
in all probability	probably

Avoid lazy beginnings

Although it may not always be possible, try to avoid beginning sentences with *It is . . .* or *There is (are) . . . .* Your sentences will be crisper and more concise:

> **orig.**   It is rare for people to see giant lobsters in Maine.
>
> **rev.**   People rarely see giant lobsters in Maine.

Lazy writing is pretty easy to detect. Too many sentences starting with either *this, that,* or *those* lend a paragraph a certain dullness. If you keep a weather eye on these words, you will gain much better control over your writing.

BE FORCEFUL

Developing a forceful, vigorous style simply means learning some common tricks of the trade and practising them until they become habit.

Choose active over passive verbs

An active verb creates more energy than a passive one does:

> Active: The lion <u>ate</u> the gazelle.
>
> Passive: The gazelle <u>was eaten</u> by the lion.

Moreover, passive constructions tend to produce awkward, convoluted phrasing. Writers of bureaucratic documents are among the worst offenders:

> **orig.**   It <u>has been decided</u> that the utilization of small rivers in the province for purposes of generating hydroelectric power <u>should be studied</u> by our department and that a report to the deputy <u>should be made</u> by our director as soon as possible.

The passive verbs in this mouthful make it hard to tell who is doing what. Passive verbs are appropriate in four cases:

1. When the subject is the passive recipient of some action:

   The cabinet minister <u>was heckled</u> by environmentalists.

2. When you want to emphasize the object rather than the person acting:

   The antipollution devices in all three plants <u>will be improved</u>.

3. When you want to avoid an awkward shift from one subject to another in a sentence or paragraph:

We developed our understanding of the nitrogen cycle by studying terrestrial environments but <u>were overwhelmed</u> by new information when cold seeps in the deep oceans yielded their secrets.

4. When you want to avoid placing responsibility or blame:

Several errors <u>were made</u> in the calculations.

When these exceptions don't apply, make an effort to use active verbs for a livelier style.

Use personal subjects

Most of us find it more interesting to learn about people than about things. Wherever possible, therefore, make the subjects of your sentences personal. This trick goes hand in hand with the use of active verbs. Almost any sentence becomes livelier with active verbs and a personal subject:

orig. The <u>consequence</u> of the class's experiment <u>was</u> the <u>decision</u> to abandon the next step.

rev. After the experiment, the <u>class decided</u> to abandon the next step.

Here's another example:

orig. <u>It is assumed</u> that the <u>experiment was a success</u>, since a new <u>paper was published</u> on the results.

rev. <u>We assume</u> that the <u>researchers succeeded</u> in the experiment, since <u>they published</u> a new paper on the results.

(or)

rev. Apparently the <u>researchers succeeded</u>, since <u>they published</u> a new paper on the results of the experiment.

Use concrete details

Concrete details are easier to understand—and to remember—than abstract theories. Whenever you are discussing abstract concepts, therefore, always provide specific examples and illustrations; if you have a choice between a concrete word and an abstract one, choose the concrete. Consider this sentence:

> La Pérouse sailed across the Pacific and collected scientific information.

Now see how a few specific details can bring the facts to life:

> La Pérouse sailed his two ships, the *Boussole* and the *Astrolabe*, across the Pacific and, like his admired predecessor Captain Cook, collected scientific, ethnographic, and geographic information.

Adding concrete details doesn't mean getting rid of all abstractions. Just try to find the proper balance. The above example is one instance where you can improve your writing by adding words, as long as they are concrete and correct.

Make important ideas stand out

Experienced writers know how to manipulate sentences in order to emphasize certain points. The following are some of their techniques.

PLACE KEY WORDS IN STRATEGIC POSITIONS

The positions of emphasis in a sentence are the beginning and, above all, the end. If you want to bring your point home with force, don't put the key words in the middle of the sentence. Save them for the end:

> **orig.** Humans are less afraid of losing polar bears than of losing an entire ecosystem in this era of global climate change.

> **rev.** In this era of global climate change, humans are less afraid of losing polar bears than of losing an entire ecosystem.

SUBORDINATE MINOR IDEAS

If small children were to write a lab report, they would likely connect incidents with a string of *ands*, as if everything were of equal importance:

> The pH was reached, and the titration was carried out, and the solution's colour changed.

As they grow up, however, they learn to subordinate—that is, to make one part of a sentence less important in order to emphasize another point:

Once the pH was reached, the titration was run until the solution's colour changed.

Major ideas stand out more and connections become clearer when minor ideas are subordinated:

orig. The researchers collected all of the samples and they adjusted the experimental design.

rev. After they collected all of the samples, the researchers adjusted the experimental design.

Make your most important idea the focus of the main clause, and try to put it at the end, where it will be most emphatic:

orig. The fish fry were dying due to sea lice.

rev. Due to sea lice, the fish fry were dying.

VARY SENTENCE STRUCTURE

As with anything else, variety adds spice to writing. One way of adding variety that will also make an important idea stand out is to use a periodic rather than a simple sentence structure.

Most sentences follow the simple pattern of subject–verb–object (plus modifiers):

Many <u>people</u> <u>eat</u> <u>meat</u>.
        S   V   O

A *simple sentence* such as this gives the main idea all at once, in a single clause, and therefore creates little tension. A *periodic sentence*, on the other hand, does not give the main clause until the end, after one or more subordinate clauses:

Although studies have shown the environmental consequences of widespread animal farming, and although there are other efficient sources of protein, many <u>people</u> <u>eat</u> <u>meat</u>.
  S   V   O

The longer the periodic sentence is, the greater the suspense and the more emphatic the final part. Since this high-tension structure is more difficult to read than the simple sentence, your reader would be exhausted if you used it too often. Save it for those times when you want to make a very strong point.

VARY SENTENCE LENGTH

A short sentence can add impact to an important point, especially when it comes after a series of longer sentences. This technique can be particularly useful for conclusions. Don't overdo it, though—a string of long sentences may be monotonous, but a string of short ones can make your writing sound like a children's book.

Still, academic papers usually have too many long sentences rather than too many short ones. Since short sentences are easier to read, try breaking up clusters of long ones. Check any sentence over twenty words or so in length to see if it will benefit from being split.

USE CONTRAST

Just as a jeweller highlights a diamond by displaying it against dark velvet, so you can highlight an idea by placing it against a contrasting background:

orig. Most sea mammals do not have toenails.

rev. Unlike sea cows, most sea mammals do not have toenails.

Using parallel phrasing will increase the effect of the contrast:

Although bromeliads tolerate drought, salt spray, and heat, they cannot tolerate cold.

USE A WELL-PLACED ADVERB OR CORRELATIVE CONSTRUCTION

Adding an adverb or two can sometimes help you dramatize or clarify a concept:

orig. Although this method is reliable, in my hands it was fickle.

rev. Although this method is <u>usually</u> reliable, in my hands it was <u>always</u> fickle.

Correlatives such as *both . . . and* or *not only . . . but also* can be used to emphasize combinations as well:

orig. The mass spectrometer separates ions by mass and by charge.

rev. The mass spectrometer separates ions not only by mass but also by charge.

(or)

rev. The mass spectrometer separates ions both by mass and by charge.

USE REPETITION

Repetition is a highly effective device for adding emphasis:

> According to E.O. Wilson, the inventor of sociobiology, humans need an evolutionary epic—an epic of creation, an epic of our beginnings, an epic of our place in the world—that would be as ennobling as any religious epic.

Of course, you would only use such a dramatic technique on rare occasions.

SOME FINAL ADVICE

Write before you revise

No one expects you to sit down and put all this advice into practice as soon as you start to write. You would feel so constrained that it would be hard to get anything down on paper at all. You will be better off if you begin concentrating on these guidelines during the final stages of the writing process when you are looking critically at what you have already written. Some experienced writers can combine the creative and critical functions, but most of us find it easier to write a rough draft first before starting the detailed task of revising and editing.

Use your ears

Your ears are probably your best critics; make good use of them. Before producing a final copy of any piece of writing, read it out loud in a clear voice. The difference between cumbersome and fluent passages will be unmistakable.

SUMMARY

The facts rarely speak for themselves—they usually need a writerly helping hand. As you face a highly stylized writing assignment such as a lab report or an essay, you should learn to depend on the same skills that all writers use. Remember that your goal is to provide clarity. Choose appropriate words, compose forceful sentences, and create dynamic paragraphs to support your line of reasoning. Always pay attention to adverbs, adjectives, sentence lengths, parallel structures, comparisons, and rhetorical devices such as repetition—they can all help you keep your reader interested in your writing. The benefit of learning to control style is that you will begin to write with individuality—you will find your voice. This newfound ability to express yourself will make your experience of the life sciences more personal and, not surprisingly, more creative.

CHAPTER 7

Common Errors in Grammar and Usage

OBJECTIVES

- maintaining sentence unity
- keeping subjects and verbs in agreement
- using proper verb tenses
- avoiding difficulties with pronouns
- understanding modifiers
- keeping order among pairs and parallels

This chapter is not a comprehensive grammar lesson; it's simply a survey of those areas where students most often make mistakes. It will help you pinpoint weaknesses as you edit your work. Once you get into the habit of checking your work, it won't be long before you are correcting potential problems as you write.

The grammatical terms used here are the most basic and familiar ones; if you need to review some of them, see Chapter 8 or the glossary. If you're interested in a more exhaustive treatment, consult one of the many books that deal exclusively with grammar and usage.

SENTENCE UNITY

Sentence fragments
To be complete, a sentence must have both a subject and a verb in an independent clause; if it doesn't, it's a fragment. There are times in informal writing when it is acceptable to use a sentence fragment in order to give emphasis to a point:

✓   Will the government pass legislation to prevent trophy hunting? <u>Not likely</u>.

Here the sentence fragment *Not likely* is clearly intended to be understood as a short form of *It is not likely that the government will pass this legislation.* Unintentional sentence fragments, on the other hand, usually seem incomplete rather than shortened:

✗　I enjoy living in Vancouver. <u>Being a skier who likes the sea.</u>

The last "sentence" is incomplete because it lacks an independent clause with a subject and a verb. Remember that a participle such as *being* is a verbal, or "part-verb," not a verb. You can make the fragment into a complete sentence by adding a subject and a verb:

✓　I am a skier who likes the sea.

Alternatively, you could join the fragment to the preceding sentence:

✓　Being a skier who likes the sea, I enjoy living in Vancouver.

✓　I enjoy living in Vancouver, since I am a skier who likes the sea.

Run-on sentences

A run-on sentence is one that continues beyond the point where it should have stopped:

✗　Mosquitoes and blackflies are annoying, but they don't stop tourists from coming to spend their holidays in Canada, and such is the case in Ontario's northland.

This run-on sentence could be fixed by adding a period or a semicolon after *Canada* and removing the word *and*.

Another kind of run-on sentence is one in which two independent clauses are wrongly joined by a comma. An independent clause is a phrase that can stand by itself as a complete sentence. Two independent clauses should not be joined by a comma without a coordinating conjunction:

✗　Northrop Frye won international acclaim as a critic, he was an English professor at the University of Toronto.

This error is known as a comma splice. There are three ways of correcting it:

1. by putting a period after *critic* and starting a new sentence:

　　✓　. . . as a critic. He . . .

2. by replacing the comma with a semicolon:

✓ . . . as a critic; he . . .

3. by making one of the independent clauses subordinate to the other, so that it doesn't stand by itself:

✓ Northrop Frye, who won international acclaim as a critic, was an English professor at the University of Toronto.

The one exception to the rule that independent clauses cannot be joined by a comma arises when the clauses are very short and arranged in a tight sequence:

✓ I opened the tent flap, I saw the skunk, and I closed the flap.

You should not use this kind of sentence very often.

Contrary to what many people think, conjunctive adverbs—words such as *however*, *therefore*, and *thus*—cannot be used to join independent clauses:

✗ Two of the sheep developed incurable scrapie, however they were quickly quarantined.

This mistake can be corrected by beginning a new sentence after *scrapie* or (preferably) by replacing the comma with a semicolon:

✓ Two of the sheep developed incurable scrapie; however, they were quickly quarantined.

In this case, a comma is also needed to prevent the reader from misreading *however* as "in whatever way."

Another option is to join the two independent clauses with a coordinating conjunction—*and*, *or*, *nor*, *but*, *for*, *yet*, *so*, or *whereas*:

✓ Two of the sheep developed incurable scrapie, but they were quickly quarantined.

Faulty predication
When the subject of a sentence is not grammatically connected to what follows (the predicate), the result is faulty predication:

✗ The <u>reason</u> he failed <u>was because</u> he couldn't handle multiple-choice exams.

The problem with this sentence is that *the reason* and *was because* mean essentially the same thing. The subject is a noun and the verb *was* needs a noun clause to complete it:

✓ The reason he failed was that he couldn't handle multiple-choice exams.

Another solution is to rephrase the sentence:

✓ He failed because he couldn't handle multiple-choice exams.

Faulty predication also occurs with *is when* and *is where* constructions:

✗ The climax of the film is when the healed bird is released in the wild.

Again, you can correct this error in one of two ways:

1. Follow the *is* with a noun phrase to complete the sentence:

   ✓ The climax is the release of the bird in the wild.

   (or)

   ✓ The climax is the bird's release in the wild.

2. Change the verb:

   ✓ The climax occurs when the bird is released in the wild.

SUBJECT–VERB AGREEMENT

Identifying the subject

A verb should always agree in number with its subject. Sometimes, however, when the subject does not come at the beginning of the sentence or when it is separated from the verb by other information, you may be tempted to use a verb form that does not agree:

✗ The increase in harvested fish and bycatch were condemned by the biologists.

The subject here is *increase*, not *fish and bycatch*; therefore, the verb should be singular:

✓ The increase in harvested fish and bycatch was condemned by the biologists.

Either, neither, each

The indefinite pronouns *either*, *neither*, and *each* always take singular verbs:

✓ Neither duck species is found in Canada.

✓ Each of them is an endangered species.

Compound subjects

When *or, either . . . or*, or *neither . . . nor* is used to create a compound subject, the verb should usually agree with the last item in the subject:

✓ Neither the professor nor her students were able to solve the equation.

✓ Either the students or the TA was misinformed.

You may find, however, that it sounds awkward in some cases to use a singular verb when a singular item follows a plural item:

orig. Either my history books or my biology text is going to gather dust this weekend.

In such instances, it's better to rephrase the sentence:

rev. This weekend, I'm going to ignore either my history books or my biology text.

Unlike the word *and*, which creates a compound subject and therefore takes a plural verb, the phrases *as well as* and *in addition to* do not create compound subjects; therefore the verb remains singular:

✓ Spruce and birch are boreal forest trees.

✓ Spruce, as well as birch, is a boreal forest tree.

Collective nouns

A collective noun is a singular noun that comprises a number of members, such as *family, army*, or *team*. If the noun refers to the members as one unit, it takes a singular verb:

✓ The research team is awaiting renewal of its grant.

If, in the context of the sentence, the noun refers to the members as individuals, the verb becomes plural:

✓　The research team are receiving their funds tomorrow.

✓　The majority of fossils occur in sedimentary layers found just above the riverbed.

Titles

The title of a book or a movie or the name of a business or organization is always treated as a singular noun, even if it contains plural words; therefore, it takes a singular verb:

✓　*Sharks of the Pacific* was a bestseller.

✓　Goodman & Goodman is handling the legal dispute.

VERB TENSES

Native speakers of English usually know without thinking which verb tense to use in a given context. However, a few tenses can still be confusing.

The past perfect

If the main verb is in the past tense and you want to refer to something that happened before that time, use the past perfect (*had* followed by the past participle). The time sequence will not be clear if you use the simple past in both clauses:

✗　He hoped that she fixed the microscope.

✓　He hoped that she had fixed the microscope.

Similarly, when you are reporting what someone said in the past—that is, when you are using past indirect discourse—you should use the past perfect tense in the clause describing what was said:

✗　He told the TA that he wrote the essay that week.

✓　He told the TA that he had written the essay that week.

Using *if*

When you are describing a possibility in the future, use the present tense in the condition (*if*) clause and the future tense in the consequence clause:

✓ If he <u>tests</u> us on photosynthesis, I <u>will fail</u>.

When the possibility is unlikely, it is conventional—especially in formal writing—to use the subjunctive in the *if* clause, and *would* followed by the base verb in the consequence clause:

✓ If he <u>were</u> to cancel the test, I <u>would cheer</u>.

When you are describing a hypothetical instance in the past, use the past subjunctive (it has the same form as the past perfect) in the *if* clause and *would have* followed by the past participle for the consequence. A common error is to use *would have* in both clauses:

✗ If he <u>would have been</u> friendlier, I <u>would have asked</u> him to be my lab partner.

✓ If he <u>had been</u> friendlier, I <u>would have asked</u> him to be my lab partner.

Writing about literature

When you are describing a literary work in its historical context, use the past tense:

✓ Margaret Atwood <u>wrote</u> *Surfacing* at a time when George Grant's *Technology and Empire* <u>was persuading</u> people to reassess technocratic values.

To discuss what goes on within a work of literature, however, you should use the present tense:

✓ The main character <u>retreats</u> to the woods and <u>tries</u> to escape the oppressive noise of the city.

When you are discussing an episode or incident in a literary work and want to refer to a prior incident or a future one, use past or future tenses accordingly:

✓ The narrator <u>returns</u> to northern Quebec, where he <u>spent</u> his early career <u>working</u> in a field station; by the time he <u>leaves</u>, he <u>will have reawakened</u> his love of microbiology.

Be sure to return to the present tense when you have finished referring to events in the past or future.

PRONOUNS

Pronoun reference

The link between a pronoun and the noun it refers to must be clear. If the noun doesn't appear in the same sentence as the pronoun, it should appear in the preceding sentence:

✗   The <u>textbook supply</u> in the bookstore had run out, so we borrowed <u>them</u> from the library.

Since *textbook* is used as an adjective rather than a noun, it cannot serve as referent or antecedent for the pronoun *them*. You must either replace *them* or change the phrase *textbook supply*:

✓   The <u>textbook supply</u> in the bookstore had run out, so we borrowed <u>the texts</u> from the library.

✓   The bookstore had run out of <u>textbooks</u>, so we borrowed <u>them</u> from the library.

When a sentence contains more than one noun, make sure there is no ambiguity about which noun the pronoun refers to:

✗   The public wants better <u>environmental regulation</u> along with lower <u>taxes</u>, but the government does not favour <u>them</u>.

What does the pronoun *them* refer to: the regulation, the taxes, or both?

✓   The public wants better environmental regulation along with lower taxes, but the government does not advocate <u>spending increases</u>.

Using *it* and *this*

Using *it* and *this* without a clear referent can lead to confusion:

✗   Although the directors wanted to meet in January, <u>it</u> (<u>this</u>) didn't take place until May.

✓   Although the directors wanted to meet in January, <u>the conference</u> didn't take place until May.

Make sure that *it* or *this* clearly refers to a specific noun or pronoun.

Using *one*

People often use the word *one* to avoid overusing *I* in their writing. Although in Britain this is common, in Canada and the United States frequent use of *one* may seem too formal and even a bit pompous:

orig. If one were to apply for the grant, one would find oneself engulfed in so many bureaucratic forms that one's patience would be stretched thin.

While there is nothing grammatically incorrect in this example, it may strike the reader as stiff or pretentious. The best thing to do is to recast the sentence with a plural subject:

rev. If researchers were to apply for grants, they would find themselves engulfed in so many bureaucratic forms that their patience would be stretched thin.

Use *one* sparingly, and don't be afraid of the occasional *I*. The one error to avoid is mixing the third-person *one* with the second-person *you*:

✗ When one visits the Rockies, you are impressed by the grandeur of the scenery.

Using *me* and other objective pronouns

Remembering that it is wrong to say "Dorcas and me were invited to present our findings to the delegates" rather than "Dorcas and I were invited . . . ," many people use the subjective form of the pronoun even when it should be objective:

✗ The delegates invited Dorcas and I to present our findings.

✓ The delegates invited Dorcas and me to present our findings.

The verb *invited* requires an object; *me* is the objective case. A good way to tell which form is correct is to ask yourself how the sentence would sound with only the pronoun. You will know by ear that the subjective form—"The delegates invited I"—is not appropriate.

The same problem often arises with prepositions, which should also be followed by a noun or pronoun in the objective case:

✗   <u>Between</u> you and <u>I</u>, this result doesn't make sense.

✓   <u>Between</u> you and <u>me</u>, this result doesn't make sense.

✗   Eating well is a problem <u>for we</u> students.

✓   Eating well is a problem <u>for us</u> students.

There are times, however, when the correct case can sound stiff or awkward:

orig.   <u>To whom</u> was the award given?

Rather than using a correct but awkward form, try to reword the sentence:

rev.   <u>Who received</u> the award?

EXCEPTIONS FOR PRONOUNS FOLLOWING PREPOSITIONS

The rule that a pronoun following a preposition takes the objective case has exceptions. When the preposition is followed by a clause, the pronoun should take the case required by its position in the clause:

✗   The students showed some concern <u>over whom would be selected</u> as Dean.

Although the pronoun follows the preposition *over*, it is also the subject of the verb *would be selected* and therefore requires the subjective case:

✓   The students showed some concern <u>over who would be selected</u> as Dean.

Similarly, when a gerund (a word that acts partly as a noun and partly as a verb) is the subject of a clause, the pronoun that modifies it takes the possessive case:

✗   We were surprised <u>by him dropping</u> out of school.

✓   We were surprised <u>by his dropping</u> out of school.

✗   He was tired <u>of me reminding</u> him.

✓   He was tired <u>of my reminding</u> him.

MODIFIERS

Adjectives modify nouns; adverbs modify verbs, adjectives, and other adverbs. Do not use an adjective to modify a verb:

✗   He dissected good. (adjective with verb)

✓   He dissected well. (adverb modifying verb)

✓   He dissected really well. (adverb modifying adverb)

✓   He had a good style. (adjective modifying noun)

✓   He had a really good style. (adverb modifying adjective)

Squinting modifiers
Remember that clarity depends largely on word order: to avoid confusion, the connections between the different parts of a sentence must be clear. Modifiers should therefore be as close as possible to the words they modify. A squinting modifier is one that, because of its position, seems to look in two directions at once:

✗   She expected after the announcement a decline in public concern.

Was *after the announcement* the time of expectation or the time of the decline in public concern? Changing the order of the sentence or rephrasing it will make the meaning clearer:

✓   After the announcement, she expected a decline in public concern.

✓   She expected public concern to decline after the announcement.

Other squinting modifiers can be corrected in the same way:

✗   Our biochemistry professor gave a lecture on leishmaniasis, which was well illustrated.

✓   Our biochemistry professor gave a well-illustrated lecture on leishmaniasis.

Often the modifier works best when placed immediately in front of the phrase it modifies. Notice the difference that this placement can make:

Only she guessed the structure of the protein.

She only guessed the structure of the protein.

She guessed <u>only</u> the structure of the protein.

She guessed the structure of the protein <u>only</u>.

Dangling modifiers

Modifiers that have no grammatical connection with anything else in the sentence are said to be dangling:

✗   <u>Walking</u> around the campus in June, the river and trees made a picturesque scene.

Who is doing the walking? Here's another example:

✗   <u>Reflecting</u> on the results of the poll, it was decided not to announce the new tuition increases right away.

Who is doing the reflecting? Clarify the meaning by connecting the dangling modifier to a new subject:

✓   <u>Walking</u> around the campus in June, <u>Winnie</u> thought the river and trees made a picturesque scene.

✓   <u>Reflecting</u> on the results of the poll, <u>the government</u> decided not to announce the new tuition increases right away.

PAIRS AND PARALLELS

Comparisons

Make sure that your comparisons are complete. The second element in a comparison should be equivalent to the first, whether the equivalence is stated or merely implied:

✗   Today's students have a greater understanding of calculus than their parents.

This sentence suggests that the two things being compared are *calculus* and *parents*. Adding a second verb (*have*) equivalent to the first one shows that the two things being compared are *parents' understanding* and *students' understanding*:

✓   Today's students <u>have</u> a greater understanding of calculus than their parents <u>have</u>.

A similar problem arises in the following comparison:

✗   That new text is <u>a boring book</u> and so are the lectures.

The lectures may be boring, but they are not *a boring book*; to make sense, the two parts of the comparison must be parallel:

✓   The new text is <u>boring</u> and so are the lectures.

Correlatives

Constructions such as *both . . . and, not only . . . but also*, and *neither . . . nor* are especially tricky. For the implied comparison to work, the two parts that come after the coordinating term must be grammatically equivalent:

✗   He <u>not only studies</u> amphibians <u>but also mammals</u>.

✓   He studies <u>not only amphibians</u> <u>but also mammals</u>.

Parallel phrasing

A series of items in a sentence should be phrased in parallel wording. Make sure that all the parts of a parallel construction are in fact equal:

✗   We had to turn in <u>our rough notes</u>, <u>our calculations</u>, and <u>finished assignment</u>.

✓   We had to turn in <u>our rough notes</u>, <u>our calculations</u>, and <u>our finished assignment</u>.

Once you have decided to include the pronoun *our* in the first two elements, the third must have it too.

For clarity as well as stylistic grace, keep similar ideas in similar form:

✗   He <u>failed</u> mathematics and <u>barely passed</u> statistics, but plants and people was a subject he did well in.

✓   He <u>failed</u> mathematics and barely <u>passed</u> statistics but did well in plants and people.

Faulty parallelism is a common problem in bulleted or numbered lists:

✗   There are several reasons for studying this organism:

 • large <u>size</u>
 • <u>there is</u> a long history of experimentation
 • <u>medically</u> important
 • <u>detecting</u> it is quick

✓ There are several reasons for studying this organism:

- large <u>size</u>
- long <u>history of experimentation</u>
- medical <u>importance</u>
- easy <u>detection</u>

SUMMARY

Gaining control over written expression is difficult, but essential. Life sciences students frequently complain about marks docked for poor grammar. They reason that grammar is not important, or at least not as important as the science that they are describing. Yet there are a number of good reasons that you should pay attention to grammar. Every fourth-year honours student, every graduate student, and every practising scientist will tell you that without the skill to write up your results in correct English, you will find it difficult to establish a career in this field. No one will make allowances for poor communication. Native English-speaking life scientists already have a huge advantage: since the end of World War II, English has become the global language of science. By mastering the grammar of the international language of communication, you will add enormous transportability to your degree. Also, once you improve your grammar, you will find that all essays and reports—no matter the subject—are easier to write.

CHAPTER 8

Punctuation

OBJECTIVE

- learning the conventions of punctuation: *apostrophe, brackets, colon, comma, dash, ellipsis, exclamation mark, hyphen, italics, parentheses, period, quotation marks,* and *semicolon*

Punctuation causes students so many problems that it deserves a chapter of its own. If your punctuation is faulty, your readers will be confused and may have to backtrack; worse still, they may be tempted to skip over the rough spots. Punctuation marks are the traffic signals of writing; use them with precision to keep readers moving smoothly through your work.

(Items in this chapter are arranged alphabetically.)

APOSTROPHE [']

1. **Use an apostrophe to indicate possession**. To figure out where to place the apostrophe, think of the possessive as an *of* phrase. If the noun of the *of* phrase ends in s, add an apostrophe. If the noun in the *of* phrase does not end in s, add an apostrophe plus s.

the laboratory <u>of Dr. Jones</u>	→	Dr. Jones' laboratory
the writings <u>of Darwin</u>	→	Darwin's writings
the migration route <u>of the whales</u>	→	the whales' migration route
the panel <u>of the spectrophotometer</u>	→	the spectrophotometer's panel

2. **Use an apostrophe to show contractions of words**:

isn't; we'll; he's; shouldn't; I'm

Caution: don't confuse *it's* (the contraction of *it is*) with *its* (the possessive of *it*), which has no apostrophe. And remember that possessive pronouns never take an apostrophe: *yours, hers, its, ours, yours, theirs*.

BRACKETS [ ]

Brackets are square enclosures, not to be confused with parentheses (which are round). **Use brackets to set off a remark of your own within a quotation.** The brackets indicate that the words enclosed are not those of the person quoted:

Wainright maintained, "Obstacles to implementing the Kyoto Accord [in the late twentieth century] are as many as they are serious."

Brackets are sometimes used to enclose *sic*, which is used after an error such as a misspelling to show that the mistake was in the original. *Sic* may be italicized:

The systematist, in his memoirs, wrote about "these parlouse [*sic*] times of economic difficulty."

COLON [:]

A colon indicates that something is to follow.

1. **Use a colon before a formal statement or series**:

✓ The selected speakers are the following: Anna, Dieter, George, and Hugh.

Do not use a colon if the words preceding it do not form a complete sentence:

✗ The selected speakers are: Anna, Dieter, George, and Hugh.

✓ The selected speakers are Anna, Dieter, George, and Hugh.

On the other hand, a colon often precedes a vertical list, even when the introductory part is not a complete sentence:

✓   The selected speakers are: Anna Singh
                                      Dieter Goering
                                      George Turner
                                      Hugh Mackay

2. **Use a colon for formality before a direct quotation or when a complete sentence precedes the quotation**:

> The leaders of the anti-nuclear group repeated their message: "The world needs bread before bombs."

3. **Use a colon between numbers expressing time and ratios**:

> 4:30 p.m.
>
> The ratio of calcium to potassium should be 7:1.

COMMA [,]

Commas are the trickiest of all punctuation marks; even the experts differ on when to use them. Most agree, however, that too many commas are as bad as too few since they make writing choppy and awkward to read. Certainly recent writers use fewer commas than earlier stylists did. Whenever you are in doubt, let clarity be your guide. The most widely accepted conventions are these:

1. **Use a comma to separate two independent clauses joined by a coordinating conjunction (*and, but, for, or, nor, yet, so, whereas*).** By signalling that there are two clauses, the comma will prevent the reader from thinking that the beginning of the second clause is the end of the first:

✗   He sampled the fish with help of his lab partner and the technician ran the analysis.

✓   He sampled the fish with help of his lab partner, and the technician ran the analysis.

When the second clause has the same subject as the first, you have the option of omitting both the second subject and the comma:

✓   She can make gels well, but she can't run the software.

✓   She can make gels well but can't run the software.

If you mistakenly punctuate two sentences as if they were one, the result will be a run-on sentence; if you use a comma but forget the coordinating conjunction, the result will be a comma splice:

✗   We took the veterinarian to the Animal Care Unit, it was closed for repairs.

✓   We took the veterinarian to the Animal Care Unit, but it was closed for repairs.

Remember that words such as *however*, *therefore*, and *thus* are conjunctive adverbs, not conjunctions; if you use one of them to join two independent clauses, the result will again be a comma splice:

✗   She was accepted into medical school, however, she took a year off to earn her tuition.

✓   She was accepted into medical school; however, she took a year off to earn her tuition.

Conjunctive adverbs are often confused with conjunctions. You can distinguish between the two if you remember that a conjunctive adverb's position in a sentence can be changed:

✓   She was accepted into medical school; she took a year off, however, to earn her tuition.

The position of a conjunction, on the other hand, is invariable; it must be placed between the two clauses:

✓   She was accepted into medical school, but she took a year off to earn her tuition.

A good rule of thumb, then, is to use a comma when the linking word can't move.

When, in rare cases, the independent clauses are short and closely related, they may be joined by a comma alone:

✓   I came, I saw, I conquered.

2. **Use a comma between items in a series**. Place a coordinating conjunction before the last item:

✓   She finally found a gravid female snake that was large, healthy, and free of disease.

✓   Then she had to scrounge for an HPLC, 96-well plates, a centrifuge, and solvents.

The comma before the conjunction is optional for single items in a series:

✓   She kept a hawk, an eagle and a merlin.

For phrases in a series, however, use the final comma to help to prevent confusion:

✗   When we set off on our backcountry trip, we were warned about ticks, attacks by bears and lost tourists.

In this case, a comma would prevent the reader from thinking that attacks were made by bears as well as lost tourists:

✓   We were warned about ticks, attacks by bears, and lost tourists.

3. **Use a comma to separate adjectives preceding a noun when they modify the same element**:

✓   It was a rainy, windy night.

However, when the adjectives do not modify the same element, you should not use a comma:

✗   It was a pleasant, winter outing.

Here *winter* modifies *outing*, but *pleasant* modifies the whole phrase—*winter outing*. A good way of deciding whether or not you need a comma is to see if you can reverse the order of the adjectives. If you can reverse them (*rainy, windy night* or *windy, rainy night*), use a comma; if you can't (*winter pleasant outing*), omit the comma:

✓ It was a pleasant winter outing.

4. Use commas to set off an interruption (or "parenthetical element"):

✓ The lecture, I hear, isn't nearly as good as people claim.

✓ The TA, however, couldn't answer the question.

Remember to put commas on both sides of the interruption:

✗ The TA however, couldn't answer the question.

✗ The software, they claim was adapted by a previous grad student.

✓ The software, they claim, was adapted by a previous grad student.

5. **Use commas to set off words or phrases that provide additional but non-essential information**:

✓ Our TA, Sue Stephens, does her job well.

✓ The golden retriever, the imprinted duck's new companion, went with him everywhere.

In these examples, *Sue Stephens* and *the imprinted duck's new companion* are *appositives*: they give additional information about the nouns they refer to (*TA* and *golden retriever*), but the sentences would make sense without them. Here's another example:

✓ My former lab partner, who grew up in Halifax, moved to Wolfville last week.

The phrase *who grew up in Halifax* is a non-restrictive modifier because it does not limit the meaning of the term it modifies (*lab partner*). Without that modifying clause, the sentence would still specify who moved to Wolfville. Since the information the clause provides is not necessary to the meaning of the sentence, you must use commas on both sides to set it off.

In contrast, a restrictive modifier is one that provides essential information; it must not be set apart from the element it modifies, and commas should not be used:

✓ The man who runs the greenhouse was my jogging partner.

Without the clause *who runs the greenhouse*, the reader would not know which man was the jogging partner.

To avoid confusion, be sure to distinguish carefully between essential and additional information. The difference can be important:

Students, who are unwilling to work, should not receive grants. (All students are unwilling to work and should not receive grants.)

Students who are unwilling to work should not receive grants. (Only those who are unwilling to work should be denied grants.)

6. **Use a comma after an introductory phrase when omitting it would cause confusion**:

✗ On the escarpment above the researchers cored the trees.

✓ On the escarpment above, the researchers cored the trees.

✗ When he turned away the lion disappeared.

✓ When he turned away, the lion disappeared.

7. **Use a comma to separate elements in dates and addresses**:

February 2, 2010 (Commas are often omitted if the day comes first: 2 February 2010.)

117 Hudson Drive, Edmonton, Alberta

They lived in Dartmouth, Nova Scotia.

8. **Use a comma before a quotation in a sentence**:

He said, "Life is too short to worry."

"The diving certification program," he repeated, "is in your hands."

For more formality, or if the quotation is preceded by a complete sentence, you may use a colon (see page 127).

9. **Use a comma with a name followed by a title**:

> David Gunn, President
>
> Patrice Lareau, M.D.

10. **Do not use a comma between a subject and its verb**:

✗   The most common ligand of all, is vanillin.

✓   The most common ligand of all is vanillin.

11. **Do not use a comma between a verb and its object**:

✗   The research team immediately decided, what they must do.

✓   The research team immediately decided what they must do.

12. **Do not use a comma between a coordinating conjunction and the following clause**:

✗   Ellen got honours but, Daniel failed the course.

✓   Ellen got honours, but Daniel failed the course.

DASH [—]

A dash creates an abrupt pause, emphasizing the words that follow. Never use dashes as casual substitutes for other punctuation; overuse can detract from the calm, well-reasoned effect you want to create. Most often, you will use a dash to stress a word or a phrase:

> Canadian parliamentarians—as a matter of honour—vowed to serve seal meat in their canteen.
>
> Ramirez was well received in the botanical society—at first.

You can type two hyphens together, with no spaces on either side, to show a dash; your word processor may automatically convert this to a solid line as you continue typing. Alternatively, you can insert an em dash from the list of special characters in your word-processing program.

ELLIPSIS [. . .]

1. **Use an ellipsis (three dots) to show an omission from a quotation**:

    For an ellipsis within a sentence, use three periods with a space before each and a space after the last:

    > "The animal care committee reported that post-mortem tests . . . verified that poor nutrition was a factor in the deaths of the mice."

    If the omission comes at the beginning of the quotation, an ellipsis is not necessary:

    > The committee cited evidence that "verified that poor nutrition was a factor in the deaths of the mice."

    When the omission comes at the end of a sentence, use four periods with no space before the first or after the last:

    > The committee noted that "poor nutrition was a factor. . . ."

2. **Use an ellipsis to show that a series of numbers continues indefinitely**:

    > 1, 3, 5, 7, 9 . . .

EXCLAMATION MARK [!]

An exclamation mark helps to show emotion or feeling. It is usually found in dialogue:

> "Eureka!" he cried.

In academic writing, you should use it only in those rare cases when you want to give a point emotional emphasis:

> He predicted that there would be a bumper crop this year. Some forecast!

HYPHEN [-]

1. **Use a hyphen if you must divide a word at the end of a line.** Although it's generally best to start a new line if a word is too long, there are instances—for example, when you're formatting text in narrow columns—when hyphenation might be preferred. The hyphenation feature in current word-processing programs has taken the guesswork out of dividing words at the end of the line, but in the event that you use manual hyphenation, here are a few guidelines:

   • Divide between syllables.
   • Never divide a one-syllable word.
   • Never leave one letter by itself.
   • Divide double consonants except when they come before a suffix, in which case divide before the suffix:

      ar-rangement
      embar-rassment
      fall-ing
      pass-able

   • When the second consonant has been added to form the suffix, keep it with the suffix:

      refer-ral
      begin-ning

2. **Use a hyphen to separate the parts of certain compound words:**

   • compound nouns:

      sister-in-law; vice-consul

   • compound verbs:

      test-market; dive-bomb

   • compound modifiers:

      a well-considered experiment; forward-looking attitudes

Note that compound modifiers are hyphenated only when they precede the part modified; otherwise, omit the hyphen:

The experiment was well considered.

His attitudes are forward looking.

Also, do not hyphenate a compound modifier that includes an adverb ending in -ly:

✓ a well-written paper

✗ a beautifully-written paper

✓ a beautifully written paper

Spell-check features today will help you determine which compounds to hyphenate, but there is no clear consensus even from one dictionary to another. As always, consistency in your writing style is most important.

3. **Use a hyphen with certain prefixes (*all-*, *self-*, *ex-*) and with prefixes preceding a proper name.** Again, practices vary, so when in doubt consult a dictionary.

all-star; self-imposed; ex-biochemist; pro-Canadian

4. **Use a hyphen to emphasize contrasting prefixes:**

The professor agreed to have both pre- and post-operation discussions with the students.

5. **Use a hyphen to separate written-out compound numbers from one to ninety-nine, and compound fractions:**

eighty-one years ago; seven-tenths full; two-thirds of a cup

6. **Use a hyphen to separate parts of inclusive numbers or dates:**

the years 1890-1914; pages 3-10

ITALICS [*italics*]

1. Use italics for the titles of works published independently, such as books, long poems that are complete books, plays, films, CDs, and long musical compositions:

   Birdscapes is one of my favourite non-fiction books.

   For articles, essays, short poems, or songs, use quotation marks.

2. **Use italics to emphasize an idea**:

   It is important that all equipment be washed *immediately*.

   Be sparing with this use, interspersing it with other, less intrusive methods of creating emphasis.

3. **Use italics (or quotation marks) to identify a word or phrase that is itself the subject of discussion**:

   The term *peer group* is an example of sociological jargon.

4. **Use italics for foreign words or expressions that have not been naturalized in English**:

   The government was overthrown in a *coup d'état*.

   Her statement was a *cri de coeur*.

PARENTHESES [( )]

1. **Use parentheses to enclose an explanation, example, or qualification**. Parentheses show that the enclosed material is of incidental importance to the main idea. They make an interruption that is more subtle than one marked off by dashes but more pronounced than one set off by commas:

   This larch hybrid (the most recent attempt at hybridization) had good form and a high growth rate.

   Their latest plan (according to everyone) is to log that stretch of forest.

Remember that punctuation should not precede parentheses but may follow them if required by the sense of the sentence:

I like coffee before class (if it's not instant), but she prefers tea.

If the parenthetical statement comes between two complete sentences, it should be punctuated as a sentence, with the period, question mark, or exclamation mark inside the parentheses:

I finished my essay on March 30. (It was on tubeworm phylogeny.) Then I had three weeks to study for the exam.

2. **Use parentheses to enclose references**. See Chapter 11 for details.

PERIOD [.]

1. **Use a period at the end of a sentence**. A period indicates a full stop, not just a pause.

2. **Use a period with some abbreviations**. It is still common, although not mandatory, to use periods in abbreviated titles (Mrs., Dr., Rev., etc.), academic degrees (M.S.W., Ph.D., etc.), and expressions of time (6:30 p.m.).

   However, Canada's adoption of the metric system in 1970 contributed to a trend away from the use of periods in many abbreviations. State and provincial abbreviations do not require periods (BC, NT, PE, NY, DC). In addition, most acronyms for organizations do not use periods (CIDA, CBC, UNESCO, WTO).

3. **Use a period at the end of an indirect question**. Do not use a question mark:

   ✗   He asked if I wanted to try this method on another new bacterium?

   ✓   He asked if I wanted to try this method on another new bacterium.

   ✗   I wonder where the whales went?

   ✓   I wonder where the whales went.

4. **Use a period for questions that are really polite orders**:

   Will you please send him the analysis by Friday.

QUOTATION MARKS [""]

1. **Use quotation marks to signify direct discourse (the actual words of a speaker)**:

   > I asked, "What is the matter?"

   > "What have you done with the binoculars," he replied.

2. **Use quotation marks to show that words themselves are the issue**:

   > The prefix "arrheno-" comes from the Greek word for "male."

   Alternatively, you may italicize the terms in question.

   Sometimes quotation marks are used to mark a slang word or inappropriate usage to show that the writer is aware of the difficulty:

   > Several of the "experts" did not seem to know anything about the topic.

Use this device only when necessary. In general, it's better to let the context show your attitude or to choose another term.

SEMICOLON [;]

1. **Use a semicolon to join independent clauses (complete sentences) that are closely related**:

   > For five days they ran transects; by Saturday the team was exhausted.

   > His lecture was confusing; no one could understand the terminology.

   A semicolon is especially useful when the second independent clause begins with a conjunctive adverb such as *however, moreover, consequently, nevertheless, in addition,* or *therefore* (usually followed by a comma):

   > The dog ate the entire contents of the box; consequently, he felt sick.

It's usually acceptable to follow a semicolon with a coordinating conjunction if the second clause is complicated by other commas:

Penguins move about in all weather; but sometimes, especially in the Antarctic winter, movement can be fatal.

2. **Use a semicolon to mark the divisions in a complicated series when individual items themselves need commas.** Using a comma to mark the subdivisions and a semicolon to mark the main divisions will help to prevent mix-ups:

✗   He invited Professor Ludvik, the award recipient, Christine Li, and Dr. Hector Jimenez.

Is the award recipient Professor Ludvik, Christine Li, or a separate person?

✓   He invited Professor Ludvik; the award recipient, Christine Li; and Dr. Hector Jimenez.

In a case such as this, the elements separated by the semicolon need not be independent clauses.

SUMMARY

Many life sciences students are beset by punctuation problems. Some are so afraid of misusing punctuation that they write exclusively in short, sparsely punctuated sentences. Yet to explore complex scientific topics in detail, writers must use longer, carefully constructed sentences. Not having the option to follow the ancient Roman practice of using no punctuation marks whatsoever, you need to understand and follow the basic rules. When used correctly, punctuation will help you control the dynamics of your writing and guide your reader through your ideas. From the obvious emphasis provided by exclamation marks, to pauses provided by commas, to asides provided by parentheses, punctuation is powerful. By learning the rules of punctuation, you will gain the confidence to create sentences and phrases that are not only direct and unambiguous, but that have an engaging flow and rhythm.

CHAPTER 9

Misused Words and Phrases

OBJECTIVES

- differentiating between words that sound similar but have different meanings
- avoiding common spelling mistakes
- choosing the word that suits the context
- recognizing commonly confused singular and plural nouns

Here are some words and phrases that are often misused. If you're wondering about a particular word or idiom, check here for advice about correct usage.

accept, except. *Accept* is a verb meaning "to receive affirmatively"; *except*, when used as a verb, means "to exclude":

> The professor <u>accepted</u> the reason for the experiment's failure.

> The researcher <u>excepted</u> unhealthy individuals from the general trial.

accompanied by, accompanied with. Use *accompanied by* for people and animals; use *accompanied with* for objects:

> The students were <u>accompanied by</u> some pets that had tagged along.

> The instrument arrived, <u>accompanied with</u> an instruction manual.

advice, advise. *Advice* is a noun, *advise* a verb:

> He was <u>advised</u> to ignore the <u>advice</u> of others.

affect, effect. *Affect* is a verb meaning "to influence"; however, it also has a specialized meaning in psychology, referring to a person's emotional state. *Effect* can be either a noun meaning "result" or a verb meaning "to bring about":

> The eye drops affect his vision.
>
> Because he was so depressed, he showed no affect when the bell was rung.
>
> The effect of oil sands extraction is environmental damage.
>
> High temperatures can effect intense chemical reactions.

all ready, already. To be *all ready* is simply to be ready for something; *already* means "beforehand" or "earlier":

> The students were all ready for the lecture to begin.
>
> The professor had already left her office by the time Blair arrived.

all right. Write as two separate words: *all right*. This can mean "safe and sound, in good condition, okay"; "correct"; "satisfactory"; or "I agree":

> Are you all right?
>
> The student's answers were all right.

(Note the ambiguity of the second example: does it mean that the answers were all correct or simply satisfactory? In this case, it might be better to use a clearer word.)

all together, altogether. *All together* means "in a group"; *altogether* is an adverb meaning "entirely":

> He was altogether certain that the dataloggers were all together.

allusion, illusion. An *allusion* is an indirect reference to something; an *illusion* is a false perception:

> The comment about bills is an allusion to Darwin's original study of finches.
>
> He thought he saw a sea monster, but it was an illusion.

a lot. Write as two separate words: *a lot*.

alternate, alternative. *Alternate* means "every other or every second thing in a series"; *alternative* refers to a choice between options:

> The two sections of the class attended discussion groups on <u>alternate</u> days.
>
> The students could do an extra paper as an <u>alternative</u> to writing the exam.

among, between. Use *among* for three or more persons or objects, *between* for two:

> <u>Between</u> you and me, there's trouble <u>among</u> the team members.

amount, number. *Amount* indicates quantity when units are not discrete and not absolute; *number* indicates quantity when units are discrete and absolute:

> A large <u>amount</u> of timber.
>
> A large <u>number</u> of students.

See also **less, fewer**.

analysis. The plural is *analyses*.

anyone, any one. *Anyone* is written as two words to give numerical emphasis; otherwise it is written as one word:

> <u>Any one</u> of us could do that.
>
> <u>Anyone</u> could do that.

anyways. Non-standard. Use *anyway*.

as, because. *As* is a weaker conjunction than *because* and may be confused with *when*:

> ✗   <u>As</u> I was working, I ate at my desk.
>
> ✓   <u>Because</u> I was working, I ate at my desk.

as to. A common feature of bureaucratese. Replace it with a single-word preposition such as *about* or *on*:

✗   They were concerned <u>as to</u> the range of disagreement.

✓   They were concerned <u>about</u> the range of disagreement.

✗   They recorded his comments <u>as to</u> the experimental protocol.

✓   They recorded his comments <u>on</u> the experimental protocol.

bad, badly. *Bad* is an adjective meaning "not good":

The meat is <u>bad</u>.

He felt <u>bad</u> about forgetting to turn off the drying oven.

Badly is an adverb meaning "not well"; when used with the verbs *want* or *need*, it means "very much":

She thought he carried out the experiment <u>badly</u>.

I <u>badly</u> need a new lab partner.

beside, besides. *Beside* is a preposition meaning "next to":

She worked <u>beside</u> her assistant.

Besides has two uses: as a preposition it means "in addition to"; as a conjunctive adverb it means "moreover":

<u>Besides</u> recommending the changes, the scientists are implementing them.

It was time for lunch; <u>besides</u>, it was hot and we wanted to rest.

between. See **among**.

bring, take. One *brings* something to a closer place and *takes* it to a farther one:

You should <u>take</u> the diatom sampler with you when you go to the ship.

He asked his fellow researcher to <u>bring</u> him the pH meter.

can, may. *Can* means "to be able"; *may* means "to have permission":

> Can you fix the lock?
>
> May I have another sample?

In speech, *can* is used to cover both meanings; in formal writing, however, you should observe the distinction.

can't hardly. A faulty combination of the phrases *can't* and *can hardly*. Use one or the other:

> The cat can't swim.
>
> This dog can hardly swim.

cite, sight, site. To *cite* something is to quote or mention it as an example or authority; *sight* can be used in many ways, all of which relate to the ability to see; *site* refers to a specific location, a particular place at which something is located:

> You need to cite that source in your essay.
>
> A vole's sight is extremely limited.
>
> That site is perfect for a wasp's nest.

complement, compliment. The verb *to complement* means "to complete or enhance"; *to compliment* means "to praise":

> Her ability to analyze data complements her excellent research skills.
>
> I complimented her on her outstanding report.

The same rule applies when these words are used as adjectives. The adjective *complimentary* can also mean "free":

> Use complementary colours for that design.
>
> That was a complimentary comment.
>
> These are complimentary tickets.

compose, comprise. Both words mean "to constitute or make up", but *compose* is preferred. *Comprise* is correctly used to mean "include", "consist of", or "be composed of." Using *comprise* in the passive ("is comprised of")—as you might be tempted to do in the second example below—is usually frowned on in formal writing:

> These students will <u>compose</u> the group that will go overseas.

> Each paragraph <u>comprises</u> an introduction, an argument, and a conclusion.

continual, continuous. *Continual* means "repeated over a period of time"; *continuous* means "constant" or "without interruption":

> The unseasonably heavy rain caused <u>continual</u> delays in building the blind.

> Five days of <u>continuous</u> rain ruined our sampling season.

could of. This construction is incorrect, as are *might of*, *should of*, and *would of*. Replace *of* with *have*:

✗ He <u>could of</u> done it.

✓ He <u>could have</u> done it.

✓ They <u>might have</u> been there.

✓ I <u>should have</u> known.

✓ We <u>would have</u> left earlier.

council, counsel. *Council* is a noun meaning "an advisory or deliberative assembly." *Counsel* as a noun means "advice" or "lawyer"; as a verb it means "to give advice."

> The college <u>council</u> meets on Tuesday.

> We respect the undergraduate adviser's <u>counsel</u>, since she's seldom wrong.

> As a grants <u>counsellor</u>, you may need to <u>counsel</u> professors and graduate students.

criterion, criteria. A *criterion* is a standard for judging something. *Criteria* is the plural of *criterion* and thus requires a plural verb:

These are my criteria for grading the reports.

The major criterion was excellence of experimental design.

data. The plural of *datum*. The set of information, usually in numerical form, that is used for analysis as the basis for a study. Since *data* often refers to a single mass entity, many writers now accept its use with a singular verb and pronoun:

These data were gathered in an unsystematic fashion.

When the data is in we'll have a look at it.

deduce, deduct. To *deduce* something is to work it out by reasoning; to *deduct* means "to subtract or take away from something." The noun form of both words is *deduction*.

You could deduce from his statement that marmot research was at an end.

We will deduct tax from your summer student pay.

defence, defense. Both spellings are correct: *defence* is standard in Britain and is somewhat more common in Canada; *defense* is standard in the United States.

delusion, illusion. A *delusion* is a belief or perception that is distorted; an *illusion* is a false belief:

He had delusions of grandeur.

The desert pool he thought he saw was an illusion.

dependent, dependant. *Dependent* is an adjective meaning "contingent on" or "subject to"; *dependant* is a noun:

Suriya's graduation is dependent upon her passing algebra.

She has four dependants.

device, devise. The word ending in *-ice* is the noun; the word ending in *-ise* is the verb.

different than, different from. Use *different from* to compare two persons or things; use *different than* with a full clause:

> You are <u>different from</u> me.

> This landscape is <u>different than</u> it used to be.

diminish, minimize. *To diminish* means "to make or become smaller"; *to minimize* means "to reduce something to the smallest possible amount or size":

> His resolve to conduct a large research expedition will <u>diminish</u> as he gets older.

> The regulation will <u>minimize</u> the impact of higher lab chemical prices.

disinterested, uninterested. *Disinterested* implies impartiality or neutrality; *uninterested* implies a lack of interest:

> As a <u>disinterested</u> observer, he was in a good position to judge the issue fairly.

> <u>Uninterested</u> in the seminar, he yawned repeatedly.

due to. Although increasingly used to mean "because of," *due* is an adjective and therefore needs to modify something:

> ✗   <u>Due to</u> his impatience, we lost the contract. [*Due* is dangling.]

> ✓   The loss was <u>due to</u> his impatience.

e.g., i.e. *E.g.* means "for example"; *i.e.* means "that is." It is incorrect to use them interchangeably.

entomology, etymology. *Entomology* is the study of insects; *etymology* is the study of the derivation and history of words.

exceptional, exceptionable. *Exceptional* means "unusual" or "outstanding," whereas *exceptionable* means "open to objection" and is generally used in negative contexts:

> His accomplishments are exceptional.

> He was ejected from the game because of his exceptionable behaviour.

farther, further. *Farther* refers to distance, *further* to extent:

> The swans paddled farther than the ducks did.

> She developed the research plan further.

focus. The plural of the noun may be either *focusses* (also spelled *focuses*) or *foci*.

good, well. *Good* is an adjective that modifies a noun; *well* is an adverb that modifies a verb:

> He is a good plant breeder.

> The cell biology experiment went well.

hanged, hung. *Hanged* means "executed by hanging." *Hung* means "suspended" or "clung to":

> He was hanged at dawn for the murder.

> He hung the gel to dry.

> The lamprey hung on to the fish.

hereditary, heredity. *Heredity* is a noun; *hereditary* is an adjective. *Heredity* is the biological process whereby characteristics are passed from one generation to the next; *hereditary* describes those characteristics:

> Heredity is a factor in the incidence of this disease.

> Your asthma may be hereditary.

hopefully. Use *hopefully* as an adverb meaning "full of hope":

> She scanned the horizon hopefully, looking for signs of the missing boat.

In formal writing, using *hopefully* to mean "I hope" is still frowned upon, although it is increasingly common; it's better to use *I hope*:

✗   Hopefully the experiment will go off without a hitch.

✓   I hope the experiment will go off without a hitch.

i.e. This is not the same as *e.g.* See **e.g.**

illusion. See **delusion.**

incite, insight. *Incite* is a verb meaning "to stir up"; *insight* is a noun meaning "(often sudden) understanding":

His intention was to incite an uprising.

Her insight into the situation was remarkable.

infer, imply. *To infer* means "to deduce or conclude by reasoning." It is often confused with *imply*, which means "to suggest or insinuate":

We can infer from the large population density that there is a large demand for services.

The large population density implies that there is a high demand for services.

inflammable, flammable, non-flammable. Despite its *in-* prefix, *inflammable* is not the opposite of *flammable*: both words describe things that are easily set on fire. The opposite of flammable is *non-flammable*. To prevent any possibility of confusion, it's best to avoid *inflammable* altogether.

irregardless. Non-standard. Use *regardless*.

its, it's. *Its* is a form of possessive pronoun; *it's* is a contraction of *it is*. Many people mistakenly put an apostrophe in *its* in order to show possession:

✗   The cub wanted it's mother.

✓   The cub wanted its mother.

✓   It's time to leave.

less, fewer. *Less* is used when units are not discrete and not absolute (as in "less information"). *Fewer* is used when the units are discrete and absolute (as in "fewer details").

lie, lay. *To lie* means "to assume a horizontal position"; *to lay* means "to put down." The changes of tense often cause confusion:

Present	Past	Past participle	Present participle
lie	lay	lain	lying
lay	laid	laid	laying

   ✗   The beaver was <u>laying</u> in its den.

   ✓   The beaver was <u>lying</u> in its den.

   ✓   I <u>laid</u> the bone fragments on the lab bench.

   ✓   The old bull was tired and needed to <u>lie</u> down.

   ✓   The crew was <u>laying</u> the gill net out to dry.

like, as. *Like* is a preposition, but it is often wrongly used as a conjunction. To join two independent clauses, use the conjunction *as*:

   ✗   I want to improve my grades <u>like</u> you have improved yours this year.

   ✓   I want to improve my grades <u>as</u> you have improved yours this year.

   ✓   Asters are <u>like</u> chrysanthemums.

might of. Incorrect. See **could of**.

minimize. See **diminish**.

mitigate, militate. *To mitigate* means "to reduce the severity of something"; *to militate against* something means "to oppose" it:

Aloe cream can <u>mitigate</u> the skin problem.

His credentials will <u>militate</u> against the resistance to his appointment as team leader.

myself, me. *Myself* is an intensifier of, not a substitute for, *I* or *me*:

   ✗   He gave it to John and <u>myself</u>.

   ✓   He gave it to John and <u>me</u>.

   ✗   Jane and <u>myself</u> are invited.

   ✓   Jane and <u>I</u> are invited.

   ✓   I hesitate to mention <u>myself</u> here.

nor, or. Use *nor* with *neither*; use *or* by itself or with *either*:

     The leafcutter bee <u>neither</u> lives in groups <u>nor</u> stores honey.

     The plant is <u>either</u> diseased <u>or</u> dried out.

off of. Remove the unnecessary *of*:

   ✗   The fence kept the deer <u>off of</u> the tree nursery's grounds.

   ✓   The fence kept the deer <u>off</u> the tree nursery's grounds.

phenomenon. A singular noun; the plural is *phenomena*.

plaintiff, plaintive. A *plaintiff* is a person who brings a case against someone else in court; *plaintive* is an adjective meaning "sorrowful."

populace, populous. *Populace* is a noun meaning "the people of a place"; *populous* is an adjective meaning "thickly inhabited":

     The <u>populace</u> of Manitoulin Island is largely rural.

     With so many people in such a small area, Hilltop village is a <u>populous</u> place.

practice, practise. Both of these spellings have become acceptable for either the noun or the verb. Just be consistent in whatever form you choose.

precede, proceed. To *precede* is to go before (earlier) or in front of others; to *proceed* is to go on or ahead:

     The faculty will <u>precede</u> the students into the hall.

     The medal winners will <u>proceed</u> to the front of the hall.

prescribe, proscribe. These words are sometimes confused, although they have quite different meanings. *Prescribe* means "to advise the use of" or "to impose authoritatively." *Proscribe* means "to reject, denounce, or ban":

> The professor prescribed the conditions under which the equipment could be used.

> The university proscribed the feeding of the rabbits on campus.

principle, principal. *Principle* is a noun meaning "a general truth or law"; *principal* can be used as either a noun, referring to the head of a school or a capital sum of money, or an adjective, meaning "chief":

> His lack of principle is a major problem.

> Daniel Woolf is the principal of Queen's University.

> The principal reason for refusing to carry out this experiment is our lack of travel funds.

promote, inhibit. In the life sciences, the opposite of *promote* is *inhibit*:

> An analog of indoleacetic acid promotes growth of crown-gall tumour tissue.

> Heat stress inhibited the genes that regulate expression of the thaumatin-like protein.

rational, rationale. *Rational* is an adjective meaning "logical" or "able to reason." *Rationale* is a noun meaning "explanation":

> That was not a rational decision.

> The president sent around a memo explaining the rationale for her decision.

real, really. *Real*, an adjective, means "true" or "genuine"; *really*, an adverb, means "actually," "truly," "very," or "extremely":

> The pellet at the bottom of the tube was real actin.

> The sample was really valuable.

seasonable, seasonal. *Seasonable* means "usual or suitable for the season"; *seasonal* means "of, depending on, or varying with the season":

> It's quite cool today, but we can expect the return of seasonable temperatures later this week.

> You must consider seasonal temperature changes when you sample plants.

should of. Incorrect. See **could of**.

that, which. *That* introduces restrictive information that completes the meaning of a clause or sentence; *which* preceded by a comma introduces non-restrictive information that is not essential to the meaning of the clause or sentence:

> The electrophoresis rig that is on the bench needs to be grounded.

> The electrophoresis rig, which is on the bench, needs to be grounded.

In the first sentence, there is more than one rig, but the one requiring grounding is on the bench. In the second sentence, there is only one rig; it is on the bench and needs grounding.

their, there. *Their* is the possessive form of the third person plural pronoun. *There* is usually an adverb, meaning "at that place" or "at that point":

> They placed their pipettes there.

> There is no point in arguing the point with you.

tortuous, torturous. The adjective *tortuous* means "full of twists and turns" or "circuitous." *Torturous*, derived from *torture*, means "involving torture" or "excruciating":

> To avoid the female bear and her cub, they took a tortuous route home.

> The midnight sampling trip to the seashore was a torturous experience for the students.

translucent, transparent. A *translucent* substance permits light to pass through, but not enough for a person to see through it; a *transparent* substance permits light to pass unobstructed, so that objects can be seen clearly through it.

turbid, turgid. *Turbid*, with respect to a liquid or colour, means "muddy," "not clear," or (with respect to literary style) "confused." *Turgid* means "swollen," "inflated," "enlarged," or (again with reference to literary style) "pompous" or "bombastic."

unique. This word, which means "of which there is only one" or "unequalled," is both overused and misused. Since there are no degrees of comparison— one thing cannot be "more unique" than another—expressions such as *very unique* or *quite unique* are incorrect.

while. To avoid misreading, use *while* only when you mean "at the same time that." Do not use *while* as a substitute for *although*, *whereas*, or *but*:

✗   While she's getting fair marks, she'd like to do better.

✗   I headed for the lake, while she decided to stay behind to guard the equipment.

✓   He fell asleep while he was reading.

who. *Who* can be used to introduce a restrictive clause. *Who* combined with a comma can introduce a non-restrictive clause:

> The nurses gave the vaccine to expectant mothers who were most susceptible to H1N1 virus.

> The nurses gave the vaccine to expectant mothers, who were most susceptible to H1N1 virus.

In the first sentence, not every expectant mother was highly susceptible to H1N1; the nurses vaccinated only those who were highly susceptible. In the second sentence, the nurses vaccinated all expectant mothers because they were all highly susceptible.

-wise. Never use *-wise* as a suffix to form new words when you mean "with regard to":

✗   Research-wise, the company did better last year.

✓   The company's research improved last year.

your, you're. *Your* is a possessive adjective; *you're* is a contraction of *you are*:

> Be sure to take <u>your</u> lab book with you.

> <u>You're</u> likely to miss your interview.

SUMMARY

English is full of words that sound similar but have radically different meanings. Many peculiarities within the language developed over time as English evolved without strict regulations or governance. Spelling in English was fluid until the mid-eighteenth century, and this variation is still reflected in some words (e.g., *flammable* and *inflammable*). Today, English continues to evolve, with influences from around the globe. Consequently, sorting out what is standard usage in modern writing requires constant effort on the part of every writer.

CHAPTER 10

Using Illustrations

OBJECTIVES

- understanding the importance of graphs—data interpretation and display
- knowing when to use tables
- presenting frequency data—bar graphs and histograms
- plotting longitudinal data—line graphs
- exploring the significance of data—box plots and scatter plots
- interpreting and avoiding pie charts
- choosing between tables and graphs

In the life sciences, illustrations are not only useful tools for summarizing complex information in reports but also essential components of data interpretation. You should always begin your analysis by graphing your data. Graphs will help you distill the data and assess what the numbers might mean. Just looking at the data won't do—it takes a good graph or table to reveal relationships that are difficult to detect. Graphic representations allow you to analyze your data in sophisticated ways.

Illustrations can also clarify complicated systems. For examples, look at the diagrams you see every day in your textbooks. You can use similar illustrations in your own reports and papers. You might choose to create a model of electron transfer within a membrane, a diagram of the nitrogen cycles in terrestrial ecosystems, or a representation of the lock-and-key model of enzyme function—each is an example of graphic simplification. Illustrations often provide a far more effective summary than you could achieve in writing. A model can be worth a thousand words. (See Chapter 12 for more information on how you can use diagrams to enhance your content.)

As you begin to write lab reports, your instructors will likely ask you to use simple tables and graphs to illustrate your data. This chapter presents some examples of the types of graphs that you will use in your first- and second-year assignments. In particular, the examples focus on ways to graph frequency distributions (relative data displays), some types of longitudinal information (e.g., changes or variations over time), and associations between variables. These examples merely skim the surface of the ways that you can use illustrations to enhance your research, but they provide a good starting point.

When writing a report, always consider how you can present important experimental information graphically rather than verbally. Here are a few basic guidelines for using visual aids effectively:

- Information in an illustration should stand alone. It should be both complete and obvious.
- Information in the text should not simply duplicate information in the illustration.
- Simple illustrations are better than cluttered ones. The easier it is for the reader to grasp the information quickly and accurately, the better.
- As in report headings and subheadings, try to make the title of the visual reflect the point of the illustration, not just the topic. When this is not possible, at least be specific about the content. For example, a title such as "Copepod density along a shoreline in autumn at St. Andrews Marine Station" or "Shoreline gradient of copepods" is better than "Copepods in St. Andrews."
- Refer to every illustration in the text, explaining what it shows. If you have several illustrations, number each one so that you can refer to it by number in the discussion.

FREQUENCY DISTRIBUTIONS

Before you begin to create tables and graphs, you should understand what a frequency distribution represents. A *frequency* is the number of times a particular occurrence is observed within a specific set of measurements (a data set). A *frequency distribution* is a summary, in the form of a table or a graph, of all frequencies that occur within a data set. As you analyze your data, you should create tables and graphs to help you identify and interpret frequency distributions in different ways.

In your report, you may choose to include a table or a graph (most often a line graph or a histogram) to summarize your frequency data. The choice will depend on the amount and type of information you are dealing with; generally, you should use a table rather than a graph when you are dealing with many categories.

TABLES

A table can convey a large amount of information, both numerical and verbal, without losing detail. If you are giving specific information in numerical form, a table allows you to show precise data more clearly than a graph or a chart does. A table is often the best way to display data when small differences in treatments are critical, when there are too many relationships to display in a graph, or when some or all of the information is verbal. Table 10.1 illustrates the type of information that is best represented in a table. In this example, frequencies are summarized by qualitative statements (*common, frequent,* etc.).

Tables are most effective when the columns and the rows are well structured, when white space is used to separate the data, and when the title of the table is clear. It is better to structure a table by frequency than by category labels.[1] Consider the following examples. Table 10.1 lists bat species alphabetically, forcing the reader to reread the frequency column to make sense of the

TABLE 10.1   Current extent of bats in Northumberland, England (information organized in alphabetical order by species)

Species	Frequency
Brandt's bat (*Myotis brandtii*)	Rare
Brown long-eared bat (*Plecotus auritus*)	Frequent
Common pipistrelle (*Pipistrellus pipistrellus*)	Common
Daubenton's bat (*Myotis daubentonii*)	Frequent on water
Leisler's bat (*Nyctalus leisleri*)	Rare
Nathusius' pipistrelle (*Pipistrellus nathusii*)	Rare
Natterer's bat (*Myotis nattereri*)	Uncommon
Noctule bat (*Nyctalus noctula*)	Scattered
Soprano pipistrelle (*Pipistrellus pygmaeus*)	Common
Whiskered bat (*Myotis mystacinus*)	Uncommon

Source: Data from Northumberland Biodiversity Partnership, "Northumberland Biodiversity Action Plan: Bats Species Action Plan" (Northumberland Biodiversity Partnership, 2008), http://www.northumberlandbiodiversity.org.uk/documents/Action_Plans/bats.pdf

TABLE 10.2   Current extent of bats in Northumberland, England (information organized in order of decreasing frequency)

Species	Frequency
Common pipistrelle (*Pipistrellus pipistrellus*)	Common
Soprano pipistrelle (*Pipistrellus pygmaeus*)	Common
Brown long-eared bat (*Plecotus auritus*)	Frequent
Daubenton's bat (*Myotis daubentonii*)	Frequent on water
Noctule bat (*Nyctalus noctula*)	Scattered
Natterer's bat (*Myotis nattereri*)	Uncommon
Whiskered bat (*Myotis mystacinus*)	Uncommon
Brandt's bat (*Myotis brandtii*)	Rare
Leisler's bat (*Nyctalus leisleri*)	Rare
Nathusius' pipistrelle (*Pipistrellus nathusii*)	Rare

Source: Data from Northumberland Biodiversity Partnership, "Northumberland Biodiversity Action Plan: Bats Species Action Plan" (Northumberland Biodiversity Partnership, 2008), http://www.northumberlandbiodiversity.org.uk/documents/Action_Plans/bats.pdf

information. Table 10.2 lists the same information, but this time the bat species are grouped according to frequency, with added white space to separate each group. As you can see, Table 10.2 displays the information more effectively.

BAR GRAPHS

A bar graph allows you to compare distinct elements at fixed points in time. The data represented in a bar graph can also be displayed in a table, but graphs add a visual element that draws attention to the relationships among the data. As an example, compare Table 10.3 with Figure 10.1—both illustrate the same information, but the bar graph makes a stronger, more immediate impression.

When creating a bar graph, you should always set the baseline at zero to avoid misrepresenting the value of the bars. You can set the bars to be horizontal or vertical, depending on the range of data, and you can make them segmented (stacked) to show different parts of the whole. You can also cluster or group the bars to compare one category with another.

TABLE 10.3   Number of cases of hepatitis C in 2005, Canada by province or territory

Province	Number of Cases
Ontario	4494
British Columbia	2882
Quebec	2395
Alberta	1528
Saskatchewan	654
Manitoba	416
New Brunswick	275
Nova Scotia	220
Others	193

Source: Data from Public Health Agency of Canada, "Reported Cases and Rates of Hepatitis C by Province/Territory and Sex, 2005 to 2008" (Hepatitis C and STI Surveillance and Epidemiology Section, Community Acquired Infections Division, Centre for Communicable Diseases and Infection Control, Public Health Agency of Canada, 2008), http://www.phac-aspc.gc.ca/sti-its-surv-epi/hepc/hepc_pt-eng.php

While bar graphs can represent a wide variety of information, they have their limits. They don't work well for displaying highly detailed information, and they cannot clearly show *change* within a data set. If you need to show change over time or trends that run in different directions, you would do better to choose a table or a different type of graph.

HISTOGRAMS

A histogram is useful when you want to display a progression of values across a single category. Whereas the bars in a bar graph can represent distinct categories (e.g., different regions) or non-consecutive measurements (e.g., measurements taken every second year), the bars (or bins) in a histogram represent continuous values of a single variable. The frequency distribution of a histogram may be symmetric or asymmetric (if asymmetric, we call it *skewed*). The bins in a histogram are side-by-side (see Figure 10.2), not separated from one another as the bars are in a bar graph. This positioning gives greater clarity to the data. However, the clarity depends on the number of intervals you choose to use—too many intervals may make the histogram seem cluttered while too few may obscure differences within a bin. There are published rules

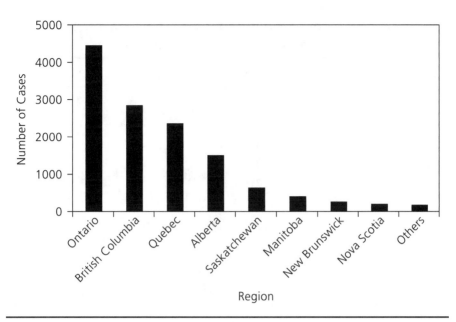

FIGURE 10.1   Number of cases of hepatitis C in 2005, Canada by province or territory

Data from Public Health Agency of Canada, "Reported Cases and Rates of Hepatitis C by Province/Territory and Sex, 2005 to 2008" (Hepatitis C and STI Surveillance and Epidemiology Section, Community Acquired Infections Division, Centre for Communicable Diseases and Infection Control, Public Health Agency of Canada, 2008), http://www.phac-aspc.gc.ca/sti-its-surv-epi/hepc/hepc_pt-eng.php

for working out how to distribute data into bins (e.g., Sturges' rule of thumb), but you should build up your judgment with experience before you consult such guides.

LINE GRAPHS

A line graph (see Figure 10.3) shows change over a period of time. It's often used to point out trends or fluctuations. In devising a line graph, put quantities on the vertical axis and time values on the horizontal axis. Try to shape the dimensions of the graph to give the most accurate impression of the extent of change. Never distort your graph to emphasize a point—for instance, by shortening the horizontal axis and lengthening the vertical axis to make a gradual rise look more dramatic. Doing so will only reduce your credibility and cause your reader to question the reliability of your information and the validity of your arguments.

TABLE 10.4   Biology 101 class lab results of optical density of water samples from Mud Creek, July 15

Optical Density	Frequency
0.30	2
0.35	3
0.40	4
0.45	4
0.50	7
0.55	5
0.60	4
0.65	3
0.70	3
0.75	4

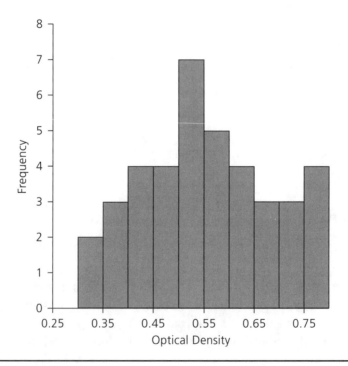

FIGURE 10.2   Biology 101 class lab results of optical density of water samples from Mud Creek, July 15

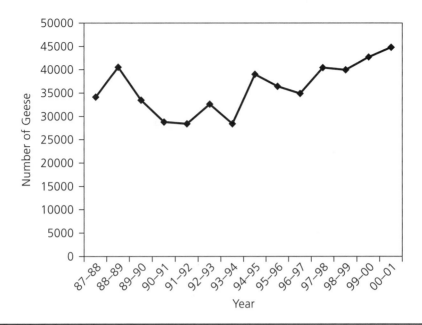

FIGURE 10.3   Line graph of abundance of adult lesser snow
geese in the Fraser and Skagit deltas assessed
from photo counts

Adapted from Environment Canada, "Lesser Snow Goose Data," Table 1 (Environment Canada, 2005), http://www.ecoinfo.ec.gc.ca/env_ind/region/snowgeese/geese_data_e.cfm#Graph1

BOX PLOTS

Also known as a box-and-whisker plot, a box plot (see Figure 10.4) is exploratory in nature. It does not assume any statistical distributions or sophistication. It highlights the median value (represented by the line that dissects the
box) and displays the remaining data by quartiles (25 per cent of the data).
The box represents 50 per cent of the data (the range between the twenty-
fifth percentile and the seventy-fifth percentile). You can gauge the depar-
tures from symmetry in the data by the relative position of the median. The
whiskers represent the remaining data that falls within the distribution (e.g.,
the data within one standard deviation above or below the mean). Although
whiskers can represent other types of distributions, such as ninety-fifth or
ninety-eighty percentiles, data found beyond the whiskers are considered
outliers in all cases.

Box plots can be very useful before you carry out any analysis because they
allow you to see obvious flaws in the data set. A box plot provides an instant

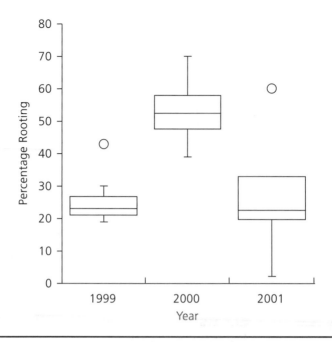

FIGURE 10.4 Box plot of rooting percentage of juniper cuttings by year

Note: Mild outliers are shown as circles.

view of outlying data points (i.e., mild and extreme outliers, represented by circles in Figure 10.4) that may be due to either variation or measurement errors. Once you identify the errors, you can eliminate them before you perform statistical analysis. Since parametric statistics depends on a number of statistical assumptions that require a data set to be free of errors, you should deal with such errors as early as possible.

Charts such as box plots provide information not only on trends over time but also on data variation. You can assess any given data point within the context of its variation. Graphing trends with variation provides you with ideas on how to test the trends statistically. Even if something looks like a trend, you must determine whether it is statistically significant according to a test. Again, this is an example of how graphing can be useful before analysis. Graphs give you a "feel" for data structure.

SCATTER PLOTS

Sometimes numerical variables can be plotted to establish patterns of association (Figure 10.5). The resulting cloud of points allows you to think about

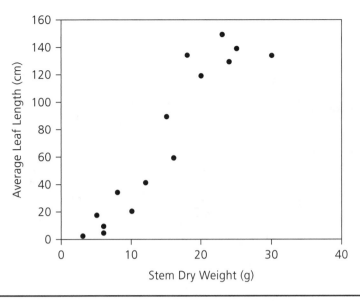

FIGURE 10.5 Average leaf length versus stem dry weight of ostrich ferns (*Matteuccia struthiopteris*)

what kind of curve would best fit the data. You will find an ample number of curve-fitting equations to help you with this task; play with these formulae and always ask whether they capture relevant information.

PIE CHARTS

A pie chart is used to emphasize proportions—to draw attention to the relative size of the parts that make up a whole. You should avoid pie charts whenever possible because they have very low data density—the only data structure is the relationship between shape and value. They also have less immediacy than the graphs discussed in this chapter, as they require the reader to look back and forth to the legend to make any sense of the diagram.

GRAPHING SOFTWARE

The number of ways to display data has increased in the last twenty years, thanks to developments in computing. Computer programs make it easy to create, format, and annotate tables, graphs, and diagrams that illustrate important points in your essay or report. Often, you can create a variety of illustrations based on a single data set. Spreadsheet programs such as Excel allow you to create simple charts and graphs, but you will likely have to use

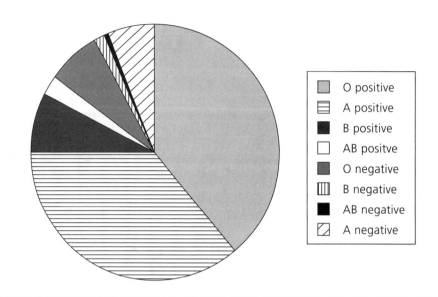

FIGURE 10.6 Pie chart of blood types in the Canadian population

Data Source: Canadian Blood Services.

more specialized programs to analyze more complex data. If you want to create a box plot, for example, you will need to use statistical software such as Minitab (a fairly simple suite of statistical programs) or SPSS (a more complex statistical program). You should be able to access programs such as these through your school's computing or statistics department. You can also use R, an excellent graphing software package that is free to download. In addition, some universities require their students to master MATLAB.

TABLES OR GRAPHS?

When deciding whether to use a table or a graph to present your data, you must always consider which will be the most effective in getting your point across. Tables have the advantage of being more exact than graphs because they provide precise numerical information, and they can include text as well as numbers. Tables are also a good choice if you have several sets of numbers that could get buried if you just listed them in the text. However, if you have data for a number of conditions that vary systematically, a graph is the best way to illustrate the information. Graphs are useful for drawing attention to relationships among the data. When the structure of the data is simple, a bar graph may do the job, but when the structure is more complex, you should use a more complex type of graph.

You might also want to consider practical implications, such as which method of presentation uses the most pixels, takes up the most space, or uses the most ink when printed. Tables are usually the most economical option, in terms of both space and printing cost, followed by box plots and line graphs; bar graphs, pie charts, and histograms can take up a lot of space and consume a lot of ink. In the end, the format you choose will often come down to nothing more than personal style or preference.

Of course, you don't always need to present your data in a graph or a table. If you're making a simple comparison in a lab report, for example, you can include your data analysis directly in the text of the *Results* section:

Understory trees in the 10–15 year age class were shorter in shaded conditions (11 ± 2 m) than those in sunny conditions (18 ± 3 m, $p < 0.001$).

THREE DANGERS IN USING ILLUSTRATIONS

- Computer programs offer a wide range of features and options for tables and graphs. These features can add visual impact and even drama to your written material, but they do make it tempting to add so much detail that you obscure the facts. Be sure that the designs you create are not too elaborate for your purpose. Visuals are meant not to dazzle but to make it easier for the reader to understand. In general, keep your presentation simple and avoid stacked bar graphs, 3-D bar graphs, and pie charts. Clarity and immediacy must always be the goal.
- Any illustration, even if it is created on a computer, can distort information. For instance, the slope of a graph line can be made to look steep or shallow depending on the graph's scale, and trend lines can begin at a time that omits unfavourable periods. Although line and bar graphs are the most susceptible to distortion, the shapes and proportions of other diagrams can also give a false picture. Be careful to present as accurate a picture as possible so that your illustrations reinforce the credibility of your words. A good test of a graph or table is whether you can imagine how the data that went into the illustration was collected. A good illustration is one that allows the reader to understand the decision-making process that led you to create the graph, table, or chart.

- You might think that you can use a picture of enzyme-folding or a graph from a scientific journal for free. After all, years of creating projects for elementary school and high school likely taught you to cut images from magazines or websites and paste them directly into your content. University is the time to leave behind these practices. Lab reports and essays are not projects but assignments created in a scientific tradition. Consequently, you must acknowledge the source for every figure and for all data that is not your own in order to avoid plagiarism. If the material is restricted by copyright, you will need to contact the copyright holder and ask for permission. If you have any questions, consult your school's policies on copyright or the federal government's Copyright Act. Reference librarians should also be able to answer any questions that you may have about using materials under copyright. Often, the best way to include information from an external source in your assignment is to re-create it in your own style, reference the source, and include the statement "modified from . . ." in a note below the illustration—for example, "modified from Grant et al. 2005."

SUMMARY

Converting raw data into a table or a graph is an essential step in data interpretation. Illustrations such as these allow you to get a feel for the data before you develop your analysis. When writing a lab report or an essay, let your textual descriptions flow from the illustrations and not vice versa. To be successful, illustrations must be easy to understand, so you should avoid using unnecessarily elaborate formatting. The tables, figures, and simple graphs covered in this chapter will help you fulfill the requirements of first- and second-year courses, but you should learn to use more complex models such as flow charts and diagrams once you are familiar with the basics. As your studies progress, you will need to analyze more complex data through more complex illustrations. To prepare yourself, begin to learn different types of graphing software that can handle more and varied types of data.

CHAPTER 11

Documenting Sources

OBJECTIVES

- understanding the purpose of documentation
- using CMS style in a life sciences essay
- using CSE style in a life sciences essay
- developing an annotated bibliography
- avoiding secondary sources

Much of the writing you do will require you to consult sources to become familiar with current research and to find support for your ideas. It's essential to acknowledge those sources, not only when you quote directly from them but also when you restate, in your own words, arguments or ideas taken from them. If you don't acknowledge your sources, you're allowing your reader to assume that the words, ideas, or thoughts are yours; in other words, you're plagiarizing, and the penalties can be severe.

The purpose of documentation is not only to avoid charges of plagiarism but also to show the body of knowledge that your work is building on. Academic writing is based on the premise that researchers are not working in a vacuum but are indebted to those scholars who came before them. By documenting your sources, you are showing that you understand this concept and are ready to make your own contribution to the body of knowledge in your field.

UNDERSTANDING WHY WE NEED DOCUMENTATION STYLES

If you were to write an assignment that contained only one quotation, one reference, or one figure based on an external source, it would hardly seem necessary for you to follow an elaborate system of rules when it comes to referencing. But most essays and lab reports involve a dozen or more references. Without stylistic consistency, a writing assignment with many references would likely frustrate the reader as he or she tried to sort through haphazardly presented references to get to the purpose of the assignment.

The purpose of an essay is to explore a theme or a thesis; the purpose of a lab report is to explore a hypothesis. External sources of information, or references, are not central to the purpose of these writing assignment—they serve only to bolster the arguments. Consequently, writers try to draw attention away from references by reducing their visibility on the page. A citation style is a system that allows writers to keep their writing clear by using an in-text shorthand to refer readers to a reference, usually listed in full at the end of the document.

A consistent style of citation also forces the writer to include all information that the average reader would need in order to retrieve the cited source. Many professionals, academics, and students like to record interesting references as they read an essay because these articles may prove to be interesting. In professional articles, references can not only provide evidence for an argument but also, on occasion, point the reader to an article or study that has been forgotten, neglected, or underappreciated.

DOCUMENTING YOUR SOURCES

There are many systems of documentation. The style you use will depend on the subject you are writing about as well as the preference of your instructor, your department, or your employer. Students who write essays for English follow the guidelines set out in the *MLA Handbook for Writers of Research Papers*. Students who write essays for psychology adhere to the rules of the *Publication Manual of the American Psychological Association*. In science, writers follow the guidelines set out in *Scientific Style and Format*, published by the Council of Science Editors, and *The Chicago Manual of Style*, published by the University of Chicago Press. (Both CSE style and Chicago style are discussed in detail in this chapter.)

In addition, some science journals use their own style of referencing. If you are asked to write your essay following the style of a particular journal, then you will have to look at articles published in that journal to determine that journal's conventions. Often journals have a website that spells out their requirements on a page entitled "Advice to Authors" or something similar. You will find that most journal-specific styles are similar to those discussed in this chapter.

If you don't need to follow a specific department- or company-wide documentation style, you should consider following one of the two most common systems of documentation used in the life sciences. Remember, though, that style guides are constantly undergoing revision, especially with the wealth of online information currently available. It's always safest to check the latest edition of the relevant manual or the appropriate website to be sure that you have the most up-to-date information available.

Note also that the latest version of your word-processing software is likely able to automatically format endnotes, footnotes, and citations as well as bibliographies and lists of works cited according to MLA, APA, and Chicago styles. It's worth your while becoming familiar with these features, as they are fast and accurate and can save you a great deal of time and effort.

CSE STYLE

The Council of Science Editors (CSE) is the recognized authority on documentation styles in all areas of science and related fields. The following guidelines are based on *Scientific Style and Format: The CSE Manual for Authors, Editors, and Publishers* (7th ed., 2006).

The CSE manual outlines three major systems for documenting sources: name–year, citation–sequence, and citation–name. A brief description of each system follows.

Name–year

In the name–year system, in-text references consist of the surname of the author and the year of publication enclosed in parentheses. Complete bibliographical information is given in a list of references, organized alphabetically by author surname, at the end of the paper. In the following examples, note that CSE style emphasizes simplicity, avoiding formatting such as italics and minimizing the use of punctuation.

IN-TEXT REFERENCE

Monte Carlo simulations were carried out to compute the escape flux of atomic nitrogen for the low and high solar activity Martian thermospheres (Bakalian and Hartle 2006).

END REFERENCE

Bakalian F, Hartle RE. 2006. Monte Carlo computations of the escape of atomic nitrogen from Mars. Icarus. 183(1):55–69.

Citation–sequence

In the citation–sequence system, superscript numbers in the text correspond to numbered references in a *References* or *Cited References* section at the end of the document. These references are listed in the order in which they are first cited in the text. Thus, the first reference used in the text will be 1, the next new reference cited will be 2, and so on. Once a source has been assigned a number, it is referred to by that number wherever it appears in the text:

> Labossière's groundbreaking study[1] was first challenged by Gormon[2] and later disputed by Huang[3]. In fact, Gormon gained considerable notoriety for her particularly harsh criticism[2] of Labossière's interpretation of the results[1].

If several sources are being referenced at once, all relevant reference numbers should be given in the same citation. Reference numbers should be separated by commas with no spaces. When using a sequence of three or more citation numbers (e.g., 7, 8, 9), use only the first and last number in the sequence, separated by a hyphen:

> Several studies[1,5,12-15] have shown . . .

IN-TEXT REFERENCE

> Self-incompatibility (SI) prevents inbreeding through specific recognition and rejection of incompatible pollen[1].

END REFERENCE

> 1. Thomas SG, Huang S, Li S, Staiger CJ, Franklin-Tong VE. Actin depolymerization is sufficient to induce programmed cell death in self-incompatible pollen. J Cell Biol. 2006;174(2):195–207.

Citation–name

In the citation–name system, the list of end references is compiled alphabetically by author surname. The references are then numbered in that sequence, with Aaronsen number 1, Babcock number 2, and so on. These numbers are used for in-text references regardless of the sequence in which they appear in the text. If Mortensen is number 38 in the reference list, the in-text reference is number 38, and the same number is used for subsequent in-text references.

When several in-text references occur at the same point, place their corresponding reference-list numbers in numerical order. In-text reference numbers not in a continuous sequence are separated by commas with no spaces. For more than two numbers in a continuous sequence, connect the first and last with a hyphen.

. . . are illustrated in studies [2,7-11,16,25] that corroborate . . .

Formats for end references are similar to those used in the citation–sequence style as shown above.

End references

The following examples illustrate end references for the citation–sequence and citation–name systems of documentation. The name–year system differs by placing the year of publication directly after the author name(s).

Note that if you cite material from a publication that you have not read but have seen cited by others you should cite the source that you actually read; do not cite the original (see page 179 for more details).

BOOK WITH ONE AUTHOR

1. Tomasello M. Constructing a language: a usage-based theory of language acquisition. Cambridge (MA): Harvard University Press; 2003. 388 p.

Note that the last element of the entry ("388 p.") indicates the total number of pages in the book. Although this is an optional component of a book reference, it can provide useful information to the reader.

BOOK WITH TWO OR MORE AUTHORS

If the book you are referencing has more than one author, give the names of all authors up to a maximum of ten; after ten, replace additional authors' names with "et al." Names should be inverted and separated by commas. Note that "and" is not used:

2. Peterson CM, Russell AF. Active and passive movement testing. New York (NY): McGraw-Hill; 2002. 418 p.

BOOK BY AN ORGANIZATION AS AUTHOR

3. National Advisory Committee on Immunization. Canadian immunization guide. 7th ed. Ottawa (ON): Public Health Agency of Canada; 2006. 398 p.

BOOK WITH AN EDITOR IN PLACE OF AN AUTHOR

4. Case-Smith J, editor. Pediatric occupational therapy and early intervention. 2nd ed. Boston (MA): Butterworth-Heinemann; 1998. 324 p.

CHAPTER OR OTHER SELECTION IN A BOOK

5. Rogers AG. Understanding changes in girls' relationships and in ego development: three studies of adolescent girls. In: Westenberg PM, Blasi A, Cohn LD, editors. Personality development: theoretical, empirical, and clinical investigations of Loevinger's conception of ego development. Mahwah (NJ): Erlbaum; 1998. p. 145–162.

ARTICLE IN A JOURNAL

6. Baranski JV, Petrusic WM. Testing architectures of the decision–confidence relation. Can J Exp Psychol. 2001;55(3):196–206.

Note that CSE abbreviates the names of journals.

ARTICLE IN A MAGAZINE

7. Hollingham R. In the realm of your senses. New Scientist. 2004 Jan 31: 40–43.

ARTICLE IN A NEWSPAPER

8. MacDonald G. CBC on trial. Globe and Mail. 2001 Jul 28;Sect. R:12 (col. 4).

9. Woman again registers her cows as voters. Toronto Star. 2004 Feb 22; Sect. F:2 (col. 6).

LECTURE OR PAPER PRESENTED AT A MEETING

10. Reinson G, Drummond K. Past exploration, resources, and reserves in the Arctic. Proceedings of the 2007 Gussow Geoscience Conference; 2007 Oct 15–17; Banff, AB.

ARTICLE IN AN ONLINE JOURNAL

11. Pethe V, Bapat B. Molecular genetic etiology of prostate cancer. Open Genomics J [Internet]. 2008 [cited 2010 May 29]; 1:13–21. Available from: http://www.bentham.org/open/togenj/openaccess2.htm doi:10.2174/1875693X00801010013

WEBSITE

12. Preventing skin cancer [Internet]. Ottawa (ON): Health Canada; 2006 May [updated 2006 Aug; cited 2010 March 19]. Available from: http://www.hc-sc.gc.ca/hl-vs/iyh-vsv/diseases-maladies/cancer-eng.php

CHICAGO STYLE

The Chicago Manual of Style (15th ed., 2003) outlines two methods of documentation.

1. The notes and bibliography method, also known as the humanities style, is preferred by those in literature, history, and the arts. It uses superscript numerals to direct the reader to footnotes at the bottom of the page or endnotes on a separate page at the end of the document.
2. The author–date system, preferred in the physical, natural, and social sciences.

For more information on either method, consult the manual itself or the online "Chicago-Style Citation Quick Guide" (http://www.chicagomanualof style.org/tools_citationguide.html), which gives examples of CMS references.

Author–date system

The following sections outline the author–date system, broken down into in-text citations (T) and reference-list entries (R).

BOOK WITH ONE AUTHOR

T: (Decter 2002, 47)

R: Decter, Michael. 2002. *Four strong winds: Understanding the growing challenges to health care*. Toronto: Stoddart.

BOOK WITH TWO OR THREE AUTHORS

T: (Price and Comac 2000, 94–6)

R: Price, Ira Marc, and Linda Comac. 2000. *Coping with macular degeneration*. New York: Penguin Putnam.

Note that with four or more authors, in-text references give just the first author followed by "et al." The reference list, however, lists all authors' names.

BOOK WITH AN ORGANIZATION AS AUTHOR

T: (University of Chicago Press 2003, 656)

R: University of Chicago Press. 2003. *The Chicago manual of style*. 15th ed. Chicago: University of Chicago Press.

BOOK WITH AN EDITOR IN PLACE OF AN AUTHOR

T: (Gontarski 2001, iv)

R: Gontarski, S. E., ed. 2001. *The Grove Press reader 1951–2001*. New York: Grove.

BOOK WITH AN EDITOR OR TRANSLATOR IN ADDITION TO AN AUTHOR

T: (Baillargeon 1999, 43)

R: Baillargeon, Denyse. 1999. *Making do: Women, family and home in Montreal during the great depression*. Trans. Yvonne Klein. Waterloo, ON: Wilfrid Laurier University Press.

CHAPTER OR OTHER SELECTION IN A BOOK

T: (Salinger 2000, 88)

R: Salinger, J. D. 2000. Slight rebellion off Madison. In *Wonderful town: New York stories from "The New Yorker,"* ed. David Remnick, 87–90. New York: Modern Library.

ARTICLE IN A JOURNAL

T: (Kuzio 2000, 77)

R: Kuzio, Taras. 2000. Nationalism in Ukraine: Towards a new framework. *Politics* 20 (2): 77–86.

ARTICLE IN A MAGAZINE

T: (Teitel 2008, 44)

R: Teitel, Jay. 2008. Failure to fail. *The Walrus*, April.

ARTICLE IN A NEWSPAPER

Newspapers may be cited in running text. They do not require parenthetical references, and they are typically omitted from a reference list. If a more formal citation is required, follow the guidelines for magazine articles but do not include page numbers.

T: (Singer 2008)

R: Singer, Peter. 2008. The god of suffering. *Toronto Star*, May 17, Ideas section.

LECTURE OR PAPER PRESENTED AT A MEETING

T: (Hahn 2007)

R: Hahn, Thomas. 2007. East and west: Cosmopolitan and imperial in the Roman Alexander. Paper presented at the annual conference of the Centre for Medieval Studies, March 8–10, in Toronto, Canada.

ARTICLE IN AN ONLINE JOURNAL

T: (Go et al. 2001)

R: Go, Alan S., Elaine M. Hylek, Kathleen A. Phillips, YuChiao Chang,
      Lori Henault, and Joe Selby. 2001. Prevalence of diagnosed atrial
      fibrillation in adults. *Journal of the American Medical Association*
      285, no. 18 (May 9), http://jama.ama-assn.org/cgi/content/
      full/285/18/2370.

WEBSITE

Websites may be cited in running text instead of in an in-text citation
("The *Canadian Musician* website lists several . . ."). Websites are often
omitted from reference lists as well. If you are required to give a more formal citation, follow the example below. Note that an access date, if required,
should be given in parentheses at the end of the citation.

T: (CBC)

R: CBC. Recruiting: Canadian astronauts. *CBC News*. http://
      origin.www.cbc.ca/news/polls/canadian-astronauts.html.

WEBLOG

As in the case of websites, blogs are often cited in running text only
("In a comment posted to the CBC News Editors' Blog on November 3,
2007 . . .") and are omitted from a reference list. If you are required to provide more formal documentation, follow the example below. If an access date
is required, include it in parentheses at the end of the citation.

T: (Saeed Geele, CBC News Editors' Blog, comment posted
      November 3, 2007)

R: CBC News Editors' blog. http://www.cbc.ca/news/canada/
      editorsblog/2007/11/the_life_of_a_journalist.html.

WRITING AN ANNOTATED BIBLIOGRAPHY

Some research assignments require an annotated bibliography, which is a
standard list of sources accompanied by descriptive or evaluative comments
on each item in your list.

If you are asked for an annotated bibliography, begin by arranging your list of entries just as you would for a standard bibliography. Then include a brief comment about the source—for example, the quality of the information it contains, the approach of the author, a brief analysis of the paper's strengths and/or weaknesses, or its relevance to your subject.

Consult whatever style guide you are using for details about the specific format recommended for an annotated bibliography.

AVOIDING SECONDARY REFERENCES

A common mistake in essays and lab reports is referring directly to a work that has been quoted in one of your reference sources but that you haven't actually read. Whenever possible, you should find the original source, read it, and make your own assessment of the material. Occasionally, you will find that a critically important reference is unavailable or, more likely, it is in a foreign language that you cannot read. In such a case, you must reference both the original source and the source in which you read the quotation.

For example, if you are writing about the evolution of plant form, you may wish to refer to Goethe's ideas on adaptability of form. In a modern book on the history of botany by A.G. Morton, you found a quotation that you would like to use in your assignment. You noticed that Morton has quoted Goethe's 1790 book *Versuch die Metamorphose der Pflanzen zu erklären*. If you were using Chicago's author–date system for your citations, you would use the following format:

In-text citation: (Goethe 1790)

Reference: Goethe, J.W. von. 1790. *Versuch die Metamorphose der Pflanzen zu erklären*. Gotha, DE: C.W. Ettinger. Quoted in A.G. Morton, *History of Botanical Science* (New York: Academic Press, 1981), 344.

The seventh edition of *Scientific Style and Format* recommends that you never include in your reference list an entry for a document that you have not actually seen. If you are using one of the styles outlined by the CSE and you can't avoid referencing such a document, cite the source in which you found the quotation:

As Morton has noted, Goethe had identified principles of organization in above-ground lateral plant parts as early as 1790: "Whether the plant produces leaves, flowers or fruit, it is always only the same organs which, in manifold determinations and often in changed forms, fulfill nature's demands"[1].

Reference: 1. Morton AG. History of botanical science. New York (NY): Academic Press; 1981. 474 p.

SUMMARY

Documentation can take various forms depending on the discipline, but all documentation styles share some common benefits. A consistent documentation style makes it easy for a reader to retrieve a source, allowing him or her to verify the facts and opinions you have obtained from external sources. A consistent style also gives your assignment an organized, professional look, making the content more readable. In the life sciences, the most common styles are Chicago and CSE. These styles cover everything from formatting quotations to adding citations and references to organizing footnotes and endnotes. You may feel overwhelmed by style points the first time you confront such a battery of conventions, but with practice, you will save time. Ultimately, using a style manual will make your life easier because you won't have to spend time deciding on the best way to cite a particular piece of information—the guide makes all of the decisions for you.

CHAPTER 12

Giving Oral Presentations and Poster Presentations

OBJECTIVES

- preparing and delivering a talk
- answering questions
- handling pressure
- improving your delivery—using a script
- creating effective visuals
- preparing a poster
- improving your poster graphic design
- learning by example—three sample posters

To master the art of giving presentations, you must learn to *prepare*. When you give a talk, you will most often make a single presentation to a group of people, and each member of the audience will have his or her own interests and listening style. In such a presentation, preparing exactly what to say and how to say it will help you address the needs of your audience members and keep their attention. When you give a poster presentation, on the other hand, you will likely present your information many times to individual listeners. In this case, your oral presentation will essentially take the form of a question-and-response discussion, and you will be able to tailor each interaction to the interests of the individual listener. Therefore, you don't need to structure your poster presentation as precisely as you do for a talk. Rather, your success will depend largely on the strength of your poster; to create a successful poster, you must master visual layout and graphics.

ORAL PRESENTATIONS

For some students the prospect of standing in front of a class to give a seminar can be terrifying. The dread of having to speak to a group is almost always rooted in the fear of appearing foolish by not knowing what to say or how to answer questions. There are people to impress—including friends, fellow students, colleagues, and an instructor or professor—in the audience. Even when the audience is completely made up of strangers, there is the pressure to perform well. If it's any consolation, this fear is nearly universal. But there is no reason you can't give a good presentation even if you're nervous when you begin—you just have to be prepared.

If you think about all the bad seminars you've heard in class, you'll probably find that the reason you couldn't follow what was going on was that the speaker jumped from topic to topic, or missed crucial segments of an argument, or took for granted things that you didn't know about. The good seminars you have heard were more likely well organized and systematic, leading you through the material being discussed in a logical manner. Some individuals are naturally more comfortable in front of an audience than others, and these students do have a slight advantage. However, you will find that even if public speaking is not one of your natural talents, you can still achieve decent grades by following a few simple rules. The two most important of these are *be prepared* and *be organized.*

Before you plan your first presentation, you should know what will be involved. You can break the presentation process into three parts: making preparations, giving your talk, and responding to questions. You should also be prepared to deal with the pressure involved. The sections below offer advice to guide you through the presentation process.

Making preparations

KNOW YOUR TOPIC

For the purposes of an in-class seminar, you are the expert and will probably know more about your topic than any of the other students. You need to show your audience that your grasp of the subject matter goes beyond what you include in your talk. If you know more than what you present, you will be better able to answer questions. The more background reading you do, the more information you will have to fall back on when someone asks a question. This extra preparation will also boost your confidence.

CONSIDER YOUR AUDIENCE

Never prepare a seminar based solely on what you know about your topic. In fact, you should approach the talk from precisely the opposite direction: put yourself in the position of your audience. If you were sitting in class instead of standing up at the front, what would you expect of the speaker? How much will the typical audience member know about this topic? What will the typical audience member find most interesting? Most relevant? What can you take for granted as common knowledge in the context of the course? If you combine these with your own question—What do I want my audience to know?—then you have the basis for setting up your talk.

PLAN YOUR PRESENTATION

Giving a presentation involves much more than writing an essay and then reading it out to the class. By the time you are asked to give an in-class presentation, it is likely that you will have sat through hundreds of lectures. Think about the ones you enjoyed most and what it was about them that made them interesting. If you do that, you will realize that your best lecturers were the ones who seemed the most prepared, who spoke without reading directly from their notes, who used a range of visual aids, and who seemed animated and interested in what they were talking about. You can be just as interesting by following some of these suggestions:

- **Decide how much material you need to script in advance**. Some students, particularly those who are already skilled orators, find it useful to fully script their presentations in advance (see pages 191–6). Other students, especially those with less presentation experience, find that writing out their whole talk makes their presentations sound laboured and monotonous. If you are one of these students, draw up an outline that will serve as a guide as you move through your talk. You should also prepare point-form notes—perhaps on index cards—for each of the points that you are planning to discuss. Because you can't read rough notes to your audience, you will be forced to use your own words and, likely, a more natural speaking style. If you are worried that you may freeze when you begin, write out the first paragraph of what you want to say, just to get you started.
- **Prepare an outline for your audience**. An outline will give your audience members something to follow as you talk. Typically, you will base this outline on the one you use to organize your talk, but

you may want to include additional details and a bibliography for your audience.

- **Use visual aids**. Having visual aids serves several purposes. First, visual aids can attract and focus the audience's attention. If you are likely to become self-conscious when standing in front of a group, you will be more at ease when all eyes are on your visual aids and not on you. Second, visual aids provide another form of lecture notes to remind you of what you need to say. If you create a PowerPoint presentation, you will have considerable flexibility to present your information in a variety of ways for maximum effect. (See pages 196–9 for more information on preparing visual aids.)

- **Rehearse your talk**. The more you rehearse your talk, the smoother your presentation will be when you deliver it to your audience. A couple of practice runs will show you where the weak points in your seminar are and will also let you know if you are running over or under time.

Giving Your Talk

DRESS COMFORTABLY

Dressing comfortably means not overdressing but also not dressing down for the occasion. For most student presentations, you should wear your normal clothes. When in doubt, find out what your instructor expects. Scientists are hardly known for their sartorial elegance, so you likely won't need to put a great deal of effort into your appearance to look good. Just don't go too far with informal dress: ripped jeans and an old T-shirt can seem disrespectful to the audience.

GIVE YOURSELF TIME AT THE BEGINNING

If you have equipment to set up or other preparations to make, try to do this before the class begins. If everything is ready, you won't get flustered trying to resolve technical problems with your classmates looking on.

BEGIN WITH AN OVERVIEW

If the audience knows how the talk is structured, they will be able to understand what you are doing as you move from one point to another. Introduce your topic and then give a brief statement of the main areas you will discuss. An overhead or handout with the presentation outline is useful because the audience can refer to it as your talk progresses.

PROJECT YOUR VOICE

When you speak, be sure you're loud enough so that everyone in the classroom can hear you. Try looking at the back row of the class and projecting your voice. Also, try to put some feeling into what you say. It is difficult for an audience member to remain attentive to even the most interesting presentation delivered in a monotone. If you've written a dynamic talk, with many short sentences punctuated by a few long sentences, you can develop a rhythm in your speech. However, if you tend to think and speak in long sentences, you will need to put more effort into escaping the trap of monotony.

DON'T BE APOLOGETIC

The worst way to start a talk is by saying, "You'll have to forgive me, I'm really nervous about this" or "I hope this projector is going to work properly." Even if you are nervous, try to create an air of confidence. A common fault is trying to break the ice with a joke. While many aspects of the life sciences lend themselves well to humour, opening with a joke or a humorous story can sound apologetic, as it implies that the material needs an entertaining boost. Also, jokes often backfire, and they usually sound strained.

MAINTAIN EYE CONTACT WITH YOUR AUDIENCE

Look around the room as you speak. When you look at individuals, you involve them in what you are saying. Also, as you scan the faces in front of you, you can monitor for signs of boredom or incomprehension and can adjust your talk accordingly.

WORK WITH YOUR VISUAL AIDS

If you have visual aids, take advantage of them; just remember that the visual material should enhance your talk, not deliver it for you. When you are making a point from your overhead or slide, try to use different words and expand on what is there.

Make it as easy as possible for your audience to interpret each visual. As you present each item, give your audience enough time to read through the content. They will find it frustrating to see images, overheads, or slides flash by before they've had a chance to take in all of the information. When creating slides, keep your text to a minimum—no more than two or three points per slide. Figure 12.1 provides an example of how you can outline the goals of your talk on a simple, easy-to-read slide. In general, try to use plain backgrounds and simple fonts for all visual aids.

Outline of talk

Goal 1: to study multiple hormone profiles of
lodgepole pine during cone production, both
in natural and experimental conditions

Goal 2: to study efficacy of cone induction treatments

FIGURE 12.1 Sample slide outlining a talk

If you're presenting figures or graphs, remember to explain the significance of each one. For a graph, describe what the x- and y-axes represent, and then explain what the graph shows. Inevitably, your explanations will take more time than you expect. Consider Figure 12.2. While it may be tempting to simply say "ABA and ABA-GE have identical patterns" and move on to the next slide, you need to provide a more complete explanation. In this example, you could start by saying that the slide shows a comparison of the concentrations of two hormones over the course of a year, indicated by months on the x-axis. You should also explain that the hormone concentrations are measured in micrograms per gram dry weight of plant material and that each data point is an average of samples gathered from nine different genotypes selected from VSOC, which you would have to explain as well (it's the Vernon Seed Orchard Company in Vernon, British Columbia). You would then explain that the two hormones show similar patterns with ABA and ABA-GE concentrations rising to a high in winter and dropping with the spring renewal of plant growth. Once you have described these basics, you can move on to add your interpretations, such as whether this is a typical pattern and whether it's true of all plants or just typical of this one.

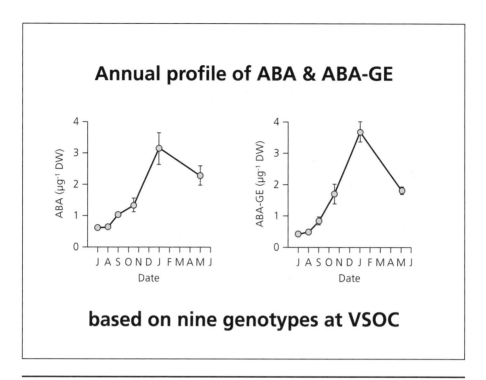

FIGURE 12.2 Sample slide presenting two graphs

If you're presenting a diagram, take the audience through it step by step; you may be familiar with the material, but your audience might not be. Figure 12.3 shows a slide that illustrates a complex catabolic pathway. The slide contains a lot of information, but the point of it is that ABA—a plant hormone—is catabolized by a particular pathway, just one of the five known for this hormone. In this case, you wouldn't need to explain each pathway, as the audience doesn't need to examine each one to understand your point. Rather, you would only have to say that this slide displays the five known pathways and that the one relevant to your presentation is indicated by the curved arrow. ABA breaks down into 8'OH-ABA, then into PA, and finally into DPA and DPA-GS. As you explain this process, you could add the full names of the compounds (e.g., 8 hydroxy-ABA) and the major enzyme in the path (CYP707A). While this description is shorter than the description of the graphs in Figure 12.2, it requires a similarly methodical elucidation.

Later in this chapter you will find some tips on how to prepare visual materials to make the strongest impression (see pages 196–9).

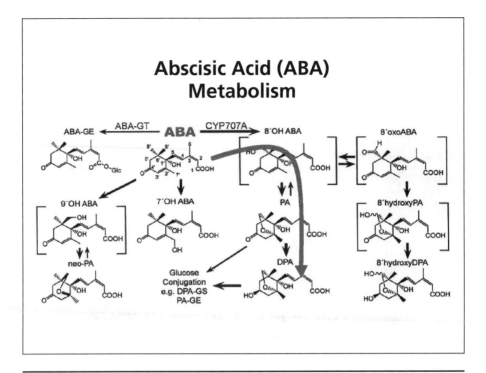

FIGURE 12.3   Sample slide presenting a diagram

Don't Go Too Fast

A good talk is one that is well paced. If you're discussing background information that everyone is familiar with, you can go over it a little faster; if you're describing something complex or less familiar, go slowly. It often helps to explain a complicated point a couple of times in slightly different ways. Don't be afraid to ask your audience if they understand. Almost certainly, someone will speak up if there is a problem.

Pacing is difficult to master, but you should take time to practise, as good pacing can drive your message home. Try to pause before a main point—for example, a conclusion of an experiment—and then spell it out slowly and clearly. Pause again after your explanation to give the audience a moment to reflect on what you have said. Pauses can also make your talk sound more calm and collected. Just as a dynamic combination of notes and rests can enhance a good piece of music, a well-planned combination of discussion and pauses can enhance a good presentation.

MONITOR YOUR TIME ALLOTMENT

As well as pacing your delivery, you should try to ensure that you aren't going to finish too quickly, or worse, go over your allotted time. If you've rehearsed your talk, you should know roughly how long it will take. Rehearse all of your talk. A common mistake during practice sessions is not practising figure descriptions. These generally take about a minute each and should be done slowly and systematically. Well-explained figures make for much better talks.

Remember to allow extra time for questions that people might ask during your talk. Ideally, you should plan to make your talk a little shorter than the prescribed length so that you have some leeway to answer questions.

END STRONGLY

Don't let your talk fade away at the end. You should finish by summarizing the main points you have made and drawing some conclusions. These conclusions should be available on your visual material so that they can be left there for the discussion. If you can raise some questions in your conclusions, this will set you up for the question period to follow.

Responding to questions

The question period is a time when you can really make a good impression. This is an opportunity for you to demonstrate your thorough understanding of the topic and even to reinforce one or two points that you think you may have missed. If you know your material well, you should have no problem dealing with the content of the questions, but the manner in which you answer the questions is important, too:

- It's a good idea to repeat a question if you are in a large room where everyone may not have heard it. This should also solidify the question in your mind and give you a few extra moments to consider it before answering.
- If you didn't hear or didn't understand a question, don't be afraid to ask the questioner to repeat or clarify it.
- Keep your answers short and to the point. Rambling answers are not helpful to anyone.
- Pause before you answer a question. If you know the answer, a pause makes you look thoughtful. It also makes you appear considerate of the questioner. A pause is a particularly useful device when the question is unexpected, awkward, or even

annoying. The pause provides a calm moment in which you can gather yourself.

- If you don't know an answer, say so. It's okay to admit that you don't know everything—as long as you don't do this for every question. And, certainly, it's better to admit that you don't know an answer than to guess or to make up a response that everyone will know is not correct. If you have no clue, don't admit it openly or be apologetic. It is far better to count silently to three, then ask, "Could you put that question differently?" or, if you're really unsure, "I just can't remember at the moment. I'll look that up and get back to you."
- Never answer before someone has completed a question, no matter how long-winded it might be or how certain of the answer you are. It is very important to treat all questions with equal respect.
- If you are asked a question that is aggressive, hostile, or clearly unfair, then simply say, "We can discuss this afterwards."

Dealing with pressure

THE NERVOUS SPEAKER

First of all, being nervous is not always a bad thing. It can sharpen the mind remarkably. If you find that you're very nervous just before a talk, take a few deep breaths to lower your heart rate. Then consider what you're going to do about controlling the most obvious signs of nervousness. Don't worry about the signs you can't control, such as skin flushing, nervous tics, and the quaver in your voice—with practice, they will disappear. Rather, focus on what you can control: your hands and your movement. If you're visibly shaky, try placing your hands on a solid surface such as a table or a podium. Keep them there until you need to point to a visual. If you're nervous and your hands aren't steady, avoid using a laser pointer. Laser pointers are small and light; in the hands of a nervous person, the little red dot will jump and careen around the screen, highlighting the speaker's nervousness. If your mouth goes dry, try the simple trick known to every actor: pass your tongue over your teeth.

THE SENSITIVE SPEAKER

As hard as you try to be informative and entertaining in your talk, not everyone will respond enthusiastically. Indeed, students sometimes roll their eyes, yawn, look bemused, act bored, or even fall asleep during the presentations of their peers. If you're overly sensitive about your audience's reaction to your talk, you might even perceive a neutral gaze as displaying a lack of interest. If you find yourself distracted by such reactions, try to direct your talk to a few audience members who show keen interest. Avoid looking them straight in the eyes—this can be distracting as well—but focus on a point between their brows. If you're still worried about keeping your audience's attention, try moving around: walk to the projection screen, point something out on one of your slides, walk back to the podium. Such movement will force you to think more about what you're doing than about who is or isn't listening; it may also draw the attention of some audience members who were starting to drift away from your presentation.

Improving your delivery

It takes a long time to become an effective public speaker. One helpful way to build your skills is to set yourself a goal in each talk. Initially, your goals will probably be simple: finishing on time or finishing on a strong note. Later, you will incorporate more advanced goals: mastering a new technology in the presentation, trying a new organizational style, incorporating feedback on a previous talk, or trying to present from a script. With time, as you adjust your presentation style, you will progress and build confidence. Trying new styles will also help you keep your talks fresh and exciting, both for yourself and for the audience.

Many students wonder whether it is better to be spontaneous or calculated. To take a page out of music, consider the difference between playing jazz and playing classical music. Jazz requires spontaneity and improvisation, while classical music demands calculation and precision. Some musicians prefer jazz over classical music, while others choose classical over jazz. Neither form is inherently *better* than the other, and both can be equally compelling with practice. Similarly, some presenters are able to give expert presentations spontaneously, while others need to plan each step carefully.

As you play around with different presentation styles, consider creating a script as a tool for self-improvement. You may find that you work better with less structure, but creating a detailed script will help you think about how you present and identify your weaknesses.

TRY CREATING A SCRIPT

Scripts are easy to put together. Essentially, a script is a written plan of everything that you will say and do in your presentation. The process of scripting may seem counterintuitive, as it would seem to constrain spontaneity. However, once you have created a script, you don't need to read directly from it. Rather, you should memorize it and practise it until it flows naturally.

When it comes time to give your talk, you should bring the script along—if you get lost, you can always pick up your script, get your bearings, and move on with the assurance that you know where you're going. You should set the script in an 18-point font so that you can easily skim the words from a distance (e.g., so that you can read it from the podium without squinting). Large type is also easier to read when you're practising. You should highlight prompts that you can refer to quickly without reading the entire script (see the boldface text in the sample script, below).

The main virtue of a script is that it forces you to think about delivery. Once you have planned *what* you want to say, you can focus on *how* you want to say it. A script provides a structure around which you can place rhetorical devices. These can be elements of timing, repetition (yes, you can repeat yourself to marvellous effect in a lecture), or dynamic clusters of ideas. Winston Churchill's famous war-time speech "We shall fight them on the beaches" has just such a cluster:

> . . . we shall fight on the beaches,
> we shall fight on the landing grounds,
> we shall fight in the fields and in the streets,
> we shall fight in the hills;
> we shall never surrender . . . .

If you're wondering how this method can be effective in the life sciences, consider the sample script, below. This script contains an introduction for a talk on an aspect of tulip biology given by a fictional student named Jane Goderich. Notice that Jane has set the prompts in boldface, for quick reference; she has also underlined words that must be delivered correctly and with emphasis. She repeats words such as *clones* and *cloning* multiple times. Repetition—or thematic reinforcement—is more acceptable in an oral presentation than it is in an essay. Essays and speeches have very different structures. If you want to make a point in a talk, you are welcome to use obvious repetition: "Let me repeat . . . ."

Start

Show title slide—"Beneath the tulip field"

Do not read the title

My name is Jane Goderich.
Today I'm going to explain the biology behind tulip cloning.

Pause

Show slide—"Tulip field in Holland"

In this Dutch field, every plant has the same flower colour, same size, and same leaf shape—same everything. It is a field of identical plants.

Slight pause

Then slowly

It is a field of <u>clones</u>.

Cloning is very common in biology, especially in plant biology.
A big clone is hard to miss—in Utah, there is a single poplar clone that covers 81 ha and weighs in excess of 6,000 t. We think this is the largest organism on earth.

Show slide—"Utah poplar clone"

Another sign that cloning is common can be found in our own language. The rich vocabulary of cloning includes dozens of terms: here are just a few.

Show composite slide I—"hyacinth, tiger lily, fern, gladiolus,"

Say rhythmically, while pointing to each one

bulb, bulbil, corm, cormil

Show composite slide II—"strawberry, ginger, potato, fern,"

stolon, runner, tuber, rhizome

Show composite slide III—"moss, hazelnut, poplar, spruce,"

gemma, stool, cutting, ramet

Pause

and my personal favourites

Show composite slide IV—"black cherry, tobacco, cycad"

root sucker, shoot sucker, pup

Slight pause

Tulips clone themselves by offsets.

Show slide—"Tulip with offsets"

Don't rush the next sentences

The development of just such an offset
—from initiation to maturity—
will be the subject of my talk.

This the story of a beautiful clone.

This introduction places tulip cloning within the larger context of plant cloning. It works because it is well organized and structured; it also adds rhythm to what could otherwise be a deadly list of terminology. Notice the small details with which the presenter has described her every step—a good script should contain enough detail that almost anyone could pick it up and make the presentation.

Since we have a pretty good idea that the body of the talk will be about the biology of offsets, let's skip to the ending.

You should always try to create a strong ending. The most effective way to end a presentation is with a final sentence that has a sense of closure. You want to let your audience know that the structured presentation is over and open the floor to questions. Usually, you won't need to put up a slide at the end entitled "Questions?" or ask for queries from the audience—questions are inevitable after every talk. Also, don't worry about thanking the audience—this type of social nicety can sound apologetic, thus weakening your conclusion. The sample ending that follows neither asks for questions nor apologizes. Instead, it gives an example of how audience members might connect the topic to their everyday lives. Of course, there are many ways to end a presentation, and you might have very good reasons for finishing differently.

So, in conclusion . . .

Show slide—"Conclusions": 1. Clones are produced by offsets; 2. The biology of offsets is understood; 3. Only virus-resistant and virus-free clones are selected; 4. Three billion bulbs are exported every year from Holland

Tulips must be bred, then multiplied by offsets, resulting in uniform bulb crops ready to be exported to market.

Pause

The biology of offset growth is relatively simple and lends itself well to large-scale production techniques.

Pause

The strategy in tulip clonal biology is, of necessity, based in combating viruses and other diseases that would otherwise rip through plants of such singular genetic makeup.

Pause

Next time you buy a variety of tulip called Douglas Bader, Toronto, or Pink Diamond, just remember that it is only one of the three <u>billion</u> certified disease-free bulbs that are exported every year from Holland.

Tulips truly do get by with a little help from their friends—humans.

Slide—"Tulip border"

As you gain experience working with scripts, you may find that you like having a map of your presentation before you at all times. You may also find that you prefer to work without a set plan. Either way, you will be one step closer to developing your own personal presentation style.

Preparing visual aids for an oral presentation

With the availability of graphic presentation software, as well as laptop computers and video projectors, your ability to use visual aids in a presentation is limited only by your own ingenuity and your instructor's willingness to let you use the technology in class. For instance, you could develop a PowerPoint presentation that includes video clips and sound as well as animated diagrams. Even if you don't have access to PowerPoint or similar software, you can type up the main points of your talk and print them on transparencies along with any pictures and diagrams you have.

KEEP IT SIMPLE

One cardinal rule applies to every aspect of a visual aid—keep it simple. It is much better to put too little material on a slide than too much.

- **Use plain fonts**. Unless you need a fancy one for a specific reason, stick with fonts that are easy to read. Avoid fonts that are too elaborate, since they have reduced readability and can become irritating after a few slides. Sans-serif fonts, such as Helvetica and Arial, work well.

- **Use sentence case throughout**. Avoid using ALL CAPS and Title Case (first letters in caps). These styles obscure scientific naming conventions (Latin binomials) and are hard to read from the audience's perspective.
- **Use italics for emphasis**. Words set in italics are generally easier to read than words that are underlined.
- **Choose an appropriate font size**. The last thing you want on your slides or overheads is text that is too small for the audience to decipher. The 12-point font you use for written assignments will almost certainly be too small when it is projected on a screen. The minimum size you can use will depend to some extent on how far the projector is from the screen, but one rule of thumb suggests 36 points for titles and 24 points for body text. It's always a good idea to test drive your presentation in the room where you'll be presenting your talk so that you can make adjustments if necessary.
- **Use a simple, light-coloured background**. If you're using PowerPoint to make your slides, choose a plain background and use the same one on every slide. Graphics show up better on lighter backgrounds, so try to avoid using dark backgrounds.
- **Be aware of colour sensitivities**. A biological limitation that you might want to consider is that about 8 in 100 males and 1 in 200 females have colour blindness—you might even have a colour sensitivity yourself. In general, avoid using red and green in close proximity to one another.
- **Limit the amount of colour or animation**. Unless you have a good reason for doing so, you should avoid using multicoloured slides or animation effects that are too busy or distracting.
- **Limit the amount of information per slide**. A good rule of thumb is to stick to only four lines of text per slide, not including a heading. White space on a slide is important because it lifts your graph, table, and text, so keep a lot of it in each slide. Also, if you treat your slides as a script, then you'll be tempted to read directly from them. Instead, make your point briefly on the slide and then expand on the material as you talk. This will make your presentation sound much more natural and professional.

- **Follow the rule of one slide per minute of talk**. Using too many slides can suggest that you are unable to talk without a prop. Take time to establish a rapport with your audience by addressing them in your own words. At the beginning, even if you open your presentation with a slide, try to introduce your topic without pointing to the visual. At the end, after you present your last slide, take a moment to put the focus back on you as a person talking to other people.

- **Keep graphs and tables clear and simple**. Tables and graphs should always have a title and clear labels. If you have space, set the text label for the y-axis horizontally—it will be much easier to read. Graphs should be plain, without fill colour, boxes, grid lines, or 3-D effects that could obscure interpretation. If you must show a complex graph or table, describe the overall outcome in brief, then use a blow-up of a part of the graph or table to illustrate your point.

- **Complete a computer-based presentation on a single platform**. If possible, avoid transferring your files to multiple computers when using presentation software. Most importantly, avoid switching between a PC and a Mac, even if the computers have compatible software. Transferring between such different platforms can cause formatting, video, and animation effects to go awry.

KEEP IT ORGANIZED

The second fundamental rule of using visual aids is to make sure your material is well organized. If you use a consistent organizational scheme, the audience will become used to it and will be able to follow along more easily.

- **Begin with a title slide**. A title slide sets the tone and orients the audience to your topic. It should contain the title, your name, and the name of the course.

- **Create an outline slide**. An outline slide gives the order of the major sections of your talk so that your audience knows what to expect.

- **Use clear headings**. Headings will help your audience identify the most important point on each slide.

- **Consider section breaks**. If your talk falls naturally into several sections, you could start each one with a new title slide. Anything that allows the audience to see the structure of your talk is worth including.

- **Keep your overheads in order**. If you are using overhead transparencies, make sure that they are in the correct order—and in the correct orientation—before you start, and be sure to place your transparencies in an ordered pile as you use them. You may have to refer to one later, and you don't want to be shuffling through a disorganized pile in order to find the one you want.
- **Consider passing samples to audience members**. If you're talking about a subject that lends itself to samples, such as snake skins or pine cones, passing them around can be a very effective way to engage the audience in your talk.

POSTER PRESENTATIONS

Posters are becoming increasingly popular in life sciences courses. Posters can describe everything from life cycles to complex models in cell biology. They commonly focus on the results of experimental tests of hypotheses.

Poster presentations are a form of oral presentation—at some point you will stand by your poster and provide a detailed explanation to interested passersby. Most students find poster presentations less intimidating than talks. There's nothing nerve-racking about describing your work one-on-one with someone who's genuinely interested. Besides, poster sessions are big informal social mixers. Their atmosphere is relaxed.

Your main goal in creating a poster is to make a visually engaging display. Posters are never put up alone, but in the company of many other posters. Assuming that all participants are presenting equally gripping data or phenomena, how can you make your poster stand out from the crowd? While you are restricted by the limitations of the media—posters are two-dimensional surfaces, most commonly one metre square in size—you should be creative with the visual layout. Focus on using illustrations to replace textual information, providing enough white space for your content to stand out, and choosing an eye-appealing colour scheme. The three examples in this chapter (pages 201–6) will give you a starting point.

Using software programs

When you begin to create posters, you will likely use PowerPoint, as it is easy to use, requires few formatting decisions, and is commonly available. As you progress, you should look into more advanced computer software. The best programs for creating posters are those designed for producing graphics that will be printed at publishing industry standards—for example, InDesign, LaTeX, and QuarkXPress. These programs are wonderful because they allow you to fully manipulate and integrate text and graphics in a single document. In addition, you can make lovely posters with other graphics packages—for example, CorelDRAW, OmniGraffle, Inkscape, Illustrator, FreeHand, and PosterGenius—some of which are freeware. You will also find *many* poster templates available on the Web—just type "poster template" into your web browser and add the name of the program you are using. Note that the same design principles apply no matter what software you choose.

Creating poster content

Most often, you will create a poster to display the results of an experiment. You should include information that is similar to what you would include in a lab report, but emphasize visual appeal over extensive written descriptions.

- **Introduction**. As in a lab report, you should use the introduction to build up to your hypothesis. Try to keep this section short (under 150 words), and provide just a few references. You can also add an image to draw attention to this section.
- **Material and Methods**. In posters, you don't need to supply the amount of detail that you would put in a lab report. Flow charts and other illustrations will help you to minimize the text and maximize the clarity of your *Material and Methods* section. You can always supply the missing details when you describe your poster to an interested viewer.
- **Results**. Lead with your most important result, then add any necessary explanations of the figures and tables you include in this section. This is also the place to discuss difficulties you came across in your experimental design. This section will take up the most space on your poster, as it includes the most figures.
- **Conclusions**. In a lab report, this would be your discussion section. Make sure your conclusions are short and to the point. State whether your hypothesis was supported. Consider your results in terms of a handful of published papers and then state the implications your work might have to the field.
- **References**. You can cite—using standardized formats—the references in the poster, but keep the number low, as a *References* section will take up space that you could have put to better use. One way to avoid this section altogether is to provide full reference

information in the text—for example, (Brant & Littlethwaite, 2009. J Poster Graphics 45:11). Toying with a reference forces you to decide whether you really need it. This has the beneficial effect of forcing you to make your text brief, clear, and precise.

- **Acknowledgments.** You will need to thank funding sources, supervisors, and people who provided access to equipment—in short, everyone who made the experiment possible.

Notice that you do not need to include an abstract in a poster. If you are attending a student conference, a specialized conference, or even an international conference, you will need to submit your abstract in advance, and it will be published in the conference booklet. By the time you present, most attendees will have already read your abstract.

Sample posters

All three of the following sample posters contain worthwhile scientific information, but the second two are far superior in their aesthetic appeal. As you read through each case, try to think about how you would improve upon the poster.

CASE 1

This poster was created in PowerPoint. While this program is easy to use, it can be unstable, and professional printers will grimace when told you're giving them a PowerPoint file. Yet the advantage lies in speed: doing a poster in PowerPoint is fast, especially if you use a ready-made template.

The main problem with this poster is that it contains too much written information. If you were to present this poster at a conference, you would soon learn why too many details can detract from your poster presentation. Little joy comes from having to explain—*ad nauseam*—the contents of an overly detailed poster. Remember: if you give a bad talk, you only have to do it once and it's over; if you create a bad poster, you have to present it many, many times over the course of a conference.

What's good?
- The title, at first blush, appears clear.
- The schematic diagrams are clear and exhibit good use of colour.
- The text fonts are large enough to read (32 points for text, 44 points for figures, and 60 points for the title) and set in a sans-serif font (Arial).

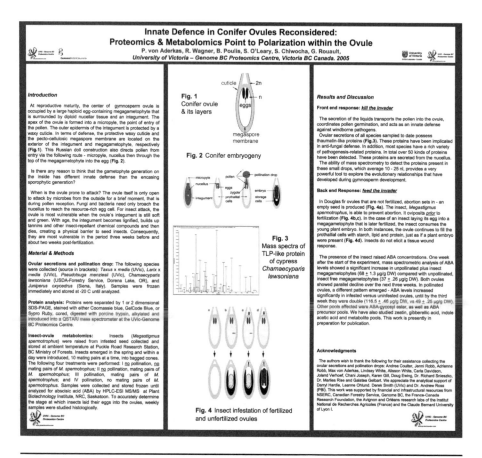

FIGURE 12.4   Poster for Case 1

What's bad?

- The title has a colon. Subtitles are almost always unnecessary and a sign of laziness. Always try to make your title as concise as possible. A better title would have been "Polarized defences within conifer ovules."

- There are too many logos. Whenever possible, avoid displaying logos on your posters. Logos are institutional branding; they're designed to attract attention, and they're usually graphically superior to your own illustrations. Therefore, don't let these unnecessary illustrations draw your viewer's attention away from your poster's significant content.

- The layout seems unplanned. It looks as though the poster's creator has merely plugged the information into a template without any further attention to achieving dynamic brevity. For example, bulleted lists would have made the text blocks seem less dense. To avoid this problem, take the time to edit your content for conciseness. If you're having trouble seeing the poster objectively, draw up a draft form and have someone else critique its assembly, text, readability, attractiveness, and clarity.

- Some headings are both underlined and set in italics. Underlining makes text difficult to read. When you think you need to underline, use italics instead.
- There is too much text. Each section should have no more than 150 to 200 words.
- There is too little white space. For ease of reading, approximately 30 per cent of the poster's surface area should be free of text and illustrations.
- It's boring. Imagine yourself as a viewer who is pressed for time. Now imagine standing in front of *this* poster. Would you take the time to examine the content? This is an acid test the poster would not pass.

CASE 2

This poster was created in InDesign. Notice how the text flows evenly around the graphics—a layout feature not offered by PowerPoint. This illustrates how you can use advanced software tools to create a better poster.

What's bad?
- It lacks references and acknowledgments.
- There is not enough white space.

What's good?
- The poster is easy to read and clear in its goals.
- The title is big and clear—it's an unambiguous question.
- The introduction is illustrated, providing a pair of contrast schematics that explain a critical aspect of the topic without having to reference external literature.
- Rows of dots effectively divide the content into sections.
- Uniformly constructed illustrations of seeds model experimentally derived information.
- The question in the title is linked to the suggested solution at the bottom of the poster. The text in the bottom panel interprets the

Do gymnosperm ovules divide defence between sporophyte and gametophyte?

Patrick von Aderkas, Graduate Centre for Forest Biology, Department of Biology, University of Victoria, Victoria BC V8W 3N5, Canada. email pvonader@uvic.ca

Introduction

Gymnosperm megagametophytes are homologous with angiosperm embryo sacs. However, ovules of these two seed types differ in gametophyte-sporophyte communication. Megagametophytes have a megaspore wall (Fig. 1) largely made up of the tough polymer sporopollenin. Embryo sacs usually lack walls (Fig. 2). If present, walls lack sporopollenin. I propose that megaspore walls may affect nutrient transport, defence and communication within the gymnosperm ovule at time of fertilization.

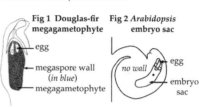

Fig 1 Douglas-fir megagametophyte
Fig 2 *Arabidopsis* embryo sac

- egg
- megaspore wall (*in blue*)
- megagametophyte
- no wall
- egg
- embryo sac

Generations are separated

EM of wall

SEM of wall

no plasmadesmata between sporophyte & megagametophyte

megaspore wall that covers most of megagametophyte is impenetrable to all but water

no wall

wall

The wall restricts transport

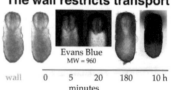

Evans Blue
MW = 960

wall   0   5   20   180   10 h
minutes

Compounds can only enter (or leave) via megaspore wall-free areas near the apex. Communication is highly polar and may be severely restricted.

Sporophyte defence

At fertilization, the sporophyte has many lines of defence

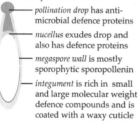

- *pollination drop* has antimicrobial defence proteins
- *nucellus* exudes drop and also has defence proteins
- *megaspore wall* is mostly sporophytic sporopollenin
- *integument* is rich in small and large molecular weight defence compounds and is coated with a waxy cuticle

Megagametophyte defence

Megastigmus spp. parasitize fertilized and *unfertilized* conifer megagametophytes

Is there any defence?
1. complete absence of wound reactions
2. failure to abort parasitized megagametophytes
3. the megagametophyte invests resources to feed insect larva. Red = lipids, proteins, carbohydrates

Seed evolution

An overlooked reason for the evolutionary success of seed habit may be the role played by division of labour within the ovule. The sporophytic portion appears to be charged with the defensive role, freeing the gametophyte to invest resources. A transcriptomic analysis is in order.

FIGURE 12.5   Poster for Case 2

original question, drives the question forward, and ultimately provides a potential method to resolve the main question.

- The text fonts are perfect: a non-serif font (Helvetica) for all the big stuff (title, subheadings) and a nice serif font (Adobe Garamond) for the main text and the figure titles. The text font size (48 points) is much bigger than in the previous poster, which makes the content more readable.

CASE 3

Another InDesign project, this poster will stand out from its neighbours because it is simple and highly visible.

What's bad?
- It lacks references and acknowledgements.

What's good?
- The white space is sufficient to draw attention to the illustrations and the text.

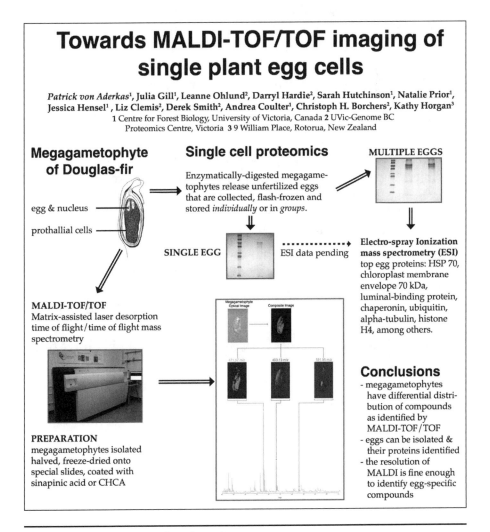

FIGURE 12.6　Poster for Case 3

- The arrows provide easy-to-follow visual paths. These visual tools would also guide the presenter through the presentation steps and help the listener to follow the discussion.
- The illustrations effectively display experimentally derived information, with minimal accompanying text.
- The purpose of the poster is adequately summarized by the title combined with the *Conclusions* section. If you only read the title and the final section, you would get the message of the whole poster in less than thirty seconds.
- The *Introduction* section is reduced to one picture, *Material and Methods* is summarized by a few words and a photo, and *Results* is reduced to two pictures and less than thirty words. As you have probably noticed, there isn't even a need for these traditional subheadings.
- The *Conclusions* section consists of an easy-to-skim bulleted list.

SUMMARY

According to some evolutionary psychologists, standing up in front of strangers and talking is a fear that we all share. With experience and practice, you can overcome this fear. Learning how to prepare an organized, articulate, and succinct talk is one important step in this process. Another is learning effective delivery. As in an acting or musical performance, rehearsal and repetition are essential. If you're nervous, you can gain control by taking a few deep breaths and placing your hands on a steady surface. Remember that talks also involve answering questions, and your answers provide a lasting impression. You should always prepare strategies for answering questions of varying difficulty. If you wish to get better at giving oral presentations, you should experiment with different delivery styles (e.g., scripting). If you want to get better at creating posters, you should learn about the principles of graphic design. Poster presentations, compared to oral presentations, are less stressful in the delivery, but you must put much more thought into the visuals.

CHAPTER 13

Working in Groups

OBJECTIVES

- learning to work in a group
- making lab partnerships work
- keeping a lab book
- studying in groups
- working as a group in a lecture class

Group work is important to the development of every young scientist. Think of it as science socialization. The goal of group activity is to teach students how to work together to perform experiments, solve problems, master complex subject matter, and think creatively. Group learning draws on multiple perspectives, leading to greater objectivity, and objectivity is one of the cornerstones of modern science. Group learning has a number of practical advantages: when performing hands-on exercises, we can learn more effectively if we observe the successes and failures of others; when compiling large data sets, we can collect information more quickly if we work with others; when solving complex problems, we can reach solutions more easily if we consider many different perspectives.

Group work may involve conducting experiments, researching literature, creating reports on controversial subjects, preparing presentations, or putting together many-faceted projects. In the first years of university or college, you will most often participate in group work in lab courses. Although learning scientific facts is often a lonely pursuit, learning to do experiments is more often than not a joint venture. To work effectively as a group, you must collectively decide how to divide labour among the group and appoint one member as the leader who will guide the project to completion. Normally, your lab instructor or professor will provide ample advice on how to set up and maintain an effective group.

GROUP DYNAMICS

Groups that work well together have a strong advantage when it comes to completing assignments in full and on time, so it is always in your best interest to get along with your fellow group members. Dysfunctional groups are the product of personality conflicts, mutual distrust, incompatible goals, varying abilities, general frustration, and at times bad luck. Sometimes a single person will dominate the discussion—either through arrogance, defiance, or extreme enthusiasm—causing others to become reluctant and withdrawn. In other cases, certain students may be unable to stick to the subject, engaging in unproductive social chatter or recounting loosely related anecdotes for the entertainment of the group. Whatever the problem, you should work to resolve it as soon as possible so you don't waste valuable time.

You can avoid most problems merely by listening to one another—after all, listening is half of the art of conversation. If you find that you are being too forceful in supporting your own opinions, try backing down to give other students a chance to voice their thoughts. You can also build cohesion within your group by openly assessing each other's work. If everyone approaches this task with objectivity and fairness, you should be able to identify the strengths and weaknesses within the group. These assessments will help you to get to know your partners and learn how to work together as a team.

If the problem stems from a general frustration resulting from a seemingly unresolvable problem, try attacking the issue from a different angle to generate new ideas. This process is easier if you appoint a group leader to pose questions and direct the discussion. Try not to give up; most often, banging away at the substance and subtleties of an issue will lead to a breakthrough. If you have enough time and all members of the group are motivated to succeed, you will find that you and your peers can work your way around almost any impasse.

Of course, if you find that you are in a dysfunctional group and you cannot resolve the issues on your own, it is best to tell your instructor. He or she can reshuffle the class into new groups, either by randomly reassigning students or by matching students who have similar personalities and skills.

LAB PARTNERSHIPS AND GROUPS

As a student, your main objective in participating in lab-based group work is to learn the techniques that will allow you to work and think as a scientist. Your instructor's objective is to guide you and your classmates through this process by directing questions and sharing advice. This is an apprenticeship style of learning—you and your lab partners are novices who share the desire to learn from a master, your instructor. Consequently, everyone involved must work together. You must not only pay close attention to your instructor's directions but also listen carefully to your peers.

Generally, your instructor will assign you a lab partner (or partners) at random. You might think that this practice is unfair, as lab partners can vary in quality, personality, and appeal. Indeed, the most frequent complaint among science students reflects these concerns: "My lab partner is not pulling his or her own weight." While you might fear that your lab partner's work will drag down your own grades, you should always approach a lab partnership with an open mind.

Is randomly grouping students together for lab work an effective team-building method? The answer is unequivocally *yes*. Working with assigned partners—often people who are virtually strangers—dictates that you find new ways to get along for the three or four hours it takes to perform a task, not to mention the hours it takes to prepare a lab report. Working with different groups of people will also help you expand your comfort zone as you learn to trust the abilities of your peers. You will find that the skills you develop in class for getting along with people of diverse abilities and backgrounds will continue to be useful after you graduate.

Achieving success in lab experiments

Before you begin a lab exercise, you should prepare your strategy. First, read up on the methods, visualizing how you will perform each step, and jot down questions. Second, discuss with your lab partners a division of labour and a plan of execution. Who will record the process? When will you meet to prepare for the experiment? Who will carry out each step? Who will present the results to your instructor?

Once your experiment is underway, stay calm and focussed. This doesn't mean that you can't socialize with your partners; some steps take longer than others, and it is natural to chat. Stay on track by appointing someone to be the human alarm clock whose job it is to bring the group's attention back, for example by saying, "Let's focus now. The next step requires some concentration." This same person should also be responsible for identifying when the group is stuck by asking, "What do we do next?"

Before each class, be sure to prepare for questions that your instructor might ask. Preparation will help the questioning process move along smoothly, making the collective learning process more effective. Instructors pose lab-related questions either to individual groups or to the whole class. Some typical examples include the following:

- When you did this, what happened?
- How do you count, measure, or assess . . . ?
- What is your goal in the next part of the experiment?
- What does this term mean?
- What relationship does this result have to what you did earlier?
- What possible mistakes occur with this type of measurement or method?
- Is the sample size big enough?

Assign a member of your group to record the questions and their answers. These questions are not spontaneous; rather, they are designed as teaching tools (i.e., instructors are told to ask these questions), and the answers will be useful to you when you write the lab report.

Polishing group work for good grades

Getting good grades on group work can be challenging. To minimize the possibility of handing in an inadequate assignment, you should formulate a plan that builds in time at the end of the process during which you can edit your work and correct any oversights. Try to leave a day or two to unite the various elements in a clear manner. One member of the group should check through your entire assignment to make certain that your group has addressed and properly integrated all of the requirements. Putting the final polish on these joint efforts is always rewarded. If you're a very organized, detail-oriented person, you should volunteer to do this. If you're not the most organized person of the group, find out who is and ask them to do it. You can still learn from this final step by offering to help that person put everything together.

Separating your work from their work

Often, your instructor will specify exactly what he or she means by "individual effort" in a group project. Every lab course—and sometimes every lab project within a course—will come with its own requirements. If you are uncertain about what you are responsible for, you should immediately contact your instructor. Not doing so may have dire consequences.

However you carry out the experiment, each member of the group must produce individual work showing personal interpretation. Although you are free to discuss a data set, a problem-solving method, or any other aspect of a lab exercise with the other members of your group, you are not free to copy another student's work. To avoid copying, you and your lab partners should each prepare a draft report of the entire assignment. Next, sit down with your group to discuss each person's interpretation. You can still revise your report to reflect important points in this discussion, and you may find that the discussion leads you to a more objective interpretation as you consider the different perspectives of your lab partners. Since you prepared the work individually to begin with, the individual touches will still be apparent after revision.

In labs, it's common for one person to record data while another performs a step in the experiment. Nevertheless, each partner should keep separate notes in his or her own lab book. This way, everyone will have a complete copy of the data when they prepare their individual student reports.

Keeping a lab book

An intact lab book is an important element in recording your experiment. A lab book provides a reliable and undisputable record of what your experiment accomplished. It is a personal record of what you have done, what you have found, and how you have interpreted your findings. It also provides an indication of what each person in a lab group contributed to an experiment.

Your instructors may ask you to keep a separate lab book for each course. In addition, you will need to keep lab books if you work in a lab as a project student, co-op student, Honours project student, or summer assistant, and you will continue to use lab books to record your research after you graduate. The only difference between a lab book that you use in class and one that you use as a paid lab worker is that the former belongs to you, while the latter belongs to the laboratory. Note that in some labs, you might be required to have a supervisor sign off on each page in order to validate the authenticity of the content.

Lab books are taken very seriously among members of the scientific community. Scientists use lab books to keep results, analysis, and protocols that they will use to write future papers or to train future scientists. Lab books contain the details of how scientists turn ideas into experiments that generate data. They are the records of scientific experience.

In most industrial and academic labs, failure to keep a lab book is grounds for dismissal. Lab books are almost always kept in the lab and never go home with the researcher. They are irreplaceable and need to be securely stored.

CHOOSE A GOOD LAB BOOK

Only use books with a stitched, glued binding. Never use spiral-bound books, binders, or other loose-leaf options in which pages can be easily replaced. Such books call into question the reliability of the information they contain, as undesirable data could be removed and replaced with falsified information and no one would be the wiser. The best lab books lay flat when they are opened. This type of book may be more expensive to buy, but you will come to love the lay-flat feature. Choose a lab book that has numbered pages. For lab work, make sure that the pages in your book are wide enough to allow you to paste in data printouts without folding them. For fieldwork, choose a smaller book that is more convenient to carry around with you.

KEEP YOUR RECORDS NEAT AND ORGANIZED

When you first get a lab book, write your name on the spine; put your name, address, and phone number inside the front cover; and write "Table of Contents" at the top of the first few pages, reserving these for a running record of the contents of the book.

Always write in ink and be sure to choose a pen that won't bleed or run. If you are doing fieldwork, you might have to record data in pencil or in indelible ink, because rain can cause havoc with ink. Do not use pencil in a lab book, because it can easily be erased. Erased entries in lab books will cause readers to question your motives for obscuring information.

Write dates out in full. Abbreviated forms such as 10/09/10 can be very ambiguous. In Canada, the standard form is day, month, year (e.g., 10 September 2010), but some Canadian scientists use the American form of month, day, year (e.g., October 9, 2010).

Always write legibly, especially when writing numbers. In the event of an error, never erase, white out, or otherwise obscure an entry. Instead, use a ruler to draw a thin line through what you have written. This way you will still be able to read the mistake. Blotting information out completely is as good as never having recorded it: you can't possibly go back and have a look at the errors. Also, you should *never* tear pages out of your lab book. Aside from looking untidy, torn pages call into question the validity of the remaining records.

RECORD EVERYTHING

As a rule, you should include in your lab book everything related to an experiment. Someone who reads your records must be able to repeat your work exactly. Include your initial thoughts and discussions on the experiment's goals and hypotheses in addition to any background information that you think is useful. Once you start an experiment, record all protocol details, equipment details, names of assistants and partners, sources of chemicals (not just manufacturers, but locations in the lab for your own future reference), software, names of files where you've stored data, and locations of computers that contain those files. In short, record *every* detail that you might need for your analysis. This includes any mistakes you've made, both major and minor. Why do you need to record errors? You must account for and interpret any data that contradicts the hypothesis. Are the errors false positives or false negatives? How could they have been avoided? What lessons can be drawn from the failure? The answers to these questions will be very helpful to you when you begin to analyze the results.

Your instructor, TA, or lab supervisor will usually specify the degree of detail you need to include in your records. At minimum, you should record the details of all calculations, estimations, measurements, and times (e.g., 3:50 p.m.—added tissue to enzyme digestion solution). When in doubt, think *overkill*. Something that you might think of as a picky detail—such as the brand, model type, and wattage of light bulbs in a growth room—may prove useful later on. Even the type of water you use (tap, distilled, double-distilled, deionized, reverse osmosis–purified, or Milli-Q) is significant. If you include these types of details, your professor will appreciate your efforts, as the best books are those with the most information.

Of course, there are limits to the amount of detail you should include. Personal details—for example, the fact that you conducted the experiment on your mother's birthday—are almost always irrelevant.

STUDY GROUPS

Study groups differ from in-class groups in that they are formed by students, not by instructors. As such, the purpose of a study group is not to learn how to work with your peers but to help each other understand difficult course material. Studying in groups is a highly effective way of learning complex material. Together, like-minded students can often master complex subjects more rapidly than they could on their own.

You will find many advantages in studying with a group. First, you will have the opportunity to see subjects from different perspectives. Each member of the group will likely have different strengths and interests—mathematics, biological theory, chemical structure, genetics, etc.—that complement one another, leading the group to a well-rounded understanding of the topic. Second, you will find it easier to focus on the task at hand. Most students are better able to avoid procrastination if they have support from peers who share their academic goals. Third, you will be forced to verbalize your understanding of different topics. If you can describe what you know in a way that is clear to your fellow group members, you are well on your way to grasping the topic. Fourth, your discussions will likely lead to debate, which will prepare you for argumentative questions on your exam. Fifth, you will learn, through discussion, how to pronounce the necessary terminology and use it in context. Life science jargon may appear to be another language, but once you can use a complex word such as Zosterophyllophyta in a sentence, you own it. As another benefit, learning to speak like a life scientist will help you build confidence in your position within the scientific community.

You will need to put some thought and effort into setting up a study group. Here are some tips for creating a good group:

- Keep the group small (three is a good number); larger groups tend to get distracted easily and chat more frequently.
- Include students who are of the same academic level.
- Pick students who arrive for class on time; punctuality suggests a strong commitment to learning, and these students are less likely to miss or arrive late for a study session.
- Choose students who want to contribute.

Once you choose your members, appoint one person to be in charge of organizing the meeting's location and time. The meeting place should be suitably quiet. Cafés and library study rooms are good, but dorm rooms are usually bad, as they provide many distractions. Each member of the group should turn off his or her cell phone and remain focussed on the group's discussion during each meeting. A period of one to one-and-a-half hours is optimal; any longer, and the group's concentration will fade. Decide in advance what topics you will study at each meeting—you will find that simple preplanning will noticeably improve the study group's efficiency.

GROUP ACTIVITIES IN A LECTURE CLASS

Group activities are becoming more common in lecture classes. Whether a class contains twenty students or eight hundred students, it is possible for the instructor to create group activities. Usually, lecture groups contain five or fewer members. Large classes used to be difficult to organize into smaller groups, but technological innovations (e.g., clickers and laptops) have created easier ways for groups of students to interact in a lecture setting.

The purpose of working in a class-based group is to discuss ideas. In some cases, your group will simply work on its own to discuss or debate a complex issue. In other cases, your group will need to come up with an answer to a specific problem or question and then present the solution or answer to the class. For the discussion process to work effectively, everyone in the group must be included; each member should, in turn, be allowed to venture a thought.

Once you have formed a group, the first step is for each group member to introduce him- or herself. Say your name and give some personal details, such as your major or where you're from. During this phase you should also mention whether or not you have experience with this sort of group activity. Make an effort to include the people with the least experience. The next step is to appoint someone to be the leader. This person will be responsible for speaking on behalf of the group. As a final preparatory step, appoint someone to be the recorder.

To begin the information-gathering process, the leader should set out simple guidelines:

> We need to state our ideas and evaluate them. We'll start by giving each one of you a minute to voice your thoughts. Even if you disagree with someone's opinion, let the speaker finish.

As you present your ideas, try to give an example to illustrate your point. No one should comment on any single opinion or thought until everyone has had a say. During this step, the recorder will take down all the ideas; when the last person has finished, the leader should say:

> Let's go around once more in the same order and see if we're missing anything.

Once the group has generated enough ideas, you can begin the discussion. The leader has to ensure that the group stays on track and within any time limitations; he or she must also ensure that each member of the group feels comfortable and included. The recorder should write down any dissenting opinions, as they will form part of the final response.

The next task is to sort the information. Begin by categorizing each idea as an advantage or a disadvantage (or pro or con), then rank the ideas in order of most to least important. To reach a decision, the leader should pose a series of questions to the group:

> Do we agree that this idea is the most important one? Do we stand behind our ranking? Are there any objections? Is there anything wrong with our proposal?

In the event of a disagreement, the leader should say:

> Shall we go around once more with everyone giving the reason for their opinion? We've made real progress, so let's see if we can resolve this issue.

When the group reaches a decision, the leader should thank everyone for their good work.

SUMMARY

Learning to work in a group has many benefits in the life sciences. Group work will teach you to rely on your peers and to work together to execute tasks that might be too complex or too time consuming for you to complete on your own. After all, many hands make light work. In the lab, group work will encourage you to incorporate different perspectives into formulating and interpreting an experiment, leading to greater overall objectivity. In order to benefit from a group-learning experience, you must work to get along with all members of your group. Remember to listen to your peers, work with their strengths, and plan each task in advance to avoid unnecessary frustration. The team-based skills you learn in your classes will pave the way to future possibilities. If you work in a lab, you will need to be able to work as part of a team. Basic group skills will also help you to work with people from other disciplines. This ability is essential in the life sciences, where projects are often interdisciplinary, and individuals with diverse expertise are often grouped together to take up new directions.

CHAPTER 14

Writing Examinations

OBJECTIVES

- preparing for exams
- using memory aids
- asking the right questions
- identifying special needs
- writing essay exams
- writing open-book exams
- writing take-home exams
- writing objective (multiple-choice) exams

Most students feel nervous before tests and exams. It's not surprising. Writing an essay exam imposes special pressures. You can't write and rewrite the way you can in a regular essay, you must often write on topics you would otherwise choose to avoid, and you must observe strict time limits. On the surface, objective exams may look easier because you don't have to compose the answers, but they force you to be more decisive about your answers than essay exams do and they require very detailed and precise knowledge of the subject. To do your best you need to feel calm—but how? The general guidelines provided in this chapter will help you approach any test or exam with confidence.

PREPARING FOR THE EXAM

Review regularly

Exam preparation has to begin long before the exam period itself. A weekly review of lecture notes and texts will help you remember important material and relate new information to old. If you don't review regularly, at the end of the semester you'll be faced with relearning rather than remembering.

Set memory triggers

As you review, condense and focus the material by writing down in the margin key words or phrases that will trigger whole sets of details in your mind. The trigger might be a concept word that names or points to an important theory or definition, or it might be a quantitative phrase such as "three causes of the decline in caribou populations" or "five factors in muscle degeneration."

Sometimes you can create an acronym or a learning aid that will trigger an otherwise hard-to-remember set of facts. A learning aid generally takes the form of an *aide-mémoire* (a set of summary notes) or a mnemonic device (a pattern of letters or words that helps you remember a complex series). An acronym is a common type of mnemonic. For example, the acronym PMAT stands for *prophase, metaphase, anaphase, telophase*, and it is doubly useful because it gives both the names of the phases of cell division and the order in which the phases occur. The more items you need to memorize, the more useful mnemonics become. Consider the acronym KPCOFGS, which stands for *kingdom, phylum, class, order, family, genus, species*—the hierarchy of biological classification. An equally effective way to remember this hierarchy is to memorize the nonsense sentence "King Philip came over for grape soda." Another mnemonic sentence that has saved many a student is "Can intelligent Karen solve some foreign mafia operations?" This sentence will help you remember the compounds that make up the Krebs (or tricarboxylic acid) cycle: *citrate, isocitrate, ketoglutarate, succinyl, succinate, fumarate, malate*, and *oxaloacetate*. Who thinks up this stuff? Well, students like you. You can find many more examples on the Web—just type "mnemonic" and "biology" into your web browser.

Use comparison tables

A lot of exam questions in life sciences courses revolve around comparison. You can master these types of questions by taking the time to sort comparative information into structured tables. Creating comparative tables while you study will also help you to see connections between many themes and concepts that recur throughout the course. Once you understand these connections, you will find exams easier to write.

Ask questions

Think of questions that will get to the heart of the material and force you to examine the relations between various subjects or issues; then think about how you would answer them. The three-C approach discussed on pages

13–16 may help. For example, reviewing the *components* of the subject could mean focussing on the main parts of an issue or on the definitions of major terms or theories. When reviewing *change* in the subject, you might ask yourself what the causes or results of those changes are. To review *context*, you might consider how certain aspects of the subject—issues, theories, actions, results—compare with others in the course. Essentially, the three-C approach forces you to look at the material from different perspectives.

Copies of exams used previously in the course are useful both for learning the types of questions your instructor might ask and for checking on the thoroughness of your preparation. If old exams aren't available, you might get together with friends who are taking the same course and ask each other questions. Just remember that the most useful review questions are not the ones that require you to recall facts but the ones that force you to analyze, integrate, or evaluate information. This sort of preparation works best in a study group (see pages 213–14 for advice on forming an effective study group).

Talk to your instructor

Instructors and TAs have office hours during which they are prepared to meet with students. You should take advantage of these opportunities. While you may find it more convenient to go online to search for answers, the information you find on the Internet is not always reliable. You should also remember that your instructor will create the exam. By speaking directly with your instructor, you will get a clear idea of his or her priorities—knowledge that can help you focus your studying efforts on the most important topics. Don't be shy about going to office hours or worry that you're wasting your instructor's time. Your instructor wants you to succeed, so he or she will likely appreciate your extra efforts in taking the time to discuss course material outside of the classroom.

Identify special needs

Educational institutions make a concerted effort to recognize and accommodate the special needs of students who have learning disabilities such as dyslexia or other perceptual problems or physical disabilities. If you think you fall into this category, be sure to make your instructor and the appropriate school officials aware of your situation. Professors are used to these situations and should be able to accommodate you. Most institutions also have offices dedicated to assisting students with special needs—all you have to do is contact this office and they will help set everything up. You may be able to complete an exam in a computer lab or under special conditions that will give you the best chance to demonstrate your knowledge.

Allow extra time to get to the exam

Give yourself lots of time to get to the exam. Nothing is more nerve-wracking than thinking you're going to be late because your alarm didn't go off or you got caught in traffic. Remember Murphy's Law: "Whatever can go wrong will." Anticipate any potential difficulties and allow yourself a good margin.

IF YOU ARE LATE

In large first- and second-year courses, there are usually rules about lateness. For example, you may be allowed to write only if you arrive within the first half-hour of the exam period; if you arrive any later, you may be banned from the exam. Even if you are late, it is still better to arrive and throw yourself at the mercy of the professor than to not come at all. Most profs will accommodate late students, especially if the reasons for their tardiness are compelling.

WRITING AN ESSAY EXAM

Read the exam

An exam is not a race. Finishing early, though satisfying, is not usually rewarded with higher grades. Good students tend to fully use the time available. Instead of starting to write immediately, take time at the beginning of the exam to read through each question and create a plan. A few minutes spent on thinking and organizing will bring better results than the same time spent on writing a few more lines.

Apportion your time

Read the instructions carefully to find out how many questions you must answer and to see if you have any choice. Subtract five minutes or so for the initial planning, and then divide the time you have left by the number of questions you have to answer. If possible, allow for a little extra time at the end to reread and edit your work. If the instructions on the exam indicate that not all questions are of equal value, allocate your time accordingly.

Choose your questions

Decide on the questions that you will do and the order in which you will do them. Your answers don't have to be in the same order as the questions. If you think you have lots of time, it's a good idea to place your best answer first, your worst answer in the middle, and your second-best answer at the end, in order to leave the reader on a high note. If you think you will be rushed, though, it's wiser to work from best to worst; that way you will be sure to get all the marks you can on your good answers, and you won't have to cut a good answer short at the end.

Stay calm

If your first reaction on reading the exam is "I can't do any of it!" then force yourself to be calm: take several slow, deep breaths to relax, then decide which question you can answer best. Even if the exam seems impossible at first, you can probably find one question that looks manageable; that's the one to begin with. It will get you rolling and increase your confidence. By the time you have finished your first answer, you will probably find that your mind has worked through to the answer for another question.

Read each question carefully

As you turn to each question, read it carefully and underline all the key words. The wording will probably suggest the number of parts your answer should have. Be sure you don't overlook anything—this is a common mistake when people are nervous. Since the verb used in the question is usually a guide for the approach to take in your answer, it's especially important that you interpret the key words in the question correctly. For advice on how to interpret the verbs *outline*, *trace*, *explain*, *discuss*, *compare*, and *evaluate*, see pages 16–17.

Make notes

Before you begin to organize your answer, jot down key ideas and information related to the topic on extra paper provided or on the spare pages of your answer book. These notes will save you the worry of forgetting something while you are writing. Next, arrange those parts you want to use into a brief plan.

Be direct

Get to the points quickly and use examples to illustrate them. In an exam, as opposed to an essay, it's best to use a direct approach. Don't worry about composing a graceful introduction; simply state the main points that you are going to discuss and then get on with developing them. Remember that your paper will likely be one of many read and marked by someone who has to work quickly; the clearer your answers are, the better they will be received.

For each main point, give the kind of specific details that will prove you really know the material. General statements will show you are able to assimilate information, but you need to support these statements with examples to get full marks.

Write legibly

Poor handwriting makes readers cranky. When the person marking your paper has to struggle to decipher your ideas, you may get poorer marks than you deserve. If for some special reason (such as a physical disability) your writing is hard to read, you should be able to make special arrangements to use a computer. If your writing is not very legible, consider printing. Also, write on every second or third line of the booklet; this will not only make your writing easier to read but also leave you space to make changes and additions if you have time later on.

Stick to your time plan

Stay on schedule and don't skip any questions. Try to write something on each topic. Remember that it's easier to score half marks for a question you don't know much about than it is to score full marks for one you could write pages on. If you find yourself running out of time on an answer and still haven't finished, summarize the remaining points and go on to the next question. Leave a large space between questions so that you can go back and add more if you have time.

Reread your answers

No matter how tired or fed up you are, reread your answers at the end if there's time. Check especially for clarity of expression; try to get rid of confusing sentences and improve your transitions so that the logical connections between your ideas are as clear as possible. Revisions that make answers easier to read are always worth the effort.

WRITING AN OPEN-BOOK EXAM

If you think that permission to take your books into the exam room is an "open sesame" to success, be forewarned: do not fall into the trap of relying too heavily on your reference materials. You may spend so much time riffling through pages and looking things up that you won't have time to write good answers. The result may be worse than if you had been allowed no books at all.

If you want to do well, use your books only to check information and look up specific, hard-to-remember details for a topic you already know a good deal about. For instance, if your subject is biology, you can look up names and functions; for a biochemistry exam, you can look up reactions; for an exam in health sciences, you can check some references and find the authors' exact definitions of key concepts—if you know where to find them quickly. In other words, use the books to make sure your answers are precise and well-illustrated, but never use them to replace studying and careful exam preparation.

Most instructors will allow you to prepare your book to some degree. This preparation can include slipping in Post-it Notes, adding marginalia (notes pencilled in the margins of the book), and highlighting passages. Some instructors may even allow you to take your own notes into an open-book exam. When this occurs, it pays to take along the comparative tables that you created while studying for the exam.

WRITING A TAKE-HOME EXAM

The benefit of a take-home exam is that you have time to plan your answers and to consult your texts and other sources. The catch is that the amount of time you have to do this is usually less than you would have for a research essay. Don't work yourself into a frenzy trying to respond with a polished essay for each question; instead, aim for well-written exam answers. Keep in mind that you were given this assignment to test your overall command of the course material; your reader is likely to be less concerned with your specialized research than with evidence that you have understood and assimilated the material.

The guidelines for a take-home exam are similar to those for a regular exam; the only difference is that you don't need to keep such a close eye on the clock:

- Keep your introductions short and get to the point quickly.
- Organize your answers in such a way that they are straightforward and clear and the reader can easily see your main ideas.
- Use concrete examples to back up your points.
- Where possible, show the range of your knowledge of course material by referring to a variety of sources rather than constantly using the same ones.

- Try to show that you can analyze and evaluate material—that you can do more than simply repeat information.
- If you are asked to acknowledge the sources of any quotations you use, be sure to jot them down as you go rather than trying to track down sources at the end.

WRITING AN OBJECTIVE EXAM

In your first- and second-year life sciences courses, most of your exams will consist of objective questions. If you are studying at a large university, objective exams may also constitute the bulk of assessment in your upper-year courses. Although objective exams sometimes contain true-false questions, they usually feature multiple-choice questions. The main difficulty with these exams is that the questions are designed to confuse the student who is not certain of the correct answers. If you tend to second-guess yourself or if you are the sort of person who readily sees two sides to every question, you may find objective exams particularly hard at first. Fortunately, practice almost always improves performance.

Preparation for objective exams is the same as for other exams. Here, though, it's especially important to pay attention to definitions and unexpected or confusing pieces of information, because these are the kinds of details that instructors often use to create questions for objective exams. Although there is no sure recipe for doing well on an objective exam—other than a thorough knowledge of the course material—the following suggestions may help you do better.

Do the easy questions first
Go through the exam at least twice. On the first round, don't waste time on troublesome questions. Since the questions are usually of equal value, it's best to get all the marks you can on the ones you find easy. You can tackle the more difficult questions on the next round. This approach has two advantages: first, you won't be forced, because you have run out of time, to leave out any questions that you could easily have answered correctly; second, when you come back to a difficult question on the second round, you may find that in the meantime you have figured out the answer.

Find out the marking system
If marks are based solely on the number of right answers, you should pick an answer for every question even if you aren't sure it's the right one. For a

true-false question, you have a 50 per cent chance of being right. Even for a multiple-choice question with four possible answers, you have a 25 per cent chance of getting it right, more if you can eliminate one or two of the wrong answers.

On the other hand, if there is a penalty for wrong answers—if marks are deducted for errors—you should guess only when you are fairly sure you are right or when you are able to rule out most of the possibilities. In this case, don't make wild guesses.

Make your guesses educated ones

Before you guess, check that you have read the question correctly. The number one problem on first-year exams is misinterpretation of questions. The cure for this problem is to take your time. If you need to, write reminders to read carefully on every page of the exam; this is time well spent and will teach you to approach all questions with careful attention.

Once you think you know what the question is asking, look at the answers. You can approach the choices in one of two ways: (1) decide which answers are truly wrong and see what's left or (2) if you have studied really well, decide which answers are closest to the correct answer and make your choice from there. The first approach generally works better—if you can eliminate more than half of the options, you'll have a more manageable number of choices. Once you've narrowed down the options, step away from the question, reread it, and see which one of the remaining answers fits best.

Don't ever make a wild guess unless you're completely stumped by the question itself. Guessing as a regular strategy is *really* bad, because you start guessing at questions that, with a little bit of patience, would have become completely obvious. Guessing is the handmaiden of surrender.

If you have to guess, forget about intuition, hunches, and lucky numbers. More importantly, forget about so-called patterns of correct answers—the idea that if there have been two "A" answers in a row, the next one can't possibly be "A" as well, or that if there hasn't been a "true" for a while, "true" must be a good guess. Many question-setters either don't worry about patterns at all or else deliberately elude pattern-hunters by giving the right answer the same letter or number several times in a row.

Remember that constructing good objective exams is a special skill that not all instructors have mastered. In many cases the questions they pose, though sound enough as questions, do not produce enough realistic alternatives for answers. In such cases the question-setter may resort to some less realistic options, and you can spot them if you pay attention. James F.

Shepherd[1] has suggested a number of tips that will increase your chances of making the right guess:

- Start by weeding out all the answers you know are wrong rather than looking for the right one.
- Avoid any terms you don't recognize. Some students are taken in by anything that looks like sophisticated terminology and may assume that such answers must be correct. In fact, these answers are usually wrong; the unfamiliar term may well be a red herring, especially if it is close in sound to the correct one.
- Avoid extremes. Most often the right answer lies in between. For example, suppose that the options are the numbers 800,000; 350,000; 275,000; and 15: the highest and lowest numbers are likely to be wrong.
- Avoid absolutes, especially on questions dealing with people. Few aspects in the life sciences are as certain as is implied by such words as *everyone, all, no one, always, invariably*, or *never*. Statements containing these words are usually false.
- Avoid jokes or humorous statements.
- Avoid demeaning or insulting statements. Like jokes, these are usually inserted simply to provide a full complement of options.
- Choose the particular statement over the general (generalizations are usually too sweeping to be true).
- Choose "all of the above" over individual answers. Question-setters know that students with a patchy knowledge of the course material will often fasten on the one fact they know. Only those with a thorough knowledge will recognize that all the answers listed are correct.

Reread the exam

If you have time at the end of the exam, go back and reread the questions. One or two wrong answers caused by misreading can make a significant difference to your score. On the other hand, don't start second-guessing yourself and changing a lot of answers at the last minute. Studies have shown that when students make changes they are often wrong. Stick with your original decisions unless you know for certain that you have made a mistake.

SUMMARY

Mastering the exam techniques outlined in this chapter will help you improve your grades in all of your courses. To prepare for exams, you should regularly review course material. In addition to studying on your own, studying with a group can be a very effective way of learning information. Whenever possible, try to find old examination papers to test your knowledge in advance. Comparison tables are particularly useful study tools for life sciences courses—they allow you to see how various features, functions, and concepts relate to one another. If you are writing an essay-type exam, try to answer the easiest question first. You can then tackle the remaining questions in order of increasing difficulty; if you have lots of time, you can put the most difficult answers in the middle and end with another easy question. For an open-book exam, you must study to fully comprehend the material, but you don't need to memorize specific details such as formulae, names, or models. You can prep your book in advance so that it is fingertip ready. When writing a multiple-choice exam, remember to read each question carefully and control the urge to guess. If you are given a take-home exam, you are less constrained by time limitations, but you must still assemble information efficiently to show that you have mastered the material. For each type of exam, you will do best if you prepare well in advance, remain calm and focussed during the exam period, and read each question carefully.

CHAPTER 15

Writing Resumés and Letters of Application

OBJECTIVES

- choosing what to include
- preparing a standard resumé
- preparing a functional resumé
- writing a letter of application
- applying by email

Whether you are looking for a summer job, applying to graduate school, or seeking permanent employment, eventually you will have to write a resumé and a letter of application. You may even need to write an application letter for some courses or programs, including those with work placement. The person who reads your application will not have time to read reams of material, so you will need to be brief yet precise.

WRITING A RESUMÉ

Choosing the best content

Think of a resumé as more than just a summary of facts; think of it as a marketing strategy tailored to specific employers. You will need to supply some basic information, but how you organize it and which details you emphasize are up to you. One good strategy is to put your most important or relevant qualifications first, so that the reader will notice them at first glance. For most students this means leading with educational qualifications, but for others it may mean starting with work experience. Within each section of your resumé, use reverse chronological order so that the most recent item is at the beginning.

Whatever arrangement you choose, your goal is to keep the resumé as concise as possible while including all the specific information that will help you "sell" yourself. A reader will lose interest in a resumé that goes on and on, mixing trivial details with the pertinent ones. On the other hand, experience or skills that may seem irrelevant to you may in fact demonstrate an important attribute or qualification, such as a sense of responsibility or a willingness to work hard. For example, working as a part-time short-order cook may be significant if you state that this was how you paid your way through university or college.

The tone of your resumé should be upbeat, so don't draw attention to any potential weaknesses you may have, such as lack of experience in a particular area. Never list a category and then write "None"—you don't want to suggest that you lack something. Remember to adjust your list of special skills to fit each job you apply for so that the reader will see at a glance that you meet the job requirements. Finally, never claim more for yourself than is true; putting a falsehood into a resumé can be grounds for firing, or even legal action, if it is discovered later.

You are not required to state anything about your age, place of birth, marital status, race, religion, or sex. Keep in mind, though, that if you are completing an application form with set questions it is a good idea to provide all the information requested; if you don't, your application may be ignored.

Here is a list of common resumé information, along with some suggestions on how to present it. The examples on pages 232–5 show the two different ways of presenting this information depending on the kind of background and experience you have. Most word-processing programs contain a number of templates that will also help you format your resumé.

- **Name.** Typically, you should type your name in capital letters and centre it at the top of the page, although there are many variations on this format.
- **Contact information.** This can include your mailing address with postal code, phone and fax numbers, and email address. If you have a temporary student address, remember to indicate where you can be reached at other times.

- **Career objective** (optional). It's often helpful to let the employer know your career goal, or at least your current aim for employment—for example, "a technician position with opportunity for advancement."
- **Education.** Include any degrees, diplomas, or certificates you have earned, along with the institution that granted them and the date. If it will help your case and if you are short of other qualifications, you may also list courses you have taken that are relevant to the job. In a functional resumé, you may include any training that is additional to your degree under a heading such as "Skills" or "Abilities" (see page 234).
- **Awards or honours.** These may be in a separate section or included with your education details.
- **Work experience.** Give the name and location of your employer, along with your job title and the dates of employment. You don't need to outline all of your duties, but you should list any specialized tasks that you performed. You should focus on listing your accomplishments on the job, using point form and action verbs, for example:

  - Designed and administered a public awareness survey.
  - Supervised a three-member field crew.

  In a functional resumé in the life sciences, you may choose to include work experience under a heading such as "Technical Background" or "Relevant Experience."
- **Research experience or specialized skills.** This section gives you a chance to list information that may give you an advantage in a competitive market, such as experience with certain computer programs or knowledge of a second language. If you have worked as a research assistant, be sure to state the type of work you did and the name of your employer, for example:

  - Assisted Professor Larry Peterson in a laboratory research project, "Root endophytes of pines," University of Guelph, Summer 2010.
- **Other interests** (optional). Depending on the employer and the amount of information you have already included, you may choose

to omit this section. Including a few achievements or interests (e.g., travel or athletic accomplishments) will show that you are well rounded; hobbies that require specialized or technical skills (e.g., playing an instrument or building small robots) will suggest coordination, discipline, and attention to detail. If the employer shares some of your interests, they can be a valuable trigger during an interview. Never include a long list of items that merely show passive or minimal involvement.

- **Volunteer activities** (optional). Time spent volunteering is a strong measure of community involvement. You should always indicate what positions you held, what kind of work you did, and the amount of time you spent with an organization.
- **References** (optional). Some applicants prefer to wait until they are asked before providing a list of references to employers. This is acceptable provided that you do actually have a list available. If you are granted a job interview, prepare to be asked to provide references on the spot. Have your list neatly typed and ready to hand to an interviewer; this avoids any delay during which your name could drop down on the list, giving other candidates an advantage. You must contact potential references ahead of time to ensure that they are willing to act in this capacity. Obtain their contact information, including complete email and mailing addresses and phone number. Since reference information is one of the elements that you can control in the hiring process, only provide contacts who you know will give you a good reference. Never use people who will not disclose to you what they would say if contacted as a reference.

Preparing a standard resumé

If you're a recent graduate without a great deal of work experience, the standard resumé format will probably show your qualifications in their best light. It includes separate headings for education and work experience and uses a reverse chronological order within those sections. At first, you may need to include all summer and part-time jobs, even if they aren't particularly related to your field. As you gain more experience, you can begin dropping some of the less relevant positions and focussing on those that are significant for the kind of job you're seeking.

ELIZABETH D. LEARNER

Current Address (Until 15 May 2011):   Permanent Address:
Solin Hall   2694 Arbutus Road
3510 Lionel-Groulx   Victoria BC V8N 3M2
Montreal QC H4C 1M7   tel. 250-214-4423
tel. 514-653-9989
email: liz.d.learner@gmail.com

Career objective: An entry-level position with the World Wildlife Fund
where my degree in biology would be an asset

Education:

- BSc (Hons) Biology, McGill University (expected June 2011)
  (Honours thesis: "Predation rates of guppies in Trinidad")

Honours and awards:

- Dean's List, 2009–10, McGill University
- Hugh M. Brock Scholarship ($3,000), 2006, McGill University
- BC Scholarship ($1,500), 2006, British Columbia Scholarship
  Society

Work experience:

Summer 2010—NSERC USRA research assistant for Professor Brian
  Falstaff, McGill University, Montreal (Project title: "Nanotechnology
  of wafer-thin bacterial biscuits")
- Collected bacteria from biofilm surfaces
- Devised, designed, and applied bacteria to nanochips
- Helped design protein calibration technique for method
- Acquired proteomics experience

Summer 2009—research technician, Cellfor Inc., Victoria
- Tissue-cultured Mexican long-leaf pine embryos
- Trained summer students in media preparation

Summer 2008—Server, Ickey Wicket, Victoria
- Waitressed and occasionally tended bar

Specialized skills and experience:

- Aseptic technique in microbiology and biotechnology. Ability to make media, test for contamination, and isolate bacteria as well as plant cells at a proficient level.
- Computer literate. Extensive knowledge of MASCOT; Microsoft Word, Excel, and PowerPoint; and Adobe Photoshop and InDesign. Rudimentary knowledge and interest in using R.
- Statistical knowledge. Extensive experience with SPSS; moderate experience with R.

Other interests and achievements:

- Trumpeter in Fight Band, McGill, 2008–10
- Member of the intramural women's lacrosse league, McGill, 2008–10
- Musician (bagpipe and tam-tam) at local festivals, 2005–10

Volunteer activities:

- Volunteer for Montreal Children's Hospital, assisting children with disabilities every Saturday since 2006
- Volunteer for SADD (Students Against Drunk Driving) booth at McGill's student orientation, 2009

References (letters available upon request):

Professor Brian Falstaff
(Summer Research Supervisor)
Stewart Biology Building
McGill University
1205 Docteur Penfield
Montreal QC H3A 1B1
Tel. 514-398-0090
brian.falstaff@mcgill.ca

Dr. Diana Tod
(Honours Supervisor)
Redpath Museum
859 Sherbrooke Street West
Montreal QC H3A 2K6
Tel. 514-398-4094
diana.tod@mcgill.ca

Preparing a functional resumé

If your background is less conventional, with a wide range of experience or a change in direction, a functional resumé may be the best format, as it gives greater flexibility to stress transferable skills. Most functional resumés include categories for different areas of expertise (e.g., Research, Administration, Computer Skills). Others may focus on personal attributes such as initiative, teamwork, analytic ability, or communication skills.

ELEANOR L. PAINTER

Apt. B - 4210 Quimpool St.
Halifax NS B3H 3A6
tel. 902-653-9989
email: eleanor.lp@gmail.com

Career objective: Work as a consultant in a marine consulting firm

Profile: Researcher with diverse experience in marine biological systems

Relevant experience:

- Research director for Benthic Directions Inc. (Dartmouth NS) responsible for day-to-day assignment of work to a team of five research technicians (January 2007–present)
- Technician with Bedford Institute of Oceanography (Dartmouth NS) in marine bacteriology group (June 2005–December 2006)
- Microbial genomicist with Cranberry Cove Research Inc. (Halifax NS) responsible for developing chip assays (May 2004–June 2005)

Related skills:

- Certification as a professional diver, Deepwater Diving Inc. (July 2005; certificates available upon request)
- Currently enrolled part-time in Master of Information Management program, Dalhousie University (begun September 2009)

Education:

BSc Biochemistry and Molecular Biology, Dalhousie University (2004)

Other achievements and activities:

- Work on marine bacteria in Bedford Basin featured in *The Nature of Things* TV program (March 2009)
- Founder of the St. George's Island Charity (begun in 2007)—last year we raised over $55,000 for habitat protection in Halifax Harbour

References:

Available upon request

WRITING A LETTER OF APPLICATION

You should *not* use the same letter for all applications; instead, you should craft each one to focus directly on the particular job and company in question and catch the attention of each particular reader. In a sense, both the resumé and the letter of application are intended to open the door to the next stage in the job hunt: the interview. The key is to link your skills to the position, not just to state information. What matters is not what *you want* but what the *employer needs*.

One challenge in writing a letter of application is to tell your reader about yourself and your qualifications without seeming egotistical. Two tips can help:

1. Limit the number of sentences beginning with *I*. Instead, try burying *I* in the middle of some sentences, where it will be less noticeable, for example, "For two months last summer, I worked as a . . . ."
2. Avoid, as much as possible, making unsupported, subjective claims. Instead of saying "I am a highly skilled manager," say something like, "Last summer I managed a $50,000 field study with a crew of seven assistants." Rather than "I have excellent research skills," you might say, "Based on my previous work, Professor Kimiko Sunahara selected me from ten applicants to help with her summer research work."

Here is an example (not to be copied rigidly) of an application letter that tries to connect the applicant's background with the needs of the company.

---

4 March 2010

Jim Newbaggins
Human Resources
BioInc Enterprises
150 Research Road
Manitoba MN R3C 0F4

RE: Job Application for Research Technician

Dear Mr. Newbaggins:

Your advertisement in the *Winnipeg Free Press* for a research technician caught my attention. As a recent graduate of the University of Toronto's Cell and Systems Biology program, I am confident that my qualifications match those you are seeking. The topic of my final thesis was "Proteomics of angiotensin." After completing my thesis, I was given a contract to write a small manual on how to improve handling of time-sensitive biological materials—in particular, protein samples derived from forensic applications—for use in student labs. Last year I had the opportunity to speak with your head researcher, Dr. Pantilly, when he gave a lecture for my fourth-year Methods in Genomics and Proteomics class, and she mentioned that proper handling of samples has become a growing concern as your clientele increases with each year.

Beyond my in-class studies, I have had relevant experience dealing with biosampling in a professional lab setting. For the past two summers, I have assisted Dr. Watson of the University of Toronto with her studies of proteomics of mice liver in response to certain pharmaceuticals. My job was to prepare and process liver samples for proteomic analysis. In 2008, I also worked as a summer student at UGel Inc., a Montreal-based firm specializing in surface films used in the biotechnology industry.

I would appreciate the chance to discuss with you how I could contribute to BioInc Enterprises and will call you next week to see if it is convenient to arrange an interview.

Please note that I have enclosed a resumé.

Sincerely,

Sarah M. Shelston

Sarah M. Shelston

USING EMAIL TO APPLY FOR A POSITION

Many employers now list job opportunities on the Internet and welcome email applications. Email has the clear advantage of speed, but it also has some potential pitfalls. The following guidelines will help you avoid them:

- Type your cover letter as an email message, and wherever possible address it to a specific person. Never write "Dear Professor" or "Dear Sir"—you don't want the recipient of your message to mistake it for spam. Indicate whether you are responding to a particular position the organization has advertised rather than applying for any available opportunity. If so, let the "Subject" line at the top of the email immediately tell the reader what you are applying for, such as "Application for Project Manager, file number 360."
- Include your resumé as an attachment. That way, you can be sure the format appears to the reader exactly as you have designed it. If you can, attach the file as a PDF; in this format, your resumé will look the same no matter what type of computer the recipient uses. We all know that the appearance of regular email can sometimes go visually askew at the receiver's end, where fonts, spacing, and alignment can change. An attachment, by contrast, will look the way you created it and can readily be printed and copied in that

format. Since you want the cover letter to get immediate attention, leave it as text in the email rather than an attachment.

- Print your message and look at it carefully before pressing the "Send" button. Typographical errors or missing words are often harder to catch on the screen than on the printed page. Another strategy is to send the email to yourself so that you can see how your message looks and ensure that the attachment opens as it should. Even though email is generally a quick and casual channel of communication, applications are too important to run the risk of error or accident.

From: liz.d.learner@gmail.com
Subject: Application for Research Assistant Job in Costa Rica
Date: 23 January 2011 9:34:57 AM EST (CA)
To: ayalala@procton.blue.ca

Attachment: ELD.pdf

Dear Mr. Ayala

This message contains my application for the position of research assistant to work on the fauna of bromeliads in Costa Rica, which you recently advertised in the Canadian Botanical Association Bulletin. I am nearing completion of my undergraduate Honours Biology degree from McGill University, and I will be available to go into the field as of 15 May 2011. My resumé is attached (see EDL.pdf).

Having twice collected guppies in Trinidad for my Honours thesis under Dr. Tod, I have extensive experience in the tropics. In preparing my thesis, I used various statistical methods to map guppy populations, a skill that is in line with your company's focus on combining ecology with population modelling. I also have experience working in biology labs, both at McGill and at the independent research firm Cellfor Inc. With this experience, I feel that I am well prepared and well qualified to conduct the type of research that you outlined in your advertisement.

Please do not hesitate to contact my references. In addition, I have a valid Canadian passport and a full British Columbia driver's licence.

I look forward to hearing from you.

Sincerely,

Elizabeth D. Learner

Current Address:
Solin Hall
3510 Lionel-Groulx
Montreal QC H4C 1M7
tel. 514-653-9989
email: liz.d.learner@gmail.com

FINAL WORDS OF ADVICE

When you apply for a job, your application is likely to be one of many. This means that it must pass an initial screening process before it is considered seriously. For that reason, it is absolutely essential that you submit a package that looks professional. Your application package will be judged not just by what you say but also by how you say it. Take the time to double-check for grammar and spelling errors, and make sure that your documents are well formatted. With applications, as with job interviews, first impressions count.

SUMMARY

Resumé writing is a mix of writing to template—standard or functional—and tailoring the content to the employer's needs. Your goal is to display your experience and interests in the best possible light. Towards this end, you must follow certain style conventions. Always put the most relevant information first. This might be your education, or it might be your experience. Your letter of application, whether it is a printed letter or an email, should tell the employer why you are interested in the job, preparing him or her for your attached resumé. In all cases, you should carefully edit your letter and your resumé before sending your application. When preparing an email submission, be especially careful to use a professional tone. Whereas email, Twitter, and text messages that you send to your friends are spontaneous and informal, communications with potential employers must be completely formal. Remember that appearance counts—pay attention to details such as content structure, visual layout, and grammar. Since you want to make a good impression, always assemble your application package with care.

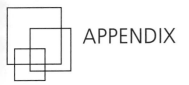

Weights, Measures, and Notation

BIOLOGY

♂   male
♀   female

STATISTICS

n   sample size
μ   mean of hypothesis
x̄   mean of sample
σ²   variance
SE   standard error
SD   standard deviation
CV   coefficient of variation
ANOVA   analysis of variance

UNITS

Quantity

ppm   parts per million
ppb   parts per billion
%   per cent
% solution   mass (g)/100 ml
1 mole (mol)   = 6.022×10^{23} objects
Avogadro's number   = number of objects in a mole (6.022×10^{23})
molar concentration   = molarity, substance concentration, amount concentration
1 molar (1 M)*   = 1 mol/L
1 millimolar (mM)   = 10^{-3} molar
1 micromolar (μM)   = 10^{-6} molar
1 nanomolar (nM)   = 10^{-9} molar
1 picomolar (pM)   = 10^{-12} molar
1 femtomolar (fM)   = 10^{-15} molar
1 attomolar (aM)   = 10^{-18} molar
1 zeptomolar (zM)   = 10^{-21} molar
1 yoctomolar (yM)   = 10^{-24} molar (~1 molecule per 1.6 litres)

Time

1 hour (h)   = 3,600 seconds (s), 60 minutes (min)
1 millisecond (ms)   = 10^{-3} seconds

Length

1 kilometre (km)   = 1,000 metres
1 metre (m)   = 1,000 millimetres
                             = 100 centimetres
1 centimetre (cm)   = 10 millimetres (10^{-2} metres)
1 millimetre (mm)   = 1,000 micrometres (10^{-3} metres)
1 nanometre (nm)**   = 10^{-9} metres
1 ångström (Å)   = 10^{-10} metres

Volume (liquid and gas)

1 litre (l or L)   = 1,000 millilitres
1 millilitre (ml or mL)   = 10^{-3} litres
1 cubic centimetre (cm³)   = 10^{-3} litres
1 microlitre (μl or μL)   = 10^{-6} litres

Mass

1 petagram (Pg)   = 10^{15} grams
1 teragram (Tg)   = 10^{12} grams, or 1 megatonne (Mt)
1 gigagram (Gg)   = 10^{9} grams
1 megagram (Mg)   = 10^{6} grams, or 1 tonne (t)
1 kilogram (kg)   = 1,000 grams
1 gram (g)   = 1,000 milligrams
1 milligram (mg)   = 1,000 micrograms
1 microgram (μg)   = 10^{-6} grams
1 kilodalton (kDa)   = 1,000 daltons
1 dalton (Da)   = 1.660×10^{-24} grams

Area

1 hectare (ha)   = 10,000 square metres
                             = 2.47 acres
1 square metre   = 10,000 square centimetres
                             = 1,000,000 square millimetres
1 square centimetre   = 100 square millimetres

*Note: free energy is measured in joules/mole (J/mol).
**Note: wavelengths (λ) are measured in nanometres (e.g., emission λ maximum for blue light is 452–475 nm).

Glossary

abstract. A summary accompanying a formal scientific report or paper, briefly outlining the contents.

abstract language. Language that deals with theoretical, intangible concepts or details: e.g., *justice*; *goodness*; *truth*. (Compare **concrete language**.)

acronym. A pronounceable word made up of the first letters of the words in a phrase or name: e.g., *NATO* (from *North Atlantic Treaty Organization*). A group of initial letters that are pronounced separately is an **initialism**: e.g., *CBC*; *NHL*.

active voice. See **voice**.

adjectival phrase (or **adjectival clause**). A group of words modifying a noun or pronoun: e.g., *the dog that belongs to my brother*.

adjective. A word that modifies or describes a noun or pronoun: e.g., *red*; *beautiful*; *solemn*.

adverb. A word that modifies or qualifies a verb, adjective, or adverb, often answering a question such as *how? why? when?* or *where?*: e.g., *slowly*; *fortunately*; *early*; *abroad*. (See also **conjunctive adverb**.)

adverbial phrase (or **adverbial clause**). A group of words modifying a verb, adjective, or adverb: e.g., *The dog ran with great speed*.

agreement. Consistency in tense, number, or person between related parts of a sentence: e.g., between subject and verb, or noun and related pronoun.

ambiguity. Vague or equivocal language; meaning that can be taken two ways.

antecedent (or **referent**). The noun for which a following pronoun stands: e.g., *cats* in *Cats are happiest when they are sleeping*.

appositive. A word or phrase that identifies a preceding noun or pronoun: e.g., *Mrs. Jones, my aunt, is sick*. The second phrase is said to be **in apposition to** the first.

article. See **definite article, indefinite article**.

assertion. A positive statement or claim: e.g., *The data are inconclusive.*

auxiliary verb. A verb used to form the tenses, moods, and voices of other verbs: e.g., "am" in *I am swimming*. The main auxiliary verbs in English are *be, do, have, can, could, may, might, must, shall, should,* and *will*.

bibliography. 1. A list of works used or referred to in writing an essay or report. 2. A reference book listing works available on a particular subject.

case. Any of the inflected forms of a pronoun (see **inflection**).
Subjective case: *I, we, you, he, she, it, they*
Objective case: *me, us, you, him, her, it, them*
Possessive case: *my/mine, your/yours, our/ours, his, her/hers, its, their/theirs*

circumlocution. A roundabout or circuitous expression, often used in a deliberate attempt to be vague or evasive: e.g., *in a family way* for "pregnant"; *at this point in time* for "now."

clause. A group of words containing a subject and predicate. An **independent clause** can stand by itself as a complete sentence: e.g., *I bought a hamburger*. A **subordinate** (or **dependent**) **clause** cannot stand by itself but must be connected to another clause: e.g., *Because I was hungry, I bought a hamburger*.

cliché. A phrase or idea that has lost its impact through overuse and betrays a lack of original thought: e.g., *slept like a log; gave 110 per cent.*

collective noun. A noun that is singular in form but refers to a group: e.g., *family; team; jury*. It may take either a singular or plural verb, depending on whether it refers to individual members or to the group as a whole.

comma splice. See **run-on sentence**.

complement. A completing word or phrase that usually follows a linking verb to form a **subjective complement**: e.g., (1) *He is my father*; (2) *That cigar smells terrible*. If the complement is an adjective it is sometimes called a **predicate adjective**. An **objective complement** completes the direct object rather than the subject: e.g., *We found him honest and trustworthy*.

complex sentence. A sentence containing a dependent clause as well as an independent one: e.g., *I bought the ring, although it was expensive.*

compound sentence. A sentence containing two or more independent clauses: e.g., *I saw the accident and I reported it*. A sentence is called **compound-complex** if it contains a dependent clause as well as two independent ones: e.g., *When the fog lifted, I saw the accident and I reported it*.

conclusion. The part of an essay in which the findings are pulled together or the implications revealed so that the reader has a sense of closure or completion.

concrete language. Specific language that communicates particular details: e.g., *red corduroy dress; three long-stemmed roses*. (Compare **abstract language**.)

conjunction. An uninflected word used to link words, phrases, or clauses. A **coordinating conjunction** (e.g., *and, or, but, for, yet*) links two equal parts of a sentence. A **subordinating conjunction**, placed at the beginning of a subordinate clause, shows the logical dependence of that clause on another: e.g., (1) *Although I am poor, I am happy*; (2) *While others slept, he studied*. **Correlative conjunctions** are pairs of coordinating conjunctions (see **correlatives**).

conjunctive adverb. A type of adverb that shows the logical relation between the phrase or clause that it modifies and a preceding one: e.g., (1) *I sent the letter; it never arrived, however*. (2) *The battery died; therefore, the car wouldn't start*.

connotation. The range of ideas or meanings suggested by a certain word in addition to its literal meaning. Apparent synonyms, such as *poor* and *underprivileged*, may have different connotations. (Compare **denotation**.)

context. The text surrounding a particular passage that helps to establish its meaning.

contraction. A word formed by combining and shortening two words: e.g., *isn't* from "is not"; *we're* from "we are."

coordinate construction. A grammatical construction that uses correlatives.

copula verb. See **linking verb**.

correlatives (or **coordinates**). Pairs of correlative conjunctions: e.g., *either/or; neither/nor; not only/but (also)*.

dangling modifier. A modifying word or phrase (often including a participle) that is not grammatically connected to any part of the sentence: e.g., *Walking to school, the street was slippery*.

definite article. The word *the*, which precedes a noun and implies that it has already been mentioned or is common knowledge. (Compare **indefinite article**.)

demonstrative pronoun. A pronoun that points out something: e.g., (1) *This is his reason*; (2) *That looks like my lost earring*. When used to modify a noun or pronoun, a demonstrative pronoun becomes a **demonstrative adjective**: e.g., *this hat*, *those people*.

denotation. The literal or dictionary meaning of a word. (Compare **connotation**.)

dependent clause. See **clause**.

diction. The choice of words with regard to their tone, degree of formality, or register. Formal diction is the language of orations and serious essays. The informal diction of everyday speech or conversational writing can, at its extreme, become slang.

direct object. See **object**.

discourse. Talk, either oral or written. **Direct discourse** (or **direct speech**) gives the actual words spoken or written: e.g., *Donne said, "No man is an island."* In writing, direct discourse is put in quotation marks. **Indirect discourse** (or **indirect speech**) gives the meaning of the speech rather than the actual words. In writing, indirect discourse is not put in quotation marks: e.g., *He said that no one exists in an island of isolation.*

ellipsis. Three spaced periods indicating an omission from a quoted passage. At the end of a sentence use four periods.

essay. A literary composition on any subject. Some essays are descriptive or narrative, but in an academic setting most are expository (explanatory) or argumentative.

euphemism. A word or phrase used to avoid some other word or phrase that might be considered offensive or blunt: e.g., *pass away* for *die*.

expletive. 1. A word or phrase used to fill out a sentence without adding to the sense: e.g., *To be sure, it's not an ideal situation.* 2. A swear word.

exploratory writing. The informal writing done to help generate ideas before formal planning begins.

fused sentence. See **run-on sentence**.

general language. Language that lacks specific details; abstract language.

gerund. A verbal (part-verb) that functions as a noun and is marked by an -ing ending: e.g., *Swimming can help you become fit.*

grammar. The study of the forms and relations of words and of the rules governing their use in speech and writing.

hypothesis. A supposition or trial proposition made as a starting point for further investigation.

hypothetical instance. A supposed occurrence, often indicated by a clause beginning with *if*.

indefinite article. The word *a* or *an*, which introduces a noun and suggests that it is non-specific. (Compare **definite article**.)

independent clause. See **clause**.

indirect discourse (or **indirect speech**). See **discourse**.

indirect object. See **object**.

infinitive. A type of verbal not connected to any subject: e.g., *to ask*. The **base infinitive** omits the *to*: e.g., *ask*.

inflection. The change in the form of a word to indicate number, person, case, tense, or degree.

initialism. See **acronym**.

intensifier (or **qualifier**). A word that modifies and adds emphasis to another word or phrase: e.g., *very tired*; *quite happy*; *I myself*.

interjection. An abrupt remark or exclamation, usually accompanied by an exclamation mark: e.g., *Oh dear! Alas!*

interrogative sentence. A sentence that asks a question: e.g., *What is the time?*

intransitive verb. A verb that does not take a direct object: e.g., *fall*; *sleep*; *talk*. (Compare **transitive verb**.)

introduction. A section at the beginning of an essay that tells the reader what is going to be discussed and why.

italics. Slanting type used for emphasis or to indicate the title of a book or journal.

jargon. Technical terms used unnecessarily or in inappropriate places: e.g., *peer-group interaction* for *friendship*.

linking verb (or **copula verb**). A verb such as *be, seem,* or *feel,* used to join subject to complement: e.g., *The apples were ripe.*

literal meaning. The primary, or denotative, meaning of a word.

logical indicator. A word or phrase—usually a conjunction or conjunctive adverb—that shows the logical relation between sentences or clauses: e.g., *since; furthermore; therefore.*

misplaced modifier. A word or group of words that can cause confusion because it is not placed next to the element it should modify: e.g., *I only ate the pie.* [Revised: *I ate only the pie.*]

modifier. A word or group of words that describes or limits another element in the sentence: e.g., *The woman with the black hat donated a million dollars.*

mood. 1. As a grammatical term, the form that shows a verb's function.
Indicative mood: *She is going.*
Imperative mood: *Go!*
Interrogative mood: *Is she going?*
Subjunctive mood: *It is important that she go.*

2. When applied to literature generally, the atmosphere or tone created by the author.

non-restrictive modifier (or **non-restrictive element**). See **restrictive modifier**.

noun. An inflected part of speech marking a person, place, thing, idea, action, or feeling, and usually serving as subject, object, or complement. A **common noun** is a general term: e.g., *dog; paper; automobile.* A **proper noun** is a specific name: e.g., *Martin; Sudbury.*

object. 1. A noun or pronoun that completes the action of a verb is called a **direct object**: e.g., *He passed the puck.* An **indirect object** is the person or thing receiving the direct object: e.g., *He passed Marcus* (indirect object) *the puck* (direct object).

2. The noun or pronoun in a group of words beginning with a preposition: e.g., *at the house; about her; for me.*

objective complement. See **complement**.

objectivity. A position or stance taken without personal bias or prejudice. (Compare **subjectivity**.)

outline. With regard to an essay or report, a brief sketch of the main parts; a written plan.

paragraph. A unit of sentences arranged logically to explain or describe an idea, event, or object. The start of a paragraph is sometimes marked by indentation of the first line.

parallel wording. Wording in which a series of items has a similar grammatical form: e.g., *At her wedding my grandmother promised to love, to honour, and to obey her husband.*

paraphrase. Restate in different words.

parentheses. Curved lines enclosing and setting off a passage; not to be confused with square brackets.

parenthetical element. A word or phrase inserted as an explanation or afterthought into a passage that is grammatically complete without it: e.g., *My musical career, if it can be called that, consisted of playing the triangle in kindergarten.*

participle. A verbal (part-verb) that functions as an adjective. Participles can be either **present**: e.g., *speaking to the assembly*), or **past** (e.g., *spoken before the jury*).

part of speech. Each of the major categories into which words are placed according to their grammatical function. Traditional grammar classifies words based on eight parts of speech: verbs, nouns, pronouns, adjectives, adverbs, prepositions, conjunctions, and interjections.

passive voice. See **voice**.

past participle. See **participle**.

periodic sentence. A sentence in which the normal order is inverted or in which an essential element is suspended until the very end: e.g., *Out of the house, past the grocery store, through the school yard, and down the railway tracks raced the frightened boy.*

person. In grammar, the three classes of personal pronouns referring to the person speaking (**first person**), the person spoken to (**second person**), and the person spoken about (**third person**). With verbs, only the third-person singular has a distinctive inflected form.

personal pronoun. See **pronoun**.

phrase. A unit of words lacking a subject-predicate combination, typically forming part of a clause. The most common kind is the **prepositional phrase**—a unit consisting of a preposition and an object: e.g., *They are waiting at the house*.

plural. Indicating two or more in number. Nouns, pronouns, and verbs all have plural forms.

possessive case. See **case**.

prefix. An element placed in front of the root form of a word to make a new word: e.g., *pro-*; *in-*; *sub-*; *anti-*. (Compare **suffix**.)

preposition. The introductory word in a unit of words containing an object, thus forming a **prepositional phrase**: e.g., *under the tree*, *before my time*.

pronoun. A word that stands in for a noun: e.g., *she*, *this*.

punctuation. A conventional system of signs (e.g., comma, period, semicolon) used to indicate stops or divisions in a sentence and to make meaning clearer.

reference works. Sources consulted when preparing an essay or report.

referent. See **antecedent**.

reflexive verb. A verb that has an identical subject and object: e.g., *Isabel taught herself to skate*.

register. The degree of formality in word choice and sentence structure.

relative clause. A clause introduced by a relative pronoun: e.g., *The man who came to dinner is my uncle*.

relative pronoun. *Who, which, what, that*, or their compounds, used to introduce an adjective or noun clause: e.g., *the house that Jack built*; *whatever you say*.

restrictive modifier (or **restrictive element**). A phrase or clause that identifies or is essential to the meaning of a term: e.g., *The book that my aunt gave me is missing*. It should not be set off by commas. A **non-restrictive**

modifier is not needed to identify the term and is usually set off by commas: e.g., *This book, which my aunt gave me, is one of my favourites.*

rhetorical question. A question asked and answered by a writer or speaker to draw attention to a point; no response is expected on the part of the audience: e.g., *How significant are these findings? In my opinion, they are extremely significant, for the following reasons. . . .*

run-on sentence. A sentence that goes on beyond the point where it should have stopped. The term covers both the **comma splice** (two sentences incorrectly joined by a comma) and the **fused sentence** (two sentences incorrectly joined without any punctuation).

sentence. A grammatical unit that includes both a subject and a verb. The end of a sentence is marked by a period.

sentence fragment. A group of words lacking either a subject or a verb; an incomplete sentence.

simple sentence. A sentence made up of only one clause: e.g., *Joaquim climbed the tree.*

slang. Colloquial speech considered inappropriate for academic writing; it is often used in a special sense by a particular group: e.g., *dope* for "good" or *diss* for "disrespect."

split infinitive. A construction in which a word is placed between *to* and the base verb: e.g., *to completely finish.* Many still object to this kind of construction, but splitting infinitives is sometimes necessary when the alternatives are awkward or ambiguous.

squinting modifier. A kind of misplaced modifier that could be connected to elements on either side, making meaning ambiguous: e.g., *When he wrote the letter finally his boss thanked him.*

standard English. The English currently spoken or written by literate people and widely accepted as the correct and standard form.

subject. In grammar, the noun or noun equivalent with which the verb agrees and about which the rest of the clause is predicated: e.g., *They swim every day when the pool is open.*

subjective complement. See **complement.**

subjectivity. A stance that is based on personal feelings or opinions and is not impartial. (Compare **objectivity**.)

subjunctive. See **mood**.

subordinate clause. See **clause**.

subordinating conjunction. See **conjunction**.

subordination. Making one clause in a sentence dependent on another.

suffix. An element added to the end of a word to form a derivative: e.g., *prepare, preparation*; *sing, singing*. (Compare **prefix**.)

synonym. A word with the same dictionary meaning as another word: e.g., *begin* and *commence*.

syntax. Sentence construction; the grammatical arrangement of words and phrases.

tense. A set of inflected forms taken by a verb to indicate the time (i.e., past, present, future) of the action.

theme. A recurring or dominant idea.

thesis statement. A one-sentence assertion that gives the central argument of an essay.

topic sentence. The sentence in a paragraph that expresses the main or controlling idea.

transition word. A word that shows the logical relation between sentences or parts of a sentence and thus helps to signal the change from one idea to another: e.g., *therefore*; *also*; *however*.

transitive verb. A verb that takes an object: e.g., *hit*; *bring*; *cover*. (Compare **intransitive verb**.)

usage. The way in which a word or phrase is normally and correctly used; accepted practice.

verb. That part of a predicate expressing an action, state of being, or condition that tells what a subject is or does. Verbs are inflected to show tense (time). The principal parts of a verb are the three basic forms from which all tenses are made: the base infinitive, the past tense, and the past participle.

verbal. A word that is similar in form to a verb but does not function as one: a participle, a gerund, or an infinitive.

voice. The form of a verb that shows whether the subject acted (**active voice**) or was acted upon (**passive voice**): e.g., *He* stole *the money* (active). *The money* was stolen *by him* (passive). Only transitive verbs (verbs taking objects) can be passive.

Notes

CHAPTER 2

1. For a more detailed discussion of heuristic procedures, see Richard E. Young, Alton L. Becker, and Kenneth Pike, *Rhetoric, Discovery and Change* (New York, NY: Harcourt Brace Jovanovich, 1970), 119–36.
2. Joseph F. Trimmer, *Writing with a Purpose*, 12th ed. (Boston, MA: Houghton Mifflin, 1998), 62–3.

CHAPTER 4

1. John R. Trimble, *Writing with Style: Conversations on the Art of Writing* (Upper Saddle River, NJ: Prentice-Hall, 2000), 22–3.
2. Sheridan Baker and Laurence B. Gamache, *The Canadian Practical Stylist*, 4th ed. (Don Mills, ON: Addison-Wesley, 1998), 55–6.
3. Baker 63–5.
4. Charles Hall, "Ecology," in *Encyclopedia of Earth* (http://www.eoearth.org/article/Ecology)

CHAPTER 10

1. Gerald van Belle, *Statistical Rules of Thumb* (New York, NY: John Wiley and Sons, 2002), 221.

CHAPTER 14

1. James F. Shepherd, *College Study Skills*, 6th ed. (Boston, MA: Houghton Mifflin, 2002) and *RSVP: The College Reading, Study, and Vocabulary Program*, 5th ed. (Boston, MA: Houghton Mifflin, 1996).

Index

The Making Sense Series

Margot Northey with Joan McKibbin
MAKING SENSE
A Student's Guide to Research and Writing
Sixth Edition • *Celebrating 25 years*

Margot Northey, David B. Knight, and Dianne Draper
MAKING SENSE IN GEOGRAPHY AND ENVIRONMENTAL SCIENCES
A Student's Guide to Research and Writing
Fourth Edition

Margot Northey and Judi Jewinski
MAKING SENSE IN ENGINEERING AND THE TECHNICAL SCIENCES
A Student's Guide to Research and Writing
Third Edition

Margot Northey, Lorne Tepperman, and Patrizia Albanese
MAKING SENSE IN THE SOCIAL SCIENCES
A Student's Guide to Research and Writing
Fourth Edition

Margot Northey and Patrick von Aderkas
MAKING SENSE IN THE LIFE SCIENCES
A Student's Guide to Research and Writing